BLACK & WHITE RECORDS

45 rpm
Stereo   **A**
℗ 2006   978 1 84502 107 8

BIG NOISE
(Kielty)
MARTIN KIELTY
Engineered by Martin Kielty

BIG NOISE
THE SOUND OF SCOTLAND

MARTIN KIELTY

blackandwhitepublishing.com

First published 2006 by
Black & White Publishing Ltd
99 Giles Street
Edinburgh
EH6 6BZ

ISBN 13: 978 1 84502 107 8
ISBN 10: 1 84502 107 X

British Library Cataloguing in publication data: a catalogue record
for this book is available from the British Library.

Set in 10 on 13pt Georgia and Helvetica Neue

Designed and produced by Martin Kielty too.

Printed and bound by
Polskabook in Poland
www.polskabook.pl

CONTENTS

ACKNOWLEDGEMENTS

Contributions:

Thanks to everyone across the world who've provided stories and pictures.
Everyone's named with their contribution – please take that as profound thanks from me as well.

Thanks:

John JC Clarke for getting the ball rolling and continued egging-on and belief
Brian Hogg, **Jim Wilkie** and **Peter Innes** for being wonderful influences
Ali Bear, Kenny Bones, Muppet, Cas, Mortal and **Frank Morgan** for putting up with the intolerable whining
The hard-working folks at papers and radio stations all over the country for helping get the word out
The guys at the **Solid**, the guys at **Fix** and the guys at the **Variety**
Tom McCartney at rockingscots.co.uk and **Tommy Devlin** at glasband80.co.uk
The steam team at **Black & White** for putting up with my, em, eccentric way of working

Special thanks to everyone who's ever worked on a fanzine. It really is worth it, innit?

Regards:

Alan Moffatt – lose the hat, you prat... **Murray** at the Record... **Ken, Russell** and **Vicky** at the Times...
Hugh, Ian and the **Trowsers**... **Carradale** and all its wonderful folk... **Cameron** at Portnellan and all at the
Ben More Lodge Hotel... **Cammie Campbell** at Northsound... **Mick Brown**... **Sweeney** if he gives me my lens back.

Dad – enjoy your retirement. Mum – you do too!

People who bought me the required amount of beer to get a mention this time:

Damien, John, Brian Mackenna, Steve Banaghan, Tim Collins, the guys at **Dunstaffnage** and the **Oyster Inn, Connell,**
Rob Davies, Kenny, Liam and Robert at the Solid, **CupTie, Scottie Douglas,** the **Cinematics** and those dodgy dodgy **Martians.**

Any errors or omissions are anybody's fault but mine.
Start with Gibby if you're looking for a blamebucket. I've taught him the word 'Sorry' especially.

Dedicated to David 'Gibby' Gibson, who, as ever, put up with and dealt with a lot more than I ever realise. Ta, mate.

Claire – what do you think of it so far? I'm sold... I'd marry you all over again. x

INTRODUCTION

Big Noise was the fanzine I ran throughout the 1990s. Some zines follow a particular band, or a genre, or a political movement. I was interested in what made Scotland's rock'n'roll different from everyone else's. I was always sure it *was* different – interviews with a wide variety of Scots artists and an equal range of folk from elsewhere only supported my belief.

The zine has run through my life ever since. Through *Big Noise* I got my first newspaper job, designed my first album cover, managed my first band and wrote my first book. Today I make my living working with words and working with musicians, including the legendary Sensational Alex Harvey Band. It's given me the opportunity to continue exploring whatever the 'Scottish music scene' was – which is a pretty damn cool thing to be doing with my life, I must admit...

So this book isn't just named after the zine – it's a new edition, which I admit I would never have got away with photocopying while the boss thought I was working late. And you can't have one for free. And you can't get your band in it. And I'm not going to harass you to write something for it.

So get strapped in: this is a rollercoaster ride. We're gonna start fast and zoom through history at a speed you wouldn't believe. Along the way we'll sneak down a couple of sidestreets and peak behind the odd set of curtains, but for most of the trip it's gonna be splat-*splat*-**splat** as we whistle-stop through fifty years of action and adventure. Jazz, skiffle, beat, prog, glam, pop, twee, dance and crossover will all make an appearance. But only for a moment, because we're moving at intergalactic velocities.

There's no way I could fit everything in, and I didn't want to try. What I did want to do, though, is what I always try to do: tell a couple of stories which share the passion and magic I've discovered underneath what some people think is nothing more than a £5-billion-per-year business. (That's what rock'n'roll is thought to contribute to the Scottish economy, incidentally.)

Before I launched *Big Noise* I suspected that, no matter when people were born, which instrument they played, which style of music they performed or how far they got with it, there's something uniting them all underneath. Something personal, something wonderful... something Scottish.

See if you reckon I was right – join the conversation at any time you like: **www.bignoisebook.com**.

Ch;M.
September 2006

REGRET

There's a story I wanted to get, tried to get but couldn't get. It's about someone very famous now, on the day he signed his life-changing record deal. He was in a posh office down south, surrounded by successful businessmen, and his eyes lit up at the collection of pre-release albums on display in the corner. On expressing an interest, the boss-types, keen to impress, said he could take whatever he wanted. Being a good Glaswegian, he took exactly three more than he could carry and effed off. Halfway down the street he was stopped by a couple of bobbies, who asked, ''Ere, wotchoo got there then, son?' In wide Scots brogue on the streets of West London, he explained, 'I've just signed a global record deal and the label boss said I could just have them for nothing...' Huckled.

As I say, I couldn't get the story confirmed, so I can't use it. Pity – I think you'd have liked it.

THE
PYTHONS
SKIFFLE
GROUP

Image of the age: the Pythons
could have been stars... anyone
could. That was the magic.

1 SCOTLAND'S FIRST PUNK

Scotland's first punk made it big in 1956 with a top ten hit that changed popular music for ever. His name was Lonnie Donegan, his hit was a cover of Leadbelly's *Rock Island Line*, and he invented skiffle. Within weeks the whole world was joining in.

Before then, your night out would have been a lot more formal than the ones which came later. The music was ballroom jazz, once itself seen as a focus for troublesome youth, but long since adopted as decent God-fearin' folks' sound. The social dancing was structured – there were a set number of ways in which you did things. In a response to the action and drama of the Second World War, people wanted a nice, calm relaxed evening's entertainment; just a tad of wholesome exertion then home to Horlicks and counting the change from your jam-jar deal.

I'm generalising, of course... it wasn't all like that. But things were certainly a darn sight more peaceful than they were going to be. The first charts of 1956 (which had only recently begun listing by record sales instead of sheet-music ones) included Frank Sinatra's *Love and Marriage*, Frank Sinatra's *Love Is the Tender Trap*, Gary Miller's *Robin Hood*, Dick James' *Robin Hood*, Bill Hayes' *Ballad of Davy Crockett*, Tennessee Ernie Ford's *Ballad of Davy Crockett* and Tennessee Ernie Ford's *Sixteen Tons*. 'One singer one song' came along later, it would seem.

In the year of the first-ever Eurovision song contest, other chart presences included Bill Haley's *Rock a-Beatin' Boogie*, Bill Haley & His Comets' *Rock Around the Clock*, David Whitfield's *When You Lose the One You Love*, the Hilltoppers' *Only You*, Eve Boswell's *Pickin' A Chicken* and Alma Cogan's *Never Do a Tango with an Eskimo*.

Truly a mixed bag – or Sheena Easton for short. But even though the hit parade represented high-falutin' romantic croonings, light-hearted ditties, boys' own TV show themes and even Tennessee Ernie's working class dirges, Lonnie's offering was completely new. That's because *anyone* could play it.

He didn't actually have a tea-chest bass – that came later – but he did have the washboard, he had a vocal delivery like you and me (if we were pretending to be American, of course) and he delivered the tune in a simplistic three-chord stylee.

Suddenly you didn't need to read music or play with advanced sophistication. It was about having soul, having a vibe, and it wasn't restricted to those who'd had the commitment to go away and learn their trade. If folk like Elvis and Bill Haley had captured the mood of a generation, Glasgow-born Lonnie had given everyone a crash course in the language.

CHAS McDEVITT, Chas McDevitt Skiffle Group: I blame George Formby, actually – so much music just after the war was dull as dishwater. Even though his stuff had been recorded in the 1930s, it made us realise music could be made very easily – and it could be bright and cheery too.

You could still buy a third-class railway ticket, and you could still get the death penalty. The first Atlantic phone cable hissed into life and the Suez Crisis came and went while the Soviet Union flattened the Hungarian revolution and promised the Western Bloc: 'We will bury you.' Round about Easter, John Lennon's shellac ten-inch 78rpm copy of *Rock Island Line* shattered like glass through overplaying. Seven-inch 45rpm discs were yet to come, as was a wee skiffle band he was thinking of calling the Quarrymen. He wasn't alone: people all over Scotland were paying anything from thirty-five bob to fifteen quid for a guitar 'Perfect For Skiffle' and playing along with Lonnie: 'Ay bee see dubya ex wy zee, cat's in the cupboard but he don't see me...'

PETER McCRAE: It really did happen overnight. My dad had a guitar and he was chuffed I was showing an interest – but I think he hoped I'd move on from skiffle... As soon as I could play those chords I got a few mates from school round the house. We had three guitars, a tea-chest bass and a washboard, and we could only play *Rock Island Line* – but in our heads we were already stars!

You can't imagine what it was like, being fourteen and knowing you could make a noise like that. There were dozens of groups like us all over New Cumnock. There were a couple of talent shows and tea-dances, and we got up to playing about a dozen songs, and even started writing our own: *Cookin' in the Kitchen* and *Uncle Tam's Tandem*... It only got better when we discovered girls.

PETE AGNEW, Nazareth: Some school mates and I got together and called our group the Spitfires, and we entered the Fife Under-fifteen Skiffle Competition at the ABC in Kirkcaldy. It was our very first gig – I was the singer and my mates had their big brothers' acoustic guitars, and they couldn't play one single chord between them. And we won the cup! It gives you an idea of the standard of musicianship at the time...

ROY KITLEY: When I was fifteen I set up the Pythons Skiffle Group – we cribbed the name from The Vipers, one of the big successful groups of the time. We were kept really busy with cinema gigs, church socials, parties and clubs. Thousands of skiffle groups sprung up from nowhere – often there were several in one street, and rivalry was pretty fierce. Songs like *In The Evening*, *Midnight Special* and *Bury My Body* are still fresh in my mind. Some of the Pythons get back together to play them and they still sound great.

ALAN MUIR: They used *Rock Island Line* in a recent TV car advert. I couldn't believe it was 1956 I'd first heard it... And the thing is, alright, it sounds a wee bit out of date, but there's still a kick in it. I heard my son jamming it on his guitar and I just thought, 'It's happening again – great!' That's Lonnie for you... still worth a listen fifty years on.

Lonnie (real name Tony) Donegan was never interested in taking credit for inventing skiffle. 'I thought I was playing American folk music,' he said. It had all come about as a way of breaking up sets when he was in the Chris Barber Jazz Band – he enjoyed it, the audience enjoyed it, and when the Barbers were in the studio he'd been allowed to lay down the track as a potential B-side, for which he was paid ten pounds. Only in 1978, when a tribute album arranged by Paul McCartney and featuring Elton John, Brian May and Rory Gallagher, did he realise the height of his achievement.

As well as turning everyone into budding musicians, he'd done for the guitar trade what Princess Diana did for Interflora: sales exploded from five thousand six-strings in 1950 to over two hundred thousandin 1956. No one wanted Meccano for Christmas that year. With fifty thousand skiffle bands across the UK, one supplier lamented not being able to serve customers who were'wandering about with fistfuls of notes, looking for guitars'. He had twenty thousand on order and wished he could get more.

Scots immigrants are credited with applying the jingly-jangliness to American folk – the *Deliverance*-style twang.

'Have ye met mah maw, paw, sister, uncle and brother?'

There's only one person there.

'Yup...'

As that influence yee-hawed its way back across the channel it fell on receptive ears in Lonnie, Chas McDevitt, Nancy Whiskey and Jimmie MacGregor – every one born in Glasgow. While Jimmie and Robin Hall were instrumental in taking the influence round into Scottish folk again, Lonnie, Chas and Nancy were the only UK skiffle acts to see any success back in the USA.

CHAS McDEVITT, Chas McDevitt Skiffle Group**:** We got the red-carpet treatment in the States when we appeared on the *Ed Sullivan Show*. There was nearly a problem because the American musicians' union didn't think our washboard was a musical instrument, meaning we wouldn't be allowed to perform – but we got away with it in the end.

The *Sullivan Show* was big news so we had TV and press people in our hotel suite the night before. Right in the middle of all this, our label boss, Chic Thompson, saw an old man hassling his wife. He went straight over, threw him to the floor, made him kiss her feet and grovel for forgiveness. A wee bit later, when it seemed like Nancy might leave the group, Chic said he'd have to kill me if I let it happen. I believed him! But asides from that it was a great experience, meeting all the people I'd only ever heard on record – Chuck Berry, the Everly Brothers, George Lewis, Tony Parenti – and Screaming Jay Hawkins. I loved the way he used the coffin in his show so much, I started to have one made for me when I got home. Fortunately, common sense prevailed and I passed the idea on to Screaming Lord Sutch.

JOHN ALLISON: Chas was based in London, playing banjo in a couple of jazz bands as well as having his Chas McDevitt Skiffle Group. I remember they used to busk in Soho to make money. They had this big big guy, Redd Sullivan, who could really belt out the numbers, and they'd all walk behind him until a group of people were following them. Then they'd stop and give the people a couple of tunes, and put the hat round before the police showed up. After they'd seen me a couple of times Chas knew I was from Glasgow too, and he'd say, 'We'll not take any money from you, son – you send it home to your mum.' I never did, of course!

CHAS McDEVITT: Most of that's true – although I don't remember offering to return any of our takings, even to a fellow Scot! Maybe Adam, the 'bottler' who took the money, thought it would be a good marketing ploy...

Lonnie Donegan: from jazz jour-
neyman to skiffle king

When I was playing the ferries years later, I came across some of the guys who'd been in Don Partridge's short-lived band, busking in Stockholm. I used to sneak provisions off the boat for them – cheese and ciggies. One day I saw one of them wandering the town looking quite glum. They'd been selling memorabilia at a rock concert – I think it was Bowie – and their banjo player had been arrested for drugs.

His banjo was still around so I offered to step in for a few hours. And once again I was busking – this time with a trio of guitar, banjo and a rather well-endowed lady tap-dancer. Phil Lynott passed by and dropped a few coins in the hat. I gave them my share of the take, but if they were taking that much every day they were on a good screw – maybe it was the tap-dancer who drew the crowds...

A recently-discovered live recording of the McDevitts, including their UK and US hit *Freight Train*, features audience reaction best described as pre-Beatlemania-mania. The kids were going wild and joining in – while the press described it as 'the sound of throttled canaries'. Now, that's punk, innit? And if you manage to find a copy, read Chas' book, *Skiffle*, which tells the whole story.

There was still room for trad-jazz in the mix, mind, with acts like the Clyde Valley Stompers still going down a treat and being impressive enough to get a Decca record deal in mid 1956. Some acts were varying their show according to the booking, so you'd be playing jazz one night and skiffle the next. Jimmy Shand had made number twenty in 1955 with *Bluebell Polka*, and that was the last of that; but as time went on jazz and skiffle remained kissing cousins. The Stompers, which usually starred Fionna Duncan on vocals, even welcomed Lonnie on their hit *Sailing Down Chesapeake Bay*.

FIONNA DUNCAN, Clyde Valley Stompers: My family's musical background was definitely jazz based – my dad, sister and brother all played jazz piano. But I started out appearing in public as a folk singer. Then I met Danny Kyle and joined a skiffle group, which to my young ears – and my personality, I suppose – seemed a lot less constricting. Then I moved on to the Clyde Valley Stompers, and Lonnie was the A&R guy behind my first recording with them.

GEOFF BOXELL: There used to be a pop panel programme on TV – I remember a Brummie girl whose 'Oi'll geeve eet foive' became a catchphrase... The Clyde Valley Stompers were on and it only got a two, because trad was starting to fade, but I didn't care what they thought – I'd been given a record token by my auntie and I went out and bought the Stompers. I think she hoped I'd spend it on Cliff Richard or something! I've never looked back.

The impact of skiffle had been as sudden as my wife's mood changes, as deep as the Loch Ness monster's cellar and as permanent as our World Cup failure. Its open-hearted spirit of joining in and sharing gave rise to outdoor gatherings where friends were made, loves were found and grassroots political movements, like the CND, began to take shape.

Good thing too – the world badly needed to change. Nat King Cole had just been attacked on stage in segregated America as a result of his all-black band touring with all-white Englishman Ted Heath's band. In England, the Archbishop of Canterbury supported the BBC in banning Don Cornell's faith-inspired pop songs, labelling the title *The Bible Tells Me So* as 'bad taste'. Haley faced allegations of 'pulling down the white man to the level of the negro' and was advised to 'ask [his] preacher about jungle music'. Against this background, skiffle celebrated a community ethic everybody could join in with.

Then, of course, there was rock'n'roll, and it was having a hard time too. Sure, it had been making waves via the admirable works of Messrs Presley and Haley, and in England it had begun to catch on with respected jazz drummer Tony Crombie seeing the Comets and starting his Rockets. Tommy Steele, classed as a variety act, made his first appearance in London, and the *Melody Maker* chortled: 'It's little short of a miracle this youth could receive such a rapturous ovation for the little talent he displayed...' People demanded their money back when respected US artist Lionel Hampton began including a bit of the wild stuff in his act. 'Spare us this trash!' appealed the *Melody Maker*. Frank Sinatra called it 'the martial music of every juvenile delinquent on earth' and US journalist John Crosby called Elvis 'an unspeakably untalented and vulgar young entertainer, who, I hope, heralds the end of rock'n'roll and a return to musical sanity.' Hear, hear – not.

The new noise didn't really explode in Scotland until the skiffle approach made it accessible to the general populace. Asides from dance moves it's tough for a nation to make an impact on a style of music until it's actually playing it, instead of other people's records.

Other people's clothes were coming into play too – when the Teddy Boy fashion was glued to teen-angst movie *The Blackboard Jungle* in London in 1955, the sharp suits and duck's-arse quiff headed north slowly but surely. The style itself was a gluing together of 'spiv' outfits worn by east end scrap merchants and the desire to cheer up drab demob suits. The kids were trying to look like Aafur Daley, strike a light guv'nor.

But while it was all the rage dahn sahth, it perhaps didn't slice right through Scottish culture the way the papers suggested. Yes indeed, the *Daily Record's* Pat Roller (back on the beat these days) carried a weekly summary of Teddy terror from coast to coast, but then the *Record* also thought the hip kids were 'zinging cats' – which, as everyone knows, is illegal. In many of Scotland's ballrooms, the bequiffed ones were a minority.

ROLLIN' JOE: I didn't see that many Teds around in Glasgow. There were a few – not Showaddywaddy Teds, just guys with long jackets, thin trousers, thick brogues shoes, the wee tie, the hair and all. But when you went to the Barrowland, the first thing you saw was people jiving. In the corner, they called it mug's alley, there were people jiving, and they knew what they were doing. Then the Teds were just jumping about – they were enjoying themselves, but not many of them were any good at dancing. I think if there were all that many Teds in Scotland, most of them were outside the cities. Most of us just wore suits. It wasn't about being flash – it was about being smart. And dancing and meeting girls.

PAT LEACH: The ted look arrived in Thurso from Glasgow – some of the boys working on the Dounreay reactor brought the gear up. I liked the look of it but it was 78 bob for a jacket. That was nearly £4, and I was earning less than £3 a week. Still, I saved up and got all the gear, and I remember feeling well smart as I went about. One Saturday afternoon I passed my dad in the street and he was talking to the local doctor – he totally blanked me! I was saying, 'Remember me? Your eldest son?' and he was acting as if I wasn't there. Even the doctor was joining in. I didn't understand – it was just fashion, I didn't go round slashing people or anything. But it was all that old tradition stuff. I still looked great though...

Let's not go near the 'first rock'n'roll record' conversation, because we're all mortals (except me – I've made other arrangements) and the argument could rage forever. We can say with some certainty that the Ricky Barnes All Stars was Scotland's first rock'n'roll band, followed shortly afterwards by acts like Butch and the Bandits, the Saints, the Kinsmen, the Falcons, at least two Crusaders and many many more. We can also say the All Stars were responsible for the country's first rock'n'roll riot. We can further say, no matter how high our eyebrows rise beyond our foreheads as we say it, that Sydney Devine stopped the first rock'n'roll riot. We can say all that because it's in the history books... but as it turns out, it's almost certainly utter bobbins.

BILL ALLISON: The town hall was always a favourite with us. Band night was usually Saturday and Jimmy McCracken was a regular – and there was a talent contest every Sunday. That Sunday we had the Ricky Barnes All Stars playing instead.

The hall was all seated except for a space between the front rows and the stage – all the girls used to crowd in there to dance. Unusually for Paisley it had been raining... There were handbags and umbrellas placed – and I mean *placed* – on the stage. The manager, Mr Edmondson, was a real gentleman. He wasn't bothered about all the stuff being put on the stage, and neither were the bouncers or the bands.

The All Stars were great. They did a song called *Skin Deep* which had a drum solo, and like many bands to this day, the rest of the musicians went off stage while the drummer did his bit. They came back on, finished the set, everyone clapped, and that was that.

Next day I picked up the paper and saw the headline 'Riot at Town Hall' across the front page. The article went on about items being thrown onto the stage, but the nearest thing to that was all the umbrellas and bags that had been *placed* on stage. Then it said the band had walked off in disgust, when they'd just gone off during the drum solo.

Sydney Devine? With the passage of time I can't say for certain he wasn't there, but I'm pretty sure there was no one else on the bill beside the All Stars. We did have an eccentric old woman in her seventies – we all called her Granny – who used to sing at the talent contests, very badly! It's more than likely she was screeching away during the interval – I can't remember.

This story about a riot has bothered me for about fifty years. It just wasn't true, and it reflected badly on the people of Paisley. I suppose it must have been a publicity stunt – or maybe just a really quiet day for the paper. But it just didn't happen.

Media panic-mongering or not, there's no doubt violence was a problem all over the nation, and there's no doubt the concept of the 'teenager' was born of a mid-fifties backlash. But no matter when you were that certain age, who doesn't remember being checked by the polis, when all you were doing was talking shite under the streetlights, and maybe daring to have a bottle of Irn Bru on the ground beside you? As ever, the problems were caused by a minority – a minority, interestingly enough, which the Duke of Wellington had formed into a world-beating force nearly two centuries previously. ('I don't know what they do to the enemy, but they scare the hell out of me,' they say he said.) When it came right down to it, for most Scots it was bollox-all about rebellion.

LIZ HAYES: Radio Luxembourg was the news channel for anyone who cared about music. You tuned into 208 or 1440 and found this crackly station that played all these magic new tunes you couldn't get in Scotland. You'd go mad for all the American music – and you'd go even madder when you lost the signal and missed the best bit of the song! But that made it all the more magical. You were listening to music from far, far away, and it just fired up your imagination. I don't think it's as easy to fall in love with a song as it was then. And it was all about falling in love with songs. I couldn't even spell 'rebellion'!

Lonnie finally hit number one with *Cumberland Gap* in April 1957, the same week Chas McDevitt and Nancy Whiskey made number five with *Freight Train*. Soon Elvis would take top place for the first time with his tenth single, *All Shook Up*. The Cavern Club was the latest buzz in Liverpool, the first video recorder was about to be created, and the USSR was preparing to send Sputnik and Muttnik into space. And just around the same time, Alex Harvey started down the road to stardom by winning a national talent contest.

The story is told in full in Martin Kielty's excellent book, *SAHB Story: the Tale of the Sensational Alex Harvey Band*, available in all good bookshops and some rubbish ones too. I'm hugely impressed by Martin's work and commend it to everyone – the average British household owns just seven books, one of which is the Bible, another of which should be *SAHB Story*, preferably on some kind of pedestal. Alongside, of course, the mighty tome you hold right now.

The contest was created by the *Sunday Mail* after the paper received one of their biggest postbags ever in response to an article which criticised Tommy Steele. People went ballistic in defence of Tommy, and even though ballroom hero Harry Margolis had condemned rock'n'roll as a fad, saying he gave it two years tops, the readership didn't agree.

The result was a national event held in heats across the county, with around 600 budding rockers aiming for a place in the grand final in Glasgow. Alex, then twenty-two, blew everyone away. He'd modified the standard ted outfit to a variant all his own, and rebuilt a cheap guitar his own way, and then gone on stage and played a set his own way.

JOE MORETTI: I was eighteen and still at school. I only knew one other guitar player – people thought you were weird if you played and sang. I had an arch-top Hofner Senator. Most guitars were arch-top then, and electric pickups were just a dream. That meant having an amplifier, and you couldn't afford that. I wanted a pickup for the contest, though, and my uncle helped me with the £7 I needed.

I went along to the audition, and there were about fifty guys in the room playing guitars. Nobody had seen that many guitarists all together before – and then I realised, one guy's got an amp! I went over, and he had a battered old acoustic with a Besson pickup like mine, and he was playing an old ballad, *St James' Infirmary*. That's how I met Alex.

He let me plug into his second input and we played *Sweet Georgia Brown* and a Django Reinhardt tune. we could hear our guitars and each other, and it was brilliant! Sounds strange now but it meant so much then.

Three of us went through to the final the next night – and Alex won, of course. He played some Little Richard and went in heavy – he just blew everyone away. Then he asked me to join his band, the Kansas City Band, and we went touring in an old 1940s car and an ex-Post Office van for the gear. We just played wherever and whenever – there was never any money, just enough for petrol and food. But we were so happy to be playing music and not stuck in some dead-end nine-to-five job.

Alex and Tommy

Joe has a new album out – there's more details on his website, www.joemoretti.org, along with a very impressive chain of stories about his time in the music business all over the world.

Sydney Devine came second in the Tommy Steele contest, and his biog *Simply Devine* has several choice tales to tell about touring with Alex, partying with girls and generally acting like a rock star. Maybe it took a while for us Scots to generate a star with global status, but we had the partying sorted from right early on. Yeah.

That contest was Alex's first step on the road to glory – and right from the word 'go' he was a rule-breaker. When he met Tommy Steele for photos, he got them both arrested by trying to break into the docks to meet some of former seaman Tommy's old shipmates. And within weeks, as the new star was added to bills across the country, he let his mates earn a few bob by pretending to be him. On any given night there might be five Alex Harveys playing across Scotland; one impostor was caught and nearly hanged when a fan brought a photo of the real deal to the show.

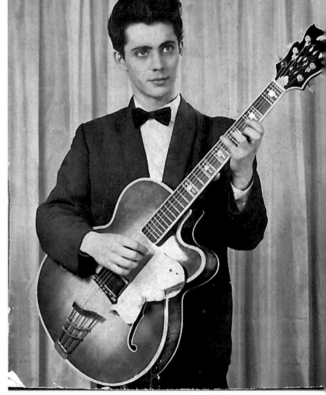

Joe Moretti

'You're no' him!'

'Em... Aye I am - I've just done my hair different!'

'Aye, and yer face – come here, you...'

Tony Crombie's Rockets split up, citing lack of industry support, despite having earned three times their jazz rates. Stereo records arrived and women were allowed to enter the House of Lords. The CND was officially brought into being as the government committed to proportional retaliation if the USSR struck first. Tommy Steele threatened to quit the music business after he was roughed up at a Dundee gig – there had been no bouncers on duty. The furious *Melody Maker* demanded an enforced end to rock'n'roll, bellowing: 'Pop Rot! Call a halt now!'

Meanwhile, the seedy scandal-merchants finally found something about rock'n'roll to get their teeth into. By the time Elvis achieved advance orders of one million for *Love Me Tender*, before the thing had even been recorded, no one thought he could be touched. The only man who came close was great ball of fire Jerry Lee Lewis – but in 1958 he burned out dramatically when it was discovered his wife was his cousin. She had been thirteen when they married and the marriage was bigamous. Disgraced and ruined, Lewis's fee fell from $10,000 to $250 a show, and he headed home after three nights of an extensive UK tour.

ROLLIN' JOE: I worked in a fitters' in Govan, and a mate of mine there had a ticket for Jerry Lee Lewis. When Lewis cancelled he gave the ticket to me, so I went along to take a look. The Treniers headlined instead – and they blew me away! I remember walking down Renfield Street with the twin brothers, Claude and Cliff, completely caught up with the music they'd just played. And that was me – a rock'n'roll fan!

Once, many *many* years ago, Scotland was a more important part of Europe than England. It happened so long ago that various raiding English kings were able to destroy the records, although there's still evidence of cultural communication moving through Italy and France, into Scotland and only then into England. In medieval times the sons of nobles spent a year on the continent to learn the rules and make business contacts, and at one point the official language of the Scottish court was French. But that was long ago. Lonnie had lived in England from an early age, as had Chas McDevitt, so as yet there was no one who'd made it out of Scotland. And as the skiffle movement began to transform into something completely different, the way to the top was the road to the south. What's more, everyone knew where they were going: the 2 I's Coffee Bar.

> **JOE MORETTI:** I knew about the 2 I's, but there I was, first time in London, standing outside it... the place where Cliff and Tommy Steele had been discovered. I asked the guy on the door – his name was Tom Littlewood – if I could play that night and he said I could. This was my chance to earn a few quid, but only if I was good. There were no rules, except you did it live and, if you couldn't cut it, you got the fuck off the stage. There were dozens of boys every night waiting to take your place.
>
> So I just went for it – cranked the volume up and just played for about forty-five minutes or so. Just good, honest rock'n'roll. Then it sank in... people are enjoying it! Maybe I *can* make it in London after all! As soon as I came off I got offered a tour with Colin Hicks, Tommy Steele's brother – and I even got a few bucks up front. I'd made it on my first night!

As the 1950s grew old, the BBC's *Six-Five Special* came and went. This important attempt at youth programming was the first time TV had broadcast between six and seven in the evening. Until then there was a tradition known as the 'toddlers' truce', when channels went off the air so that mothers across the nation could put the kids to bed – and so the set's valves could cool down. All that changed when, at five past six on a Saturday evening, presenter Pete Murray announced: 'Welcome aboard – we've got a hundred cool cats jumping here and some cool characters to give us the gas, so just get on with it and have a ball.' As the wee orange lights behind your telly's single-ply backing plate glowed just that bit brighter, it was 'time to jive on the old six-five'.

Planned to last six weeks, it ran for nearly a year, until producer Jack Good fell out with the BBC, and moved over to ABC – part of the independent network, where a lot of posh kids would never be allowed to watch his next offering, *Oh Boy!* Good's intention was to speed up the pace and delivery, so he abandoned a lot of the general-interest stuff he'd been forced to include on *Six-Five Special* and aimed to 'startle viewers with quick, lively presentation'.

The first show included Cliff Richard's TV debut at the age of seventeen, assisted by his nineteen-year-old manager, and Marty Wilde, by then a pop veteran of nearly nine months. Presented by Jimmy Henney, it was also the debut of the house band, Lord Rockingham's XI, which was fronted by Scots conductor Harry Robinson.

Although Good and Robinson later went to court over the Rockingham title – a tad dim since there actually *was* a Lord Rockingham who could object to them both – the affiliation lasted long enough for the band to go on tour and record the famous jazz spoof, *Hoots, Mon* – a take on *A Hundred Pipers* which stopped swinging long enough for everyone to shout, 'Hoots mon... there's a moose loose aboot this hoose!' Yes, isn't that grand? Here we are swinging towards the sixties with no mention of Harry

Charlie Gracie, complete with fresh wedding ring, during his first UK tour

Lauder, except that one, and it was happening all over again. And it wasn't over either. We should be proud to note that the first-ever UK rock'n'roll export to American TV was Edinburgh teenager Jackie Dennis. We should be less so that he's remembered for swinging through his hits *La Dee Dah* and *Purple People Eater*, colourfully in black and white, in full kilt and regalia. Oh boy, Jackie had wheech. Unfortunately...

ELSA KIRKWOOD: I remember seeing him on the telly – he was swinging from side to side with his arms flapping away, clicking his fingers to the beat. It looked like he was going to fall over, he was throwing himself about so much... and he had a big smile even though he was singing. I thought he looked superb in the kilt. I didn't think how tacky it was until many years later. We were all young in those days, even the producers!

He looks a bit like David Sneddon, if you ask me.

Meanwhile, back on BBC, the Scottish music programme was really piling it on. Variety star Andy Stewart had first presented *The White Heather Club* as a Hogmanay special in 1957. Then the tartan telly went weekly, backed up with its fellow production, *The Kilt Is My Delight*. There was clearly still a lot of work to be done if the kids' new noise was to become mainstream.

~~David Sneddon~~ Jackie Dennis

That work took a knock when the self-styled father of rock'n'roll came a cropper in a payola scandal. Alan Freed, who'd championed the movement via radio stations in the USA and on a pre-recorded show on Radio Luxembourg, was accused of adding his name to songwriting credits and then artificially promoting those songs, thereby making himself more cash.

It wasn't illegal – Elvis quite openly admitted he increased his income by a third by insisting that songs written for him listed him as a co-writer, or he just wouldn't perform them. It was tough for non-songwriters to make a good living; to this day, if one of your band writes hit songs and the rest of you just perform them, he'll be rich and you'll never be anything like as rich.

So there was an argument for trendsetters like Freed and Presley to have a vested interest in the songs they chose to make famous. Nevertheless, accusations of straight-out bribery led to Freed's demise, and a fair amount of innocence died in the crossfire. Even though many artists called him a hero for many years to come, the icy hand of profiteering had been seen dipping into rock'n'roll's trouser pocket, and no one liked it. Payola was made illegal in 1960.

Still, sales increased, more money was made, and record companies were able to drop single prices from six bob to four. Even the *Melody Maker* began softening ever so slightly. On one page they lamented 'the pay-day rowdies who throw chairs' while on another they reported 'a fine night's entertainment with no form of trouble whatsoever'.

CHARLIE GRACIE: I was the first solo American act to tour Britain, and I remember the Scottish audiences being very warm and passionate. I distinctly recall the welcome I and my new bride received – we'd only been married six weeks. I did two British tours. The first was supposed to last six weeks but Lew and Leslie Grade, who promoted it, extended it to ten.

I was twenty-two and my wife was just eighteen. Imagine what it felt like when we were leaving Glasgow and all these fans turned up at the train station, crying and begging us not to go! We were on the verge of tears too – it was very, *very* emotional. It was like a scene from a movie.

I've played the UK in thirty-two of the last fifty years, and I'm back again in 2006, but there are no dates in Scotland, which is a great disappointment. I'd love to come back. I visited with Van Morrison recently – he's a big fan and took me on tour with him a few years ago. He says I should play Ireland too, that I'd go over very well. Scotland and Ireland – it sounds perfect. My agent is waiting if anyone wants to book me!

Transatlantic flights were introduced by BOAC and PanAm – then Buddy Holly, Richie Valens and the Big Bopper died in a plane crash. Fidel Castro came to power in Cuba, while Alaska and Hawaii became part of the USA, and the Dali Lama escaped Chinese control by fleeing to India. And back home in Scotland, with the parochial powers flip-flopping like feck, it looked as if the crazy new craze was going to make it. But, as a matter of fact, rock'n'roll only had two years to live.

A very early Alex Harvey band (Alex is at the centre of the stage) during a traditional night out, before 'dancing apart to the beat' began

2 THE DEATH OF ROCK'N'ROLL

Looking back, you can almost taste it. Like the way the ocean recedes before a tsunami, the opening years of the 1960s seem to herald the catastrophic explosion of unseen proportions. But maybe that's just because we all know that's exactly what happened.

One thing's for certain – skiffle, jazz and rock'n'roll were all acting like A&R men. Those of us (un)lucky enough to have played a showcase in front of several label reps will know the feeling – you watch them watch each other, wondering whether it's safe to clap, wondering whether one of the other guys has made a decision or has already pounced, wondering if they'll have a job in the morning. Only if one of them is utterly, *utterly* sure of themselves will the tsunami advance. None of the three movements to come out of the fifties were sure enough.

If you'll allow me to call 1960 the beginning of the sixties (what exactly do you mean, 'pedantic'?) the decade opened to a world scene that included the discovery of the Dead Sea Scrolls, the Soviet capture of U2 pilot Gary Powers, the Israeli capture of Nazi Adolf Eichmann, and the addition of one tenth of a second to the year because explosions on the sun had slowed the earth's rotation. Mad crowds of people raced to repair shops to have two microns added to the circumference of their watches. Or something.

Back in the real world, the decade began with another pick'n'mix in the hit parade. January starred *Starry Eyed* by Michael Holliday, *Poor Me* by Adam Faith, *A Voice in the Wilderness* by Cliff and the Shadows and *Summer Set* by Mr Acker Bilk and his Paramount Jazz Band.

Oh, aye, and Elvis made it out of the army intact. Funny, that.

'Rock'n'roll is now respectable,' a TV spokesman told the music press as ABC announced the cancellation of *Boy Meets Girl* and the BBC announced the launch of *Big Beat*. 'Pop music is now the biggest force in entertainment and the wild stuff has given way to beat ballads. This is what our audiences want to hear.' Over on radio, the Light Programme got the John Barry Seven in to rock up the *Saturday Club*.

The wild stuff was far from over, of course, and thank the good Lord furrit, and anyone who tried to push the point was slapped down. Gene Vincent, for one, walked off early on a tour which began in Glasgow, when the punters heckled his rendition of *Over The Rainbow*. 'I'm going to show you that rock'n'rollers can sing,' he'd said, 'because the critics say we can't.' Maybe he could, but no one wanted him to – and that was the end of the show. Except, of course, for the finale: *The Queen*, which even Vincent wouldn't dare stay off for.

Funny to note how little time had passed since people had been shouting for *less* rock'n'roll. But the indecision was set to continue, and as the battle of the giants of the future raged, some right stupid things started happening.

Only months after believing that the kids wanted to dig the crazy sound, ABC cancelled Jack Good's new show, *Wham!* 'There's no longer a public for teenage type programmes,' they reckoned after giving it eight weeks. It had just had time, mind you, to get into hot water over Billy Fury's 'erotic gyrations', to which Good had said, 'Anything suggestive should be avoided – but these things are partially in the mind of individual viewers.' Sounding old, Jack...

The release of Ray Peterson's *Tell Laura I Love Her* was postponed because Decca Records bosses felt the kids wouldn't be able to handle the tear-jerking nature of the lyrics. Boy meets girl, boy wants to marry girl, boy meets financial problem over buying ring, boy meets stock car race with cash prize, boy meets technical issue with stock car, boy meets Grim Reaper, boy doesn't want to marry Grim Reaper, Grim Reaper has other ideas, girl cries alone in church as boy's dying words echo to fade. Three months later, Ricky Valence's version of the song, released by Columbia, made it to number one for three weeks without any problems. Decca bosses had five board meetings about their future attitudes.

ELAINE MORTON: Ooh, it was so romantic! The *Jackie* wasn't out, I don't think, but all that stuff was right up our street – photos of the pop stars you were going to marry and all that. I loved Adam Faith. I didn't know if he had a girlfriend but when our eyes met he'd know as well as I did, and that would be that! I remember looking through my mum's cook books, trying to work out the kind of cakes Adam might like me to bake for him... But *Tell Laura I Love Her* – wow! Of course we cried about it, but we were all crying about different singers. At least, my friends better not have been thinking about Adam! Imagine having someone ready to die for you! I didn't want Adam to die, of course, but it would be nice if he'd be ready to, for me...

Gentlemen, it's worth noting that I've deduced the reason women like being given flowers: they enjoy the feeling that something's died for their pleasure. Send them back to their own planet...

Gene Vincent was obviously not enjoying life in the UK any more. After the heckling episode, and allegedly collapsing backstage after a Scottish gig, he survived the car crash in which Eddie Cochran was killed. Eventually he announced that his daughter had died and he had to go home – then a week later his manager admitted it had been a hoax to get him out of the country. In an earlier interview with the *NME*, he'd said that he felt inferior to British acts: 'They know all kinds of music, they discuss keys, arrangements and so on. They try to achieve perfection. I just sing – that's all I know...' Nowadays that pattern of behaviour would set alarm bells ringing; it's a shame they weren't installed in Gene Vincent's time.

JOE MORETTI: Gene was a genuine superstar – no other word covers it. But in the short time I knew him, the person, he always seemed to be hurting inside. Loneliness was part of the bag in those days. The rock'n'roll lifestyle fed the ego, but you had nowhere to hang your hat. Forget all the movies, the magazines and TV shows and the black leather – he just wanted to be one of the guys, and when he was hanging with us, that's who he was.

There was a night in Glasgow where the Empire just became a riot – there were a couple of new acts on before us, but the audience just wanted Gene. When Billy Fury went on in his gold lamé suit, I thought it looked brilliant, but the crowd didn't. They started tearing the brass ashtrays off the seats and throwing them at the stage, shouting for Gene. In the end there were police everywhere – the auditorium, the foyer, the street – everywhere. We didn't go on that night.

But I knew Gene was hankering for some good old southern-fried chicken and corn on the cob. I also knew you could get the best in Britain at Allan's Hotel in Kelvinside. Gene didn't believe me but we went along, and the manager did us proud – gave us a private dining room, looked after every bit of detail. Proper Scottish hospitality. We had a great night, and I don't think any of us remember getting home.

As the backing band we were always skint – we never even had the money to phone home to check everything was okay, but Gene would just put it on his expenses. And that was for all twelve of us!

He didn't know about 'fag' being the British word for 'cigarette' – he knew the American meaning, 'homosexual'. So every time we talked about wanting a fag he'd say, 'Don't look at me baby – you got the wrong guy!'

I had a lot of genuine affection for him, and I was no special case. God bless your memory, Gene.

The BBC banned Nero and the Gladiators from performing a rock'n'roll version of Grieg's *Hall of the Mountain King*, stating that pop acts could not be allowed to perform versions of classical pieces. Jazz was fighting amongst itself, not for the last time, as a festival in England disintegrated into pitched battle between fans of Acker Bilk's trad and Johnny Dankworth's modern.

It was early days for the new club scene. Ballrooms were still the big power, and while one or two coffee shops were beginning to appear across Scotland, there was still a dearth of places to play. But not in Germany – it had a thriving scene, and while the Beatles made the trip to Hamburg, lived through the residencies and solidified their career, they weren't the only ones who could follow the road to Europe.

The life was hard, no doubt about it. You played as many as five sets a day, often without your usual lineup, and often without anything to eat. You almost always owed your landlord everything you earned, and your landlord was usually your club owner. Stories of soup diets and hunger pangs abound – especially if you encountered club impresario Bruno Koschmider. And you usually did.

The pre Fab Four five (you don't need that explained, do you?) made their first trek in August 1960. After falling out with Koschmider, Harrison was sent home for being underage, while McCartney and Pete Best were deported for arson. Lennon and Stuart Sutcliffe returned to Liverpool in early December – just in time to catch the first episode of *Coronation Street* – and began regular stints in the Cavern Club, which had only recently lightened up on its jazz-only rule.

FIONNA DUNCAN, Clyde Valley Stompers: All the gigs we played up and down the country, unless they were in trad-jazz clubs, were two-band sessions. We topped the bill, and the support act, then known as the interval group, was usually the big local band to bring in more kids – or an accordion and fiddle group to cater for the older members of the audience who actually thought we were too loud! I vividly remember playing the Cavern at the beginning of the sixties. We arrived at the venue early to set up and there was a massive queue at the entrance. We wondered if our new album had snuck into the hit parade without our noticing. But it wasn't that – it was the interval group, four young boys in black. I remember giggling when I heard they were calling themselves 'the Beatles'...

PETER KERR, Clyde Valley Stompers: If we had a blank in the datesheet on a Sunday, our agency would put us in the Cavern. What a shithole place that was to play. I don't think it would be allowed now. It was just a tunnel, and it got jam-packed, you couldn't breathe, you couldn't move and you

Clyde Valley Stompers

were soaked in sweat on a tiny wee stand, and the dressing room was a cupboard. The acoustics were dreadful too. But the atmosphere was electric among the punters, because they were right there in it. It was like one big punter – you didn't really have much choice!

But it was always a jazz club, and all those Liverpool bands that came out later had been our interval acts. Being jazz men – you know we can be a bit snobby – we thought they were all crap.

But because the scene was in transition you'd find a lot of those early beat groups were made to record trad songs, stuff from the 1920s and such. The record companies weren't sure what was happening next so they'd play it safe and have the beat tracks and some jazz tracks too. I don't think many of those groups would have wanted to be playing those songs...

The Clyde Valley Stompers were one of many jazz bands to enjoy an early-60s hit, scoring with their re-interpretation of *Peter and the Wolf* which, one assumes, the BBC didn't bother trying to ban. Along with Acker Bilk, the Dave Brubeck Quartet and others, there was a comfortable resurgence of the eldest of the rock'n'roll cousins.

PETER KERR: The Stompers had a very rough time, a very disruptive history of people falling out and lots of personnel changes. After about a year in London, Ian Menzies decided he'd had enough leading the band, and went off to run a boarding house in Jersey. But instead of letting us buy the name or anything, he set up a limited company with the Lyn Dutton Agency – and suddenly we were all working for them. That did a lot to the tension – a lot of the married guys went home. We lost the contract with Pye but we were picked up by George Martin at Parlophone.

The first thing we did was *Peter and the Wolf*, which was our own idea and our own arrangement. The arrangement was credited to someone else in the first pressing – this guy had said he could do better than us and gave it to the Lyn Dutton Agency – but in fact it wasn't better. It might have been technically better, but it didn't work as well. So the one that went out was ours, and that opened a lot of doors for us.

By now the beat boom was the tsunami on the horizon. 'Beat' was the word coined, Alex Harvey claimed, when tired drummers in Hamburg couldn't be bothered playing smart-ass stuff during their fifth set of the day, and concentrated on keeping four on the floor. 'Just play the beat, man.'

Beat clubs began to open all over Scotland – although some of them, converted ballrooms, kept the word in their title. In Glasgow, the Picasso, the Lindella, the Maryland; in Edinburgh, the Gamp, the Green Light, the Blue Door; in Aberdeen, the Beehive, the 62 Club and the Silver City Cafe. Whether they were beatnik bars, cool cafes or bohemian hangouts, they were all fuelling the fire, em, of the tsunami... shit. You get it.

As the space race got into full swing, with Yuri Gagarin orbiting the earth and JFK promising to put a man on the moon by the end of the decade, the Berlin Wall went up, and the Poets formed in Glasgow while the Shadettes, later to become Nazareth, formed in Dunfermline.

PETE AGNEW, Nazareth: There hadn't really been much of a music scene for us – all the dance halls still had the big bands. You'd hardly ever see a group in there, and even if they did we were too young to get in! By now you were seeing groups a lot more often, although they were only special guests and the big bands played most of the night.

Then the clubs started up. At home we had the St.Margaret's Hall, which later burned down, and they had the Vandals in residency. The Cowdenbeath Palais, which *should* have burned down, had the Hellcats and the Kinema Ballroom had The Redhawks. We wound up in the Kinema ourselves, much later on.

But no Scottish band ever really thought they'd end up making records. It just didn't happen. You did want to be a force to be reckoned with in Scotland, though. I think we achieved that – and the whole time, we never gave a thought to ever being a full-time band. Even the best-known bands on the circuit had day jobs.

Meanwhile, rock'n'roll – the true real rock'n'roll, began to die.

ROLLIN' JOE: There were incredible jive clubs all over Glasgow. Dalgleish's, Johnny Wilson's in Cathcart and later in Byres Road too, Bill Murdoch's, the Lindella – which is still going. You paid your money and they taught you to jive. Glasgow jive was unique as well – we had a lot more moves, a lot more soul.

It's important to realise rock'n'roll was a dance culture – it was about a band playing and people dancing. It wasn't really around for long. It was only 1960 or 1961 that ballrooms started taking on what you'd call rock'n'roll groups. There were the Sabres, the Chaperones, the Redhawks from Dunfermline, and one or two others. Before that it was traditional dance bands who might play a bit of rock'n'roll for the jivers.

And the thing is, rock'n'roll was about real dancing – not just throwing yourself around the room. And you didn't do it on your own either – if you tried dancing on your own the men in white coats would come!

But the twist killed it stone dead. That bastard Chubby Checker came along and totally aborted rock'n'roll. After that there were all those other cheap dances from America – and every single one of them was shite. It had been a social event – the band learned to play, you learned to dance and everyone had a night out. Then it was gone.

I remember Sol Byron at the Hamilton Town Hall – that was the first time I saw people just standing around watching the band. You went to see Chuck Berry, Jerry Lee Lewis, all the greats, and of course you watched them – they were unique. So were the Stones, the Beatles, the Kinks and Alex Harvey. But just watching any old band? Checker has a lot to answer for – stub oot yer cigarette, that's all you need to do for a night out... Within a year jive was dead, and so was real rock'n'roll.

Chubby Checker is proud to take credit for having introduced 'dancing apart to the beat'. Some point out that it was financially agreeable for venues to increase ticket sales, because with solo dancing you could stuff more people into the room. But it's also clear to see a line being drawn between the genteel social dancing events of earlier times along with the assumption that new music could be absorbed into that, and the other argument of continuing in the new exciting direction, on to success or oblivion. The world's become faster and faster ever since – and maybe even lost that extra tenth of a second.

ROLLIN' JOE: Bill Haley came to the Barrowland. Bill Haley! I nipped out of work to try to buy tickets, thinking there'd be a big queue. Nothing. Same with the show – you could wander straight in no problem. The room was about quarter full, and only about half a dozen people were jiving. You can say what you like about Bill Haley, but he was rock'n'roll. Seeing him playing to an empty room – well, you knew it was over.

Still, the rock'n'roll label lived on; unlike skiffle, which was breathing its last. Lonnie Donegan's singles were no longer guaranteed to be hits, and in order to keep his batting average up he resorted to more and more light-hearted songs. *Does Your Chewing Gum Lose Its Flavour on the Bedpost Overnight?* If a tree falls in the forest will anyone buy this single? The charts belonged to American rockers like Elvis, twisters like Chubby Checker, UK popsters like Cliff, Billy Fury and the Shadows, and jazzters like Acker Bilk.

Like the coming motorways, which would shave hours and even days off tours, the music scene was a multi-track road. A change in social trends led to new ways of thinking, which led to new ways of expressing ideas through instruments. People were thinking about the moon, Mars and galaxies, as well as nuclear holocaust, the Common Market and the coolest clubs to check out on Friday nights. And the vehicle best suited to tear up that motorway was the tsunami. Driven by the Beatles.

Note to self: never use tsunamis as an analogy for rock'n'roll again.

3 BRINGING THE BEAT

The coldest night of my life was spent in a minibus between Aberdeen and Gills Bay, heading for Orkney, during a Sensational Alex Harvey Band UK tour. It was also, as my good pal Luck would have it, the coldest night of the year, making it down to minus 20 – and the minibus wasn't entirely windproof or snowproof. I'd have burst into tears only the moisture had frozen in my eyes, and there was the added danger of getting stuck to the window – again. 'This is like the old days,' said Chris Glen. As an encyclopaedia of all things SAHB, I was able to tell him the band had never played Orkney before. 'No,' he said, 'this is like the old days going up to Dundee.'

In the motorway age, the eighty-mile Glasgow–Dundee trip can be completed legally in an hour and twenty-six minutes. In the sixties, it was a different story but it was nothing compared to the epic four-hundred-mile run from Liverpool to Elgin. And, if it was also snowing, the fun just never ended.

> **PETER KERR,** Clyde Valley Stompers: Travelling was murder. There was only one motorway, the M1, which went from the outskirts of London to Rugby. Everything else was single-lane trunk roads, so you'd spend hours and hours on end sitting behind streams of trucks. And you'd be doing runs like London to Birmingham and back again on the same night. Complete hell.

Even more of a hellish trip was experienced by the Beatles in 1963, as they set out on a five-day tour of Scotland. They completed their Hogmanay show in Hamburg then flew to London, but with the weather against them the show scheduled for 2 January was abandoned, which meant their first appointment in the north of the nation – asides from having backed Johnny Gentle in 1960, with a guest drummer because they didn't have one yet – was on 3 January, at the Two Red Shoes in Elgin.

The venue's owner, Albert Bonici, was a smart operator. Partly because bands didn't know any better, and partly because it was worth taking the risk, Bonici pressed the pre-Fab Four (now four) into a deal which made him their exclusive Scottish agent. It was a standard trick he'd continue to get away with until the London businessmen began to realise how big a market Scotland really was. They also played Dingwall Town Hall, the Museum Hall, Bridge of Allan, and the Beach Ballroom, Aberdeen, all for three shillings a ticket, before heading southward. But it was a mixed impression they left behind them.

> **COLIN McINTOSH:** You can always tell a good band, and without doubt they were that – but they didn't grab me. My girlfriend loved it, but I'd seen better. If you ask me, Alex Harvey wiped the floor

with the Beatles – I'd seen him a few months earlier and I found myself comparing everything to his show. But when they dropped the covers and did one of their own tunes, you could feel things changing. They definitely had something there. But you couldn't do a set of all your own songs in those days... and anyway, I was heading towards R&B. When I heard the Stones I knew I was right. The girlfriend didn't last either!

Nevertheless, the thirty-seven -date promotional tour propelled *Please Please Me* to the number one spot after a gradual climb, where it stayed for seven weeks. DJ Keith Fordyce told the *NME*: 'I can't think of any other group recording in this style. I shan't be in the least surprised to see the charts invaded by the Beatles.'

And, lo! The beat boom had arrived. Finally there was a convincing direction for all the young post-skiffle bands that had been springing up across Scotland – unsure of their future, they'd been influenced by a wide range of musical styles, and that was to serve them well in the coming revolution. And for those who hadn't struck a note in anger yet, there was a punk ethic at the top of the charts again, fuelled by the four-on-the-floor drum drive. Another generation of Scots reached for guitars thanks to the Liverpudlians – who once, never let it be forgotten I suppose, had a Scot in their line-up.

ALAN MAIR, Beatstalkers: Rhythm was in my blood. We lived with my gran, and I loved it when my uncles put Radio Luxembourg on. Even if I was meant to be in bed I couldn't help dancing around if I heard a song I liked. The actual sound of guitars really moved me too. My mum bought me an old acoustic one at an auction and I used to play it with my ear stuck to it, so I could hear a kind of electric sound. But when you got to thirteen or fourteen, and you were just becoming aware of yourself, you realised it was cool to be in a band. That's why everyone was doing it.

ANDY LOW: I thought the Beatles were incredible. The look, the delivery, the harmonies – it was a breath of fresh air. I'd seen so many copycat groups at the Beach Ballroom in Aberdeen, I really thought about giving up going to concerts, although God knows what else there was to do at the time. But the Beatles brought it back to life. I thought, 'Hey, maybe I can do that.' and I borrowed my mate's guitar – then bought one myself. It's been a big part of my life ever since. I never joined a band and never went on stage – never really wanted to. But it's still important to me.

ROB MITCHELL: People were screaming right the way through the songs. I thought, this is a great way to get girls! Although to be fair, they more or less did that at every gig. The other thing was, you didn't have to learn the words because of all the screaming – you just needed to know the chorus!

This time round, there was less of the doubt shown by record labels in the past. The pop machine was soon the only game in town, heralding the advance of Merseybeat across the world, and, for a while anyway, American singers trying to spoof British accents. It was also the end of the line for the musical genres who'd been pretenders to the throne.

PETER KERR, Clyde Valley Stompers: *Peter and the Wolf* had done very well for us. We ended up doing a lot of telly – *Morecambe and Wise, Thank Your Lucky Stars, Cool for Cats*... We were resident on *Young At Heart* from TTTV. We'd go up to Newcastle every Wednesday, the show went live from seven till eight, then we got pissed on Newcastle Brown because the sleeper didn't leave till half past eleven. We did the title track for a Norman Wisdom film, *On the Beat*, and even appeared in Tommy Steele's movie, *It's All Happening*.

But all through this the line-up was changing. The Lyn Dutton Agency were good in that respect – it was always a problem to find new Scottish members in London, but we managed it up until near the end. The first non-Scot we got was at least Irish, Joe McIntyre, but then the guy who'd replaced Ian Menzies left himself, and the first English guy came in. We knew the hard fans, especially in the west of Scotland, would take a dim view if we filled the line-up with Sassenachs.

We wound up with this guy who just didn't fit – it wasn't anyone's fault, it just happens. But it was social – when you're living in a van you've just got to get on. So we replaced him with someone we chose ourselves, and that's when the agency took the hump. It doesn't make any sense, looking back on it – you've got to let the band be the band.

So they called me into their office and said, 'We're firing you... We've got to get someone in who'll let us run things.' Then they offered me a job in the agency! Of course, I told them what to do with it...

I went back and told the boys. They all said, 'That's it, we're going with you.' I said, 'Don't be daft – you're earning good money here!' But the agency had tried to get at them all, and they knew you couldn't go along with that kind of thing. So there I was with a band, no name and no work – just like when I'd come back from Germany before I joined the Stompers! Their support was very touching, though.

So we called ourselves Pete Kerr's Scottish All Stars, even though we weren't all Scottish any more. But Ian Menzies and Lyn Dutton still had the name, so they got the Leathertown Jazz Band, an all-English band, back from Germany, dressed them in tartan and called them the Clyde Valley Stompers. They went out on the road – and lasted a week.

So that was very sad – but everything was about to change anyway, because of the Beatles. We'd all been thinking we were going to have to shift away from the trad stuff. We'd been getting more progressive anyway. Some of the last broadcasts we did as the Stompers were very different from the stuff we'd done before. It was the best time to lose the Stompers name.

But things were moving so fast that within a year there wasn't enough work for us to keep going, and that was the end of my career as a touring musician. No one could have seen all that coming. Not even the Beatles.

It was a momentous year, was 1963. Purchase tax on records was cut, meaning you now paid 6/3 for a single, 10/1 for an EP and 30/11 for an LP (30p, 50p and £1.60 respectively). As the US and USSR installed their leader-to-leader hotline, an anti-nuclear march in London drew seventy thousand protestors, while Martin Luther King told two hundred thousand civil rights demonstrators: 'I have a dream...' *Ready Steady Go!* announced: 'The weekend starts here!' JFK told the world with dodgy grammar, 'Ich bien ein Berliner', and months later he was assassinated. The following day, William Hartnell appeared as Dr Who. After manic crowd scenes outside the London Palladium during a Beatles' appearance, the word 'Beatlemania' entered the language. And the Great Train Robbers made off with £2.6m.

PETE AGNEW, Nazareth: When we were still the Shadettes we used to play Burntisland Palais every Saturday night. Sometimes we'd play the local cinema afterwards during the midnight horror presentations – movies with names like *The Wasp Woman*...

We had a knackered ex-gas board van, painted bright yellow, and we wore bright yellow suits with a black 'S' embroidered on the pocket. To our eternal shame, now! When we finished at about 4 a.m.

we'd be too tired to bother changing clothes, so we'd just pack up and head home. One time like that, it was the morning of 9 August 1963, and just after we chugged up the hill out of Burntisland we were pulled over by a police car. Two cops told us to get out of the van and unload it. We asked what the problem was, and they said there'd been a train robbery and a lot of money was involved.

They said it had happened a couple of hours earlier, and we thought it must have been at Aberdour or Kirkaldy or somewhere like that. But they said it was Buckinghamshire – four hundred miles away! And we're in a bright yellow van in bright yellow suits, mind you! We were probably the first, and definitely the most colourful, suspects in the Great Train Robbery...

Record labels were hungry. Starving. Ravenous. Brian Poole and the Tremeloes, Freddie and the Dreamers, Gerry and the Pacemakers, John Doe and the Kitchen Sink if they could sign them. They urgently wanted to present as many new faces as they could so they pounced. They were accused of visiting towns, cleaning them out of beat groups and leaving them empty. Except in Scotland...

A growing number of outfits north of the border felt they were better than the gunk being churned out down south. In Dunfermline, Manny Charlton and the Mark Five got so upset they decided to walk all the way to London in protest at the way Scotland was being ignored.

It may be true that they didn't walk so much as hitch, especially when there were no media types about – but it worked; the Mark Five were met in Market Harborough and offered a deal. Then, after one single, they were dropped. So, actually, it didn't work. And it's also worth noting that the group had completed three hundred and sixty miles of the journey, while the record company managed to make it a whole seventy miles out of London. Well done them.

Many Scots rock'n'rollers were establishing a sound that took a lot from beat, but was still in the line of sight with R&B. In the purest sense, then, the London labels couldn't be sure it would sell, and of course didn't see the point in taking a risk when everyone in Liverpool was playing exactly what would sell.

Still, it finally happened – Dean Ford and the Gaylords were signed by EMI. The Glaswegian five-piece, all around sixteen years old, had been hammering away for around two years by this point, inspired by Cliff and the Everlys. They'd started as the four-man Gaylords but added Tommy McAleese, alias Dean Ford, and changed the name to reflect the trend of focusing on the frontman. They quickly became the unquestioned biggest band in Scotland; but, underlining the problems with Scots having a slightly different approach, and the labels' unwillingness to spend money on risky moves, success down south continued to evade them.

Mick Jagger was making a similar observation about the developing R&B movement, in which, of course, the Rolling Stones were deeply involved. 'It's got to move out of London,' he told the *Melody Maker*. 'It has to spread to live. That's the only way it can become popular and retain its form at the same time.'

Perhaps, perhaps, perhaps – but in Scotland it applied more to the pop-based than the blues-based stuff. The black music influence had been alive and well for some time. When the Alex Harvey Soul Band headed for Hamburg in mid 63, they took with them the founding embers of the Scottish rock blaze.

FIONNA DUNCAN, Clyde Valley Stompers: I first heard the Alex Harvey Band at La Cave in Glasgow. I remember being blown away by Alex's amazing voice and the powerhouse sound of the band. I was thinking, this has got to be 50 decibels higher than us at our loudest – and people think we're loud! He also affirmed the fact that so many Scottish singers have a black sound.

PETER KERR, Clyde Valley Stompers: We also did a gig in The Place in Edinburgh – it was a series of old tea warehouses – there was us and the Alex Harvey Band. We were playing different parts of the club, and I remember going down the stairs and hearing what they were doing – it was fantastic! Absolutely bloody shit hot! There was no way we could go that far, but jazz has its roots in blues so we could certainly touch on the rhythm and blues side.

If you find the Soul Band album on sale, buy it. I managed to get one cheap in a really weaselly manner — I bought a cover without a disc on eBay for about a fiver, then, two years later, someone sold me a disc without a cover for about twenty quid. Total value when put together: approaching £120. Big tick!

The sleeve notes are a slice of perfect beat-scene schmoozery, demonstrating how unsure the labels were about who they were selling to: *The manager of one of Hamburg's leading twisteries was on the blower... I scrambled into my nitelife clothes and headed hotfoot for the Reeperbahn... The manager gave me a soft drink with a hard filling and a ringside seat at the twisting turmoil... I memorised the nifty twisted variations that were being ground out all around me... In my mind I'd already signed Harvey after eight minutes... Then came an interval, Harvey came to me, and we both came to an agreement... The result is this LP, recorded on the spot in that nitery.*

The shame is, the album doesn't demonstrate the Soul Band in all its glory, because most of the musicians are from Kingsize Taylor's band, due to the carve-up between the various recording contracts. Still, it clearly demonstrates the dramatic edge Harvey had already been working on for around eight years. Versions of *Framed* and *I Just Wanna Make Love to You*, which he'd later revisit and turn into Harvey vehicles for a new generation, show just how much of a performer he already was.

On 1 January 1964, when everything was still shut and 'Yer Uncle Michael's affy tired, son' was being slurred across the nation by slouched lumps on sofas, later-to-be-Sir Jimmy Savile launched *Top of the Pops* from a converted church in Manchester. Like all the other music shows, the bosses gave it a tentative one-season run, and of course it stayed on air for forty-two years. Episode one starred the up-and-coming Rolling Stones, the Hollies, Dusty Springfield, the Swinging Blue Jeans, the Dave Clark Five, Gene Pitney, Freddie and the Dreamers and no Beatles at all... well, except for the Beatles. A week later, more than seventy million people in the USA – that's a quarter of the population, fact fans – tuned in to watch the JohnPaulGeorgeRingo thing on the *Ed Sullivan Show*.

New forces were gathering to help the beat boom replace the baby boom: the pirate station Radio Caroline began broadcasting from the Suffolk coast, BBC2 was launched and the first experimental transmissions in stereo were made. In other music technology, Robert Moog's first synthesiser arrived, as did the Fender Rhodes electric piano, the Hohner clavinet and the Studer four-track tape recorder.

Prime Minister Nehru of India died, Canada replaced the Union Jack with the maple leaf, Nelson Mandela was jailed and the earliest kind of human, Homo habilis ('handy man') was discovered. Meanwhile, the earliest kind of music venue was dying out in Scotland – the ballrooms had finally fallen against the flood of cool new clubs, and in the frenzy of opening doors there were enough stage spots for everyone to get a gig. Stories abound of bands painting moustaches on because they were far too young to enter the club they were headlining. The Gaylords were ahead of the pack, but many others were starting to catch up, including the Beatstalkers.

ALAN MAIR, Beatstalkers: The singer, Davie Lennox, and I, both worked at Dalglish's as sheet metal draughtsmen. We'd been going for over a year by this point and we were doing really well

Eddie Johnstone from
the Hi Fi Combo

wherever we went. We'd end up sleeping in the factory sometimes – if you were coming back from a gig in Aberdeen at five in the morning it made more sense to go straight to the factory than to try going home first.

All the bosses took us in – *all* the bosses, the MD and everyone, and we were standing there with our heads bowed as they shook their fingers saying, 'It's not good enough – we know you're sleeping here. If it doesn't stop we'll have to let you go.' We told them we were going to turn pro, but it just sounded like a big joke to them. No one realised what a following we had all over Scotland.

They weren't the only band leaving school or work on Friday afternoon, playing five, six or more shows over the weekend then heading back to normality at 9 a.m. on Monday. The boys to entertain yoo-hoo included Glasgow's Pathfinders, Chevlons, Studio Six and MI5; Edinburgh's Avengers, Crusaders (at least two, one of them Golden) and Boston Dexters; Aberdeen's Facells, Diamonds, Jacobeats and Johnny and the Copycats; Ayrshire's Tones, Ancestors and Chase; Caithness' Rocking Stompers, Hunters, Federals and Talismen; Clydebank's Boleros and Dundee's Poor Souls.

Top venues included: Glasgow's Locarno, Majestic, Lindella, Elizabethan and Burns Howff; Edinburgh's Place, Gamp, McGoos and St Mary's Hall; Leith's Top Storey; Aberdeen's Looking Glass, Elte, Philemon, St K's and Double Two in Torry; Dundee's JM's; Ayr's Bobby Jones's; Peterhead's Rescue Rooms; and, of course Elgin's Two Red Shoes.

BRIAN HOGG, writer: I started going to see bands in Edinburgh when I was thirteen. In those days there wasn't the alcohol connection to music that you have now. The first club I started to go to regularly was called the Green Hill, in 1964. The main band was the Athenians, who were great. There was the Avengers, who were the first band I heard doing songs by Paul Revere and the Raiders – *Just Like Me* and *Steppin' Out*.

Then I started going to the Gonk and seeing bands like the Moonrakers and the Hippo People. The Place was also going at the same time – that was where Alex Harvey and the Boston Dexters used to play. The Dexters looked great with their gangster image and Tam White had a fantastic voice. Then there was Bungees, the all-nighter.

A lot of the Glasgow bands would play where I was staying, Galston in the west of Edinburgh, then move on to a venue closer to the city centre, and finish up at an all-nighter – so they'd be doing three gigs in the one night. There was a difference between the east and west coast bands... Edinburgh bands would do an obscure Kinks track but the Glasgow bands would do an obscure soul track. they were less kinda 'poppy', if you like.

EDDIE JOHNSTONE, Hi Fi Combo: The band was formed in 1965 by two brothers from Kilbirnie, Dick and Andy Sneddon. Dick was the drummer and Andy played bass. They recruited Glaswegian Kenny Munro on guitar, and a singer with an amazing range, Tommy Gray, from Lochwinnoch. They reckoned music on the Tamla Motown label would be the next big thing, at a time when most bands were playing chart covers. They began to search for the perfect organist to complete the line-up – and that's where I came in.

I was starting my second-year exams at Ballochmyle Hospital when they turned up at my dormitory room. They knew I'd been playing piano in my own rock'n'roll band, and asked me to play something for them. I took them to the recreation hall where there was a grand piano, and played the *Theme from Exodus*, plus a piece by Mozart. Then Dick asked in his strange brogue, 'Dae ye wahnt tae jine oor bonn? Wi'v bin searchin' furra perfect organist – but ye'll huv ti' dae...'

As they frightened me terribly, I declined their offer, but they offered me stardom in both Germany and Britain, a record deal and millions of pounds, which I felt was pretty generous considering they all looked poverty-stricken. It seemed a little better than the £2 a week I'd earn with my RGN Certificate. I resigned from the hospital and bade farewell to my nursing girlfriend Katie Girvan. Katie, wherever you are, I'm sorry about that scribbled note I put under your door...

Scotland was rockin' at long last – and was finally cutting discs. Despite having the first record deal, the Gaylords didn't have the first single. The honour went to the Athenians, whose *You Tell Me* was released by Waverley, a mainly traditional-Scottish label which was also the country's first independent. Soon came the Poets' *Now We're Thru*, which made it to number thirty, while the McKinleys released *Someone Cares For Me*; and later came the Gaylords' long-awaited first cut, *Twenty Miles*. But as Dean Ford and co settled in to their new homes in London, having marked their departure with a private party in the Picasso Club, the first proper Scottish rock'n'roll hit was recorded by none of the aforementioned heavyweights.

We-eeeeee-eeee-eee-eeeee-eeeee-eeeee-eeee-eee-ll.... you make me wanna...

Lulu and the Luvvers made number seven in mid-64 with their cover of the Isley Brothers' track *Shout!* starring fifteen-year-old Marie Lawrie's middle-aged vocal. Inspired when she'd heard Alex Harvey singing the number, she'd teamed up with a band called Gleneagles and they'd become the near-enough overnight sensation breakthrough act Scotland so badly needed. They appeared on *Top of the Pops* on 3 and 10 of June, surrounded by Brian Poole and the Tremeloes, the Dave Clark Five and the Swinging Blue Jeans – and did it all without tartan.

> **ANNE BROWN:** A girl my age on *Top of the Pops*? From my home town? Now you're talking! Watching the show was about the only time me and my big brother agreed on anything. I told him right there, 'I'm joining your group!' And they didn't have a singer so he let me! All I could do at first was Lulu's 'Weeell...' bit, but it was a start. Soon I was getting into the Stones and a whole world of music, but then my parents cut in – they wanted me to be a good little girl and not a rocker, and there was certainly no way I was going on stage. My brother stood up for me, but no one could talk them round, and that was that. I still do *Shout!* at the karaokes and family parties, but my brother gave up the guitar in the sixties. Parents! And I should know – I'm one now...

The Stones, by now, were the figurehead of rebellion, playing the Devil's music and corrupting the young the way Lulu couldn't. They'd had their first number one with *It's All Over Now* and there was no stopping them. An appearance in Hamilton had led to a full-scale riot when four thousand people tried to get into a fifteen-hundred capacity venue, and after a mighty struggle the police had given in and let them. As the newspapers lambasted them, they rolled on to a show in Blackpool during the Glasgow fair fortnight. Naturally enough, a goodly percentage of Glaswegians were holidaying in Blackpool at that time of year, and the latest Stones riot was blamed on 'drunk Scots', thanks a bigoted lot. Soon afterwards Jagger and his cronies would appear on the *Ed Sullivan Show*, and the presenter would promise never to have them back, only to do just that the following year.

In the UK, 1965 started with the abolition of the death sentence, the death of Winston Churchill, a ban on

EVENING TIMES

Newspaper Design Award Winner

No. 27,819   FRIDAY, JUNE 11, 1965.   Fourpence

● The Beatstalkers (left to right)—Ronnie Smith, Alan Mair, David Lennox, Tudge Williamson, and Eddie Campbell.

'BEAT' BEDLAM IN THE SQUARE

SCREAMING TEENAGERS swarmed on to the bandstand in George Square, Glasgow, to-day and mobbed a local beat group giving

They're really a riot

The Beatstalkers

BEATSTALKRAZY!

Police lose caps —and control— as fans go berserk

BY CORINNE CLARK

POP blew up yesterday. Like B-A-N-G! An explosion of teenage hysteria that rocked Glasgow's Kinning Park

At the centre of the blast was the city's own pop group The Beatstalkers.

Scores of police lost their caps and all control of hundreds of frenzied girls who went berserk and Beatstalkray

Fan goes...out

There to open a mods and rockers shop in Paisley Street, the group had to fight through 200 girl fans first. Singer Davie Lennox of Priesthill collapsed on the shop

floor — and had to receive treatment later at the Southern General Hospital.

Betta McCullough (21), who owns the shop, suffered a badly cut wrist as he tried to keep the fans from stampeding.

Later he looked around at the deep cut and said: "I don't know how I came to keep standing.

As the group toured the shop, excited teenage girls banged with

their fists against the windows and several leapt through the police barriers.

One dark haired head - scarved girl enthusiastically kissed each of the group in

turn. A blonde, who had been married half - consclous into the shop after collapsing in the crowd recovered sufficiently to shake hands reverently with each of her idols.

The Beatstalkers accepted the drammah nonchalantly.

"A great reception," commented 18-year-old Allan Mair, as he loosened his tie preparatory to battling his way back to the car again.

● The Beatstalkers did a hectic hour long session at the Dennistoun Palais last night minus lead singer Davie Lennox, who collapsed earlier when the group visited Kinning Park.

Said manager Joe Gaffney: "Davie was badly shaken up by the incident today and along with that is suffering from flu. The he felt he could not

Beatstalker goes...over

Anything goes...in grip of fan hysteria

Sgt. goes...und

THE BEATSTALKERS
Pictures by James Robertson

DAILY RECORD, SATURDAY

MIDDAY MADNESS AS FANS MOB

BEATSTALKERS

STORY BY NORMAN ROSS AND BOB JOYNER

A CHIEF constable, two squad cars and several mounties were involved yesterday when teenagers mobbed the Beatstalkers beat group at a lunchtime concert in Glasgow's George Square.

The group had to

escape through the City Chambers pursued by screaming fans.

It seemed peaceful enough at 12.30 p.m. when officers emptied for lunch and hundreds of teenagers gathered round the candy-striped bandstand.

By 12.45 p.m. came the first signs of impending trouble as a

dozen girls invaded the bandstand when the group finished their number.

Four policemen tried to control the crowd and both the police and the group appealed to the girls to behave.

12.50 p.m. The police called for assistance and two squad cars arrived in the Square. By then the girls were overwhelming the officers and climbing into, around, underneath and on top of the platform.

At 12.55, a constable hurried across to the City Chambers and consulted Mr. John Maine, sub-convener of the Parks Committee. The decision was made to withdraw the group.

By then the crowd had swelled to around 600. Other police, including "mounties," had been diverted to the Square.

HOUR EARLY

At 1 p.m. the group announced over the loudspeaker that they were having to leave — an hour earlier than they were due to finish. The girls pressed forward and overran the platform.

The group and police were bemused in an instant as overturned and chants of "We want the Beatstalkers" echoed round the Square.

Then the group made a 100-yard dash to the City Chambers as the girls chased them.

At 1.5 p.m. Chief Constable James Robertson stepped on to the pavement outside the City Chambers when one group of

girls caught up with a member of the beat team and his clothing.

Mr. Robertson helped to rescue him and take him into the City Chambers.

The boys were led along underground corridors that took them under John Street and through the Corporation's Health and Welfare Department—and emerged among a group of startled workmen in a yard off Montrose Street.

There they waited as a van was driven up.

MOBBED

They leaped in—but a group of keen-eyed girls had spotted them. The van was mobbed, but asked by police, drove off.

Later the group's manager, Joe Gaffney, said: "This was a riot. My boys have never experienced anything like this.

"I should imagine that today's carry-on may result in groups being banned in the Square by the city fathers."

Nursing a cut head, guitarist Ronnie Smith, 20, of 136 Tollcross Road, Parkhead, Glasgow, said: "We've experienced screaming girls trying to climb on to a stage and mob us before—but nothing like at lunch time. It was frightening.

"I had my head banged against a door. The Chief Constable came to my aid."

Mr. Maine said: "We will meet on Monday to discuss the future of beat groups being included in the afternoon music. I feel they will have to be withdrawn. That applies to all types of beat music."

The Beatstalkers have three more concerts arranged on July 14, 20 and August 4.

"It is a pity that the Beatstalkers have to suffer."

● FAN FRENZY . . . a fainting girl is held by police as the crowd presses forward.
(Pictures by 'Record' staff photographer Charles Barr)

Massacre town recaptured

George Square.

SUSTAINED South Vietnamese women wept over the bodies of their menfolk.

deadly battle of Dong Xoai.

130 Americans and South Vietnamese — are dead.

Retreat

But, where the Americans, in a single clash of the Vietnamese war, lost in Government hands.

At Dong Xoai force was probably less than the rated countryside by the next attack Government garrison, which razed a forces commerce more than 100 using testimony to the flame-throwers and

the dead were now, and children who, in the Viet Cong forced the defenders at their attacks, dried capital and as their bodies in

force of Americans and the remainder of 800 Vietnamese civil infantry defence troops were forced to pull back.

Every American was reminded of killed as they trudged to the district headquarters for a last ditch stand.

Medical evacuation helicopters managed to land for five minutes and pick the wounded out just after 2 p.m.

Rocket and machine - gun firing planes flew over while B-26 Air Force Skyraiders and B-57 bombers and Marine Phantoms strafed Viet Cong positions on the edge of the compound, only yards from the South Vietnamese Rangers.

Two helicopters were shot down during the operation and the eight Americans aboard are believed to be dead.

Government defenders joined the Rangers allowing the Viet

15 m.m. recoilless rifles and heavy calibre machine-gun in their attack.

The special forces camp and the artillery compound are a shambles of twisted, flattened buildings.

It is the monsoon season now in South Vietnam.

The Viet Cong are on the offensive.

Last night Vietnamese military leaders were reported to have voted against the continued rule of the Government of Dr. Phan Huy Quat.

It is not certain whether the Government will fall.

Dong Xoai, South Vietnam, Friday.

They run

---

600 BAPTISE

TV cigarette advertising and the appearance of plastic in every imaginable household object, and some unimaginable ones too. (There's a... *thing*... in my kitchen drawer that I daren't even mention to the wife in case it's for something evil and she's just forgotten to do it to me yet.)

There was another ban in place – the Shangri-Las' *Leader of the Pack*, because it was just so *Tell Laura I Love Her*. Although this time it was ITV (well, ABC and Rediffusion) rather than the BBC. The song was played on *Top of the Pops* and nothing too horrible happened. A few weeks later Rediffusion, makers of *Ready Steady Go!*, introduced a different kind of ban: one on miming.

The folk influence was returning to mainstream noise, assisted by several substances which translated it into psychedelia. At the very forefront in those early days was Scotland's very own Donovan, whose first release, *Catch the Wind*, very much caught the spirit of the coming years. So too did Bert Jansch, a doyen of the Edinburgh folk scene. His self-titled album displayed rare guitar prowess and songwriting ability, and was to lead to his direct influence on artists as diverse as Jimmy Page and Neil Young. Despite that, he'd made the album on a reel-to-reel tape recorder and sold it to his label for £99. Lulu's backing band were being backed and backed closer to the door, and when the album *Something to Shout About* came out, it was a Lulu solo album.

Meanwhile, Alex Harvey had given up on trying to be a beat hero, and had gone back to his roots to record *The Blues* with his brother, Les. The album features a cracking version of *St James Infirmary*, the song he'd been playing the day before he became a star, and as usual drips with character and attitude.

The Harveys are remembered as lovely members of a lovely family, but they were never far from tragedy. Les' band, the very promising Blues Council, was destroyed when members Fraser Calder and James Giffen died in a car crash on the way home from a gig. Their legacy was one single, *Baby Don't Look Down*.

With the Gaylords now visiting heroes, the jury was split between the Pathfinders and the Beatstalkers as to who was the biggest band in Scotland. Let there be no doubt – big meant big. Witness the proceedings in Glasgow's George Square, when the Beatstalkers decided to put on a free show for a couple of hundred fans.

ALAN MAIR, Beatstalkers: That was the wildest and most bizarre thing ever. My mum said I should put an advert in the *Sunday Mail*, but I said it wouldn't be right, and there'll be a few hundred people there anyway. So the day came and we were sitting in the manager's office, a few hundred yards from the square, and one of the roadies phoned: 'There's hundreds... there's *thousands* of people here!'

We knew the Tongs, one of the hardest gangs in Glasgow, and we asked them to get a few people there because there were only two policemen. But when we arrived we still had to fight our way to the stage! We got to play one number – but people were rushing the stage, pushing in every direction, and the Tongs were shouting, 'We can't hold them back!' The two police had gone to their TARDIS and phoned for more police, and there was a press helicopter above us, and the mounted police galloped in, and I'm thinking, 'Fucking hell, this is out of control!'

Then the police told us we'd need to stop playing, and that's when everyone went nuts. They must have been thinking, 'I want a piece of them before they go!' The stage started coming forward and the police told us to get out over the back and get into the City Chambers. Tudge and Ronnie ended up on the back of police horses – tally ho! We were very bedraggled by the time we made the 80 yards in to the Chambers. It was national news... all the papers covered it, front page and everything!

I got home before my mum finished work, and she said, 'How did it go?' I said, 'Aye, okay...' She said, 'You should have put it in the *Sunday Mail* – it would probably have gone better.' I said, 'Maybe – have you seen the paper?'

We were doing very well by then – we'd gone pro the year before, despite what our bosses had said. We'd bought a *Z Cars* car, the Zephyr 4. I used to never understand why people were staring at me, but I was seventeen, looked twelve, and I'm driving this really flashy car! We knew that all the bosses at the factory sat with the guys at lunchtime, so Davie and I drove up in the Zephyr 4 at just the right time. We didn't have to say anything – our faces told the story: 'See, we knew!' Great... but ridiculous!

We could go into McCormack's to buy expensive gear with cash, and we'd take even more cash in so we could wave it about and show off. There were girls sleeping outside all our flats... I remember crawling across the floor from the bedroom to the kitchen, so they wouldn't see me through the front door window, just so I could have an hour to myself before the doorbell started ringing. One night there were twenty-five girls in the close. We were recognised by grannies, young kids – mind-blowing! When you were on your own, with your wife or whatever, it was hard going, because you never got a moment to yourself... but when you were with the band it was wonderful. And the great thing is, it saw us through those problematic puberty years, when you don't know what to do with yourself.

MARTIN GRIFFITHS, Beggars Opera: I'd just joined this school group, the System, and we'd played our first gig at a birthday party. The fact I'd broken my collar bone, and the fact I only knew the words to a few songs, didn't put me off at all. Actually, I'd felt quite groovy with my arm strapped up and the empty sleeve just hanging there! I managed to groan my way through *High-Heeled Sneakers* and *Walking the Dog* – and I was hooked.

When I saw the Beatstalkers in George Square I knew I'd experienced a real pro group. Their stage presence, their songs, their equipment – they actually had a PA to sing through! I had to share an amp with our bass player and it gave my voice a strange kind of low vibrato when he plucked the strings. I don't remember anything about the things that happened around me – I walked away in a daze, and I remember I was trembling.

Race riots raged across America. The Beatles entered the record books by playing to fifty-six thousand people in Shea Stadium, New York. Bob Dylan was booed off for trying to play with an electric band. Great train robber Ronnie Biggs escaped from Wandsworth Prison and the Stones were fined £5 each for peeing against a wall. All these, and more top stories, were now broadcast across the Atlantic by the first commercial satellites. Radio Luxembourg improved its signal across Europe, just in time for the cassette tape to be introduced. The 70mph speed limit became law in Britain, and in Scotland, BP struck oil and still managed not to make us one of the richest countries in the world. Little bit o'politics there...

But the biggest and best moment for Scottish rock'n'roll in that era took place on Hogmanay 1965 – the pirate station, Radio Scotland, began broadcasting.

4 WE WILL ROCK THEM OFF THE BEACHES

The mid-atlantic accent came about when pirate DJs wanted to distance themselves from the stuffy kind of delivery you'd normally expect on UK radio. The style was a statement: we're a bit exotic; we want to be part of the rock'n'roll dream; we share your aspirations; we're like you. And we're most certainly not like *them*, you hip cats, you.

It began with Radio Caroline and there were others, but north of the border, and across much of England and Ireland, the happening sounds were broadcast from the mast of the *Comet*, a converted Clyde-built lightship from 1904. The plan was for a big party launch in the tradition of a Scottish Hogmanay, but after a trial of technical trickery the station managed to get up and running on 242 metres just minutes before 1966.

Radio Scotland is playing just for you
So beat the ban and join the clan
On station 242!

By broadcasting from international waters pirate stations were able to loop a loophole in the law, and thus play songs about people dying in car crashes if they bloody well wanted to. The *Comet* had four base locations in its time: off Dunbar, off Troon, off Ballywater, Ireland, then back to Dunbar. Being a lightship, and therefore having no engine, it had to be towed from anchorage to anchorage.

A Whole Scene Going On began its BBC TV run with Lulu, the Who and Spike Milligan guesting, while Liverpool's Cavern Club went bankrupt and closed down. Controversy raged about how much shorter miniskirts could go and the price of singles went up to 7/3 (35p). The USSR's Luna 9 landed on the moon, Luna 10 orbited the moon and Venera 3 crashed on Venus. With its magazine, its Clan Fan Club and regular Clan Balls all over the country, Radio Scotland was the big noise on the music scene.

DOUG CARMICHAEL, DJ: The *Comet* in the summer was a brilliant experience – although on the first couple of days I had to be relieved in the studio because of seasickness... It did take time to get used to the motion of a ship anchored three miles off the coast. But the craic on board was great. On Sunday afternoons we'd all lie nearly naked on the deck and fishing boats would come out with tourists and fans who wanted to see the ship. They always brought us presents – for instance, if someone mentioned on air that we liked chocolate cake, that's what they'd bring us!

JOHN KERR, DJ: I also remember many pop stars coming out to visit when they were playing Scotland – Cat Stevens and Gene Pitney were regulars. Once I got fairly excited about an upcoming visit from an Australian star, Normie Rowe. I'd compèred a lot of his shows so I'd been bragging to all the DJs about this tall, good-looking guy – I knew what a star he was, especially with the girls. He's still very popular today. Normie arrived out on the *Comet's* tender on a pretty rough-sea day, stepped onboard and promptly threw up on the deck. So much for the macho star I'd been portraying...

DOUG CARMICHAEL: Radio Scotland had a huge, loyal, following. The Clan Balls, especially at the Locarno in Glasgow, were hugely supported – especially when the Troggs starred, when there were people jumping onstage cuddling DJs, groups and everyone else. The kids wanted anything that was Radio Scotland – you had to make sure your trousers had a belt! As Promotions Manager I usually introduced the DJs, and that's when all hell would break out. I managed Stuart Hendry, and he got lots of gigs because he never went on to the ship due to chronic seasickness. He was always likened to a Scottish Jimmy Savile and he was amazingly popular with all age groups. I lived in the flat below his, and fans always seemed to find out his address, and they'd camp outside till he made an appearance.

EDDIE JOHNSTONE, Hi Fi Combo: Radio Scotland produced its own monthly magazine called *242 Showbeat*, at one shilling a copy. It showcased the many Scottish groups on the scene, and it was very well produced. It also documented what must have been one of the funniest quotes ever attributed to a Scottish pop star when the late great Alex Harvey, while still disillusioned by his experience of the English pop industry, said, 'The pop scene down south needs the lid lifted off to let people see the squalid mess that's squirming underneath.' I still have that copy of the magazine.

Lulu and the Luvvers finally went their separate ways, with the backing band failing in an attempt to keep going in their own right. The Gaylords released another single, *He's a Good Face (But He's Down and Out)*, but irritatingly, yet again, there was no chart action. Meanwhile, the Beatstalkers, also now London-based, were ending their Decca record deal after three technically unsuccessful releases, and moving on to CBS, with the taste of shite in their mouths.

ALAN MAIR, Beatstalkers: It was all ridiculous. Our gut feeling was, everything they were doing was wrong, but we didn't have the power to do anything about it. But you knew they'd had success so you were half-thinking, 'They *must* know what they're talking about...' We'd become Scotland's top band through our own work, and suddenly that had been taken away from us. We started doubting that we knew best. If we'd carried on doing it our own way we'd have broken through – almost all the songs we did in our set were hits two or three years later. We were finding songs from the States that no one else had heard yet – that's what the Stones were doing too. It was a very frustrating time. If the first single had been *Hey Girl Don't Bother Me*, like we wanted, it would have worked. And the worst of it is, we got the figures years later, and that first single, *Everybody's Talkin' 'Bout My Baby*, had sold two hundred thousand copies in Scotland. But there were only two chart-registered shops in Scotland, one in Glasgow, one in Edinburgh. So the charts reported sales of five thousand in the first week when in fact we'd done something like eighty thousand. It still went in at number thirty-seven, from those two record stores. UK sales only started kicking up when we'd done *Ready Steady Go!* But it should have been listed much higher.

We were so big in Scotland that we did a gig without even being there! They made cardboard cutouts

Radio Scotland's staff in late 1966:

Top row, Tommy Shields, Mel Howard, Tony Meehan. Middle row, Ben Healy, Drew Hamlyn, Bob Spencer. Bottom row, Cathy Spence, Jack McLaughlin.

Ray Evans' painting of the Comet, from which Radio Scotland broadcast

Ray Evans / Kenny Tosh

of us, and put them on the revolving stage at the Dennistoun Palais, and the idea was Davie would phone the fans when the stage turned round. It's not like they didn't know they were going to see cardboard cutouts! It was billed as 'Not the Beatstalkers'. When Davie phoned it was put through the tannoy. Some of the girls who were there told me they'd been screaming at the cutouts, then when Davie's voice came over people started screaming louder, fainting and stuff like that!

On the outskirts of mainstream, classic Scots vocalist Kenneth McKellar had a number ten hit, *A Man Without Love*, which had been the UK's Eurovision entry (it came ninth). But the rumblings of the next big change were beginning to be heard. The Incredible String Band released their self-titled debut album, planting the flowery flag for the hippy generation. Incredibly, the album had been born amid scenes of mad violence, when the band opened their own folk club in Glasgow. The band's Mike Heron later told *Beat Instrumental*: 'Gangs used to come and fight amongst themselves, the bouncers carried swords down their trouser-legs. We would usually sit there terrified – it wasn't exactly the ideal environment for us, tender souls that we were.'

Around the same time, Donovan's *Sunshine Superman* stuck an even bigger beatnik banner up, topping the US chart with his landmark electric debut. The first Scottish album to hit the top in the States is an undoubted classic, although some people accused him of being a Dylan copyist. The American release is the real version of the album; the UK one was changed because there were contract problems with producer Mickie Most. Along with the notable *Seasons of the Witch* and *Guinevere*, there's *Bert's Blues*, a tribute to Jansch. Even Alex Harvey, who was always going to be known as a rock artist, was experimenting with the hippy approach. His new-age band Giant Moth was an attempt at brushing off the pop and blues which had been delivered so well but received so poorly. Soon he was to join the band of the musical *Hair*, the showpiece moment of the Age of Aquarius.

But those winds of change were a'blowin' stronger still. As Pink Floyd completed a residency in London's Marquee Club, a young man by the name of Hendrix was beginning to cause a stir Stateside. Scots bass player Jack Bruce had left Manfred Mann and was starting to jam with Eric Clapton and Ginger Baker. The era of 'music ye cannae dance ti' was beginning to dawn.

There was still time to celebrate that timeless Friday feeling, and tracks by the Easybeats and Manny Charlton did just that. While Charlton was still Fife-bound, the Australian Easybeats were fronted by George Young, another Scot, who'd emigrated years before – and was to be the father, although actually being the brother, of AC/DC. His track, *Friday on My Mind*, made number six and has been covered many times since, not least by Bowie.

EDDIE JOHNSTONE, Hi Fi Combo: Our presentation each evening was quite notable, and we'd often outshine the chart-topping groups. While most of the chart groups liked to wander or run onto stage and plug in their guitars before facing the audience, this sometimes led to a delay in the show getting going, and it had no impact either. Dick, our drummer, identified this weakness and did something about it – so we were caked in orange stage make-up and pink lipstick, standing in position behind the curtains. Jim Finnie, our manager, would take the microphone side-stage and give us the big build up as we blasted out the opening chords to *Land of a Thousand Dances*. 'Ladies and gentlemen... It's the *Hi* – big chord – *Fi* – big chord – *Combo!*' As the curtains opened the audience saw us grinning, dancing and clapping along to Dick's drumbeat, and getting them to clap along while they sang that well-known lyric 'Na-na-na-na...'

Dick, would be thrashing wildly and shouting like a madman. Think of Animal from the *Muppet Show* and you're just about there. He was the motivator – if he caught me flagging he'd shout, 'Smile, ya wee bastard – ye'r oan stage!' Andy would normally be roaming around, hunched over his bass, but he had this peculiar knock-kneed stance when he was at the microphone. Vocalist Tommy was normally smooth and calm, but onstage he went that extra mile. I think he felt uncomfortable jumping about – it just wasn't his style. He was more Jack Jones than Jumpin' Jack Flash. Kenny was the only guitarist I ever knew who seemed to bar bar chords, if you know what I mean. He was also the best guitarist I've heard to this day. He was Pete Townsend before Pete Townsend, complete with swinging arm. He was the first guy in Scotland to get a fuzzbox, which he played on our record *I Wanna Hear You Say Yeah*. He was also the first guy with a gold-plated Gibson guitar – but on his first appearance with it he fell up the stairs on to the stage at Paisley Town Hall and dented it. Next day he took it back to the shop, complaining he hadn't noticed that it was bashed when he bought it. He stuck with a white Fender Telecaster from then on.

Meanwhile, I was restricted by being stuck behind my organ. I'd been instructed to rock the Farfisa Compact towards the audience with my left hand while holding chords with my right. That got me a punch on the jaw at one gig – in order to save time, the support band's organist let me use his organ. I was still obliged to do my thing on stage, and when I got off, he did his thing – he banjoed me for abusing his keyboard. If you're out there reading this, I forgive you – just please don't hit me again.

We had a really good fan base, like a family. I remember being quite blasé about signing autographs for the girls, but I imagine this was a result of my tender age. The manager always insisted it was part of being a pop star, although I never ever felt like anything other than a musician in a very good band. The fans would also turn up at the music shops and bars we frequented, as if by accident, and their lives seemed to revolve around the Hi Fi Combo.

We'd often pass many of the girls hitching to our gig, and give them a toot. If they were really lucky, we'd jam as many as possible into the back of the van beside the gear on the way home. We'd drop them off in Glasgow, at George Square, then head to a nightclub, usually the Picasso. Sometimes, the next day, without warning and usually at an unearthly hour, some of the girls would find their way to my parents' house. My father would shout, 'Eddie, there are some wee lassies here from Glasgow – get out of bed!' I'd be obliged to sit up chatting to them before they'd go home. They'd done a round trip of sixty miles just for an hour's chat and a cup of tea.

Every Saturday morning the place to be was Bath Street, Glasgow. All the bands gathered near McCormack's music shop, posing, signing autographs, buying gear or just window-shopping, and the fans would chat away with us while the nearby restaurant did a roaring trade from us all.

While the Beatles' US tour was swamped with outrage at Lennon's Bigger Than Jesus speech (made many months previously without any fuss), forcing him to apologise for the remark, Dean Ford and the Gaylords were moving everything along a little: from their former name to Marmalade, and from Friday evening to the following one. Their first release with the modern moniker was *It's All Leading Up to Saturday Night* – again, it didn't do well across the UK, but they were still the undoubted bosses in Scotland. And they had a hit in Holland with *I See the Rain* – so it wasn't all bad.

The Animals split up and bassist Chas Chandler fell in with a young man by the name of Jimmy James, and persuaded him to come to the UK. Somewhere on the way his name became Jimi Hendrix, and by the time December came the Jimi Hendrix Experience was the name to watch. They made their first TV appearance

Above: The Bo Weavles – George, Al, Davie, Ricky and Jimmy – in outfits which were almost certainly made from stolen curtains.
Right: The Beatstalkers – Davie, Alan, Tudge, Eddie and Ronnie – in outfits which really should have been stolen from them

with *Hey Joe* on the second-last edition of *Ready Steady Go!* (Lulu made an appearance on the final show on 23 December).

It's difficult to leave the year without mentioning a particular sporting event, but we're going to do just that... You think 1966 is all over? It is now. As the year of Scotland's light-hearted and effortless destruction of England's national football team began, new names on the music scene included the Bo Weavles, the Jury, the Beachcombers (featuring a mad wee drummer called Eccles, now known as bar owner Kenny McLean), the Chris McClure Section, the Power of Music and the Sleaz Band. All these and many others were able to take advantage of the fact that Radio Luxembourg's signal had been boosted all across Europe, and they could be broadcast and written about by Radio Scotland. Yeah, that's a healthy scene going on.

DAVE BATCHELOR, Bo Weavles: People said we were Scotland's first boy band, but the difference was, we could play. We could play music that really mattered to us, then shag ourselves to death!

To the backing of Donovan's *Mellow Yellow*, seven minutes of *Juke Box Jury* were censored as the panel exploded with fury over 'disgusting record' *The Addicted Man* by The Game; Donald Campbell died in his world water-speed record attempt on Coniston Water; The Anon changed their name to Genesis when Jonathan King signed them; Floyd recorded their first single, *Arnold Layne*; Joe Meek killed his landlady then himself; and Keef Richard's home was raided in a drugs bust, resulting in the arrests of himself and Mick Jagger.

The Pathfinders were now being billed as 'Scotland's Most Exciting Band'. Dressed as outlandish hipsters but founded on the Scottish tradition of R&B, they really did tear a hole right through the middle of club nights all over the country. They were fronted by Ian Clews, known universally as Clewsy, who developed a reputation for threatening to quit. There were other bands in the game at the time called the Pathfinders, at least one of which had a recording contract, so the band called themselves Jason's Flock for a while, before returning to their original name.

Then, like Marmalade and the Beatstalkers before them, they went south, changed their name to Trash, then White Trash, and still headline stadiums all over the galaxy. No, I'm joking – what actually happened was, they went south, the label tried to change their repertoire, a couple of singles did nothing, and they wound up being Marsha Hunt's backing band. Thanks again, London, you complete bastard squad...

MARTIN GRIFFITHS, Beggars Opera: There were so many bands and so many places to play at the time. We were out and about all over the place – but it was supporting the Pathfinders at the Flamingo Ballroom that changed us. Even the smell of the ballroom was electrifying. The Pathfinders played the soul standards their way and Clewsy was the perfect frontman... way ahead of his time. Offstage he was a very quiet man – but once up and running he became a big brash personality, oozing with confidence. To us they were just the epitome of what a group should be.

I waited outside after one of their gigs at Clarkston Hall. There was a bunch of girls hanging around the Pathfinders' van, and just before they set off there came a voice from inside: 'If ye fuck, ye can jump in!' And to my innocent amazement most of the girls did! Jump in, I mean...

BRIAN HOGG, writer: The Pathfinders always impressed, and they had that Glasgow soul thing while Edinburgh bands were doing more pop. Clewsy would be standing there, looking as cool as fuck, and it's like, 'This is a song called *Harlem Shuffle*... One, two, three...' Bang!

I maintain that their single, *Road to Nowhere*, is one of the greatest records of all time. When they did that live and you heard Ronnie Leahy's organ coming up it was just... wow! Scottish bands were light years ahead of most of their contemporaries in Britain at that time. Take the Poets – one of the greatest groups ever. It's a shame that, just through the politics of the industry, they lost out to the push given to the Rolling Stones.

Paul McCartney became the last Beatle to admit he'd taken LSD, and Hendrix started burning his guitar as part of his stage show. A BBC DJ called Pink Floyd 'a con – nothing more' and the Stones' Brian Jones was arrested on drugs charges, finally receiving a suspended sentence. With *Sergeant Pepper's Lonely Hearts Club Band* and *Magical Mystery Tour* both under production, the drug presence in popular culture was impossible to ignore.

The Incredible String Band returned with their second album, *5000 Spirits or the Layers of the Onion*. Man. Yeah. The lineup was now focussed on the duo of Mike Heron and Robin Williamson, whose choice of instruments and heavy Eastern influence made tracks like *My Name Is Death* and *First Girl I Loved* genuine icons of the moment. Underlining the 'head music' approach, Mike described it as 'a smoky record'.

Bette Davis fainted on live TV when the Who's appearance on a US comedy show resulted in Moonie's kit exploding. Brian Epstein was found dead of a drugs overdose, aged thirty-two. The Six Day War came and went while the Vietnam War stayed; the QE2 was launched on the Clyde, the USSR's Venera and the USA's Mariner probes went to Venus; and Che Guevara was executed by Bolivian troops.

It was also the end for Britain's pirate radio stations: the Marine Offences Act made their operation illegal. Radio Scotland had fought hard to survive, raising a petition of two hundred thousand signatures and even relocating the *Comet* after fines were imposed.

JOHN KERR, DJ: We'd been fined quite a lot of money for being in close proximity to Arran and the station had to decide whether to give up the fight and close down, stay where we were and continue to cop fines, or relocate the *Comet*. They decided to relocate. We were heading for the east coast, but the weather meant she dropped anchor off the Belfast Lough.

So the signal was great in Northern Ireland, but not great in Scotland. That didn't make much sense, so another attempt to go around the north coast was to be made and volunteers were asked for to stay onboard during the tow to broadcast whenever we were in international waters. I stayed on with Mel Howard and Bryan Vaughn. The tow was meant to take three days – but it eventually took ten.

We were hit with the worst weather imaginable, sheltering for a night in Tobermory Bay then going around the top of Britain one memorable night in gale force nine. It's not an exaggeration to say the seven of us, three DJs and four crew, genuinely all thought we were going to die that night. We could see the red light on the tug's mast cresting a monstrous wave every now and again, and we knew the tow line was taking a dreadful battering.

We did survive, of course, but it was definitely the most frightening time of all our lives. As we ran down the east coast, the weather turned round and started to hit us head on again. We sheltered for four nights in the Moray Firth, and the tow line actually did snap after the pounding it had taken round the top. When we dropped anchor in the Firth of Forth we literally had no food or water left, and the Glasgow papers were headlining the story we'd all been lost at sea. But we got there, and that's where we stayed for the last months of the station's life.

MEL HOWARD, DJ: I'll never forget one of those pirate picture-perfect early evenings. It was a warm summer day with no wind to speak of, and the *Comet* was sitting quietly on a glass sheet. It was bliss. The crew had finished dinner and had gone below to rest, read or tend to chores. I'd just started a taped programme that featured Garner Ted Armstrong bringing us *The World Tomorrow* – thirty minutes of modern religion, delivered like only GTA could.

I was sitting out over the bow, daydreaming, when I became aware of a low rumbling sound that seemed to be coming from the depths just a few yards away from me. I noticed a series of bubbles and ripples forming on the surface... then the bubbling became boiling. I'd never witnessed anything like it – it was like an undersea volcano was about to erupt right in front of me!

Then, up from this cauldron of seething water emerged a submarine! I'd only ever seen one in books, and now there it was dwarfing our little vessel. I was stuck – silently rooted to the spot. I hadn't taken my eyes off the scene, nor had I called any of the crew to join me. Then a figure appeared in a rubber suit, climbed out of the sub's tower, launched a dinghy, and began heading towards the *Comet*.

Back at the office, there was one absolute rule that *had* to be obeyed. Given the controversy that swirled around the presence of the pirates and the political beach ball it had become, our boss, Tommy Shields, demanded that, if we were challenged by any representative of Her Majesty's Government at sea, we were immediately to cease transmission. So I ran aft, calling our captain, Willie Fisher, and shouting, 'All hands on deck!' It was showdown time.

The naval officer asked for permission to come aboard and the skipper granted it. At that precise moment, Garner Ted Armstrong was silenced. We were off the air. The officer was up on our deck in an instant – I fought the urge to raise my hands. Surely I wasn't going to be arrested? That would be silly, wouldn't it? Finally, he said, 'Thanks for allowing me onboard. We've been doing manoeuvres in this area, and one of our exercises was to set foot on a place that wasn't a part of our vessel. So we chose you!' All thoughts of arrest vanished, a bottle of the ship's best rum soon materialised and Willie the skipper poured tots. Everyone had a laugh when our side of the story was told – and we were delighted to learn that Radio Scotland was often heard in the crew's quarters when the sub was in the area. What could be sweeter?

The bottle was emptied and our new shipmate waved his goodbyes. Garner Ted Armstrong returned to the air and Radio Scotland was back in business, doing what it did best: bringing the beat of the sixties to those above and below the waves.

I often dream of all those days and nights – they meant so much to me then, and even more so now. In a small way, it's a little like D Day – we rocked them off the beaches. With no loss of life.

The last broadcast of 14 August 1967 was an emotional affair, complete with piper, as were the wind-up clan balls held all over Scotland. As many DJs wound up with the new BBC pop station, Radio 1, there was indeed to be loss of life. Radio Scotland's MD, Tommy Shields, who was known as Mister 242, died six months after the Marine Offences Act became law. It was noted, 'We're supposed to have abolished the death penalty.'

Colour TV arrived, although the Christmas broadcast of the *Magical Mystery Tour* movie was in mono, leading to much confusion. Dolby unveiled their noise reduction system while the British-French team unveiled the Concorde. Marmalade released *Man in a Shop* and the Beatstalkers released *Silver Tree Top School for Boys*, written for them by a not-yet-famous Bowie. And at last, they were allowed to record one of their own songs, the B-side, *Sugar Chocolate Machine*.

ALAN MAIR, Beatstalkers: At least we were finally allowed to do something of our own. I hadn't actually written anything before, but the whole song came to me in one sitting – including the arrangement. And I didn't write anything again for years...

BRIAN YOUNG, CaVa Studios: When I left school my band, the Power of Music, had done enough gigs to allow us to buy our own van, PA, backline and instruments – mostly on HP – and we were even marginally profitable. We supported the Move and the Pathfinders at the Maryland in Glasgow in 1967, where everyone was wearing kaftans and the stage was covered with flowers. All really groovy! The Move were stunning with *Flowers in the Rain* and I remember wee Roy Wood standing on top of his
massive Vortexian amps to see the audience. The Maryland was great – I remember seeing Pink Floyd, Clapton with John Mayall, Jack Bruce with John McLaughlin, Muddy Waters, Geno Washington and loads of others. We supported loads of them too. Marmalade at their peak were something else. It's a shame the Arts Council haven't put up a plaque to the Maryland – Bill Garden and Willie Cuthbertson did it all with a non-alcohol licence. Although you were allowed to smoke.

After the Maryland you went up to Norman Solomon's Picasso Club... Thin Lizzy, Rory Gallagher, Writing on the Wall, Tear Gas, the Beings with Supertramp's Dougie Thompson and the Poets with Hamish Stuart were all regulars. Great days.

Right at the end of the year, Pink Floyd released *Piper at the Gates of Dawn* and experienced a disastrous US trip with Syd Barrett standing stock-still and staring blankly during live TV performances. Oh, and a wee band called Traffic Jam decided to change its name to Status Quo.

5 PROG-RESS

A very wise old editor once told me the best journalists were people who would be in jail if they hadn't found newspapers. Perhaps that same is true of musicians, certainly from the first quarter century of Scottish rock-'n'roll. Everyone viewed nights out at concerts as an escape from working-class drudgery – and for the guys on stage, at least, it stood a spitting chance of being permanent.

But in early 1968, for many of the lads and lassies who went home to the schemes of Scotland once the house lights came up, it was a different story. Some spoke with six strings wired into an amp – others spoke with five fingers wrapped into a fist.

> **MARTIN GRIFFITHS,** Beggars Opera: First time we experienced any of that was while we were taking group photos in Rouken Glen Park, and we came across a guy who'd been attacked with an open razor. When we started to play at youth clubs and school halls there would always be a gang presence. Their girls would take sharpened steel combs into the dance and we'd end up hanging on to our equipment while chairs and kids flew through the air.
>
> I remember at one dance at Stamperland, south of Glasgow, being approached by three members of a well-known gang and 'asked' to play *Satisfaction* by the Stones. It was lucky we knew it because, later on, the same guys threw acid at a couple walking near Clarkston Toll.

For veteran crooner Frankie Vaughan, the crowd behaviour at his Glasgow Pavillion show was enough to make him want to go down there and sort it out. 'Down there', in this case, was Easterhouse, and since Frankie was already heavily involved in boys' clubs (they'd sorted him out when he was a wean himself) he decided to spearhead a weapons amnesty.

Papers dripped with the story, and photo opportunities abounded. There's still a lot of goodwill to his memory – he died in 1999 – but, according to some of the kids involved, there was really very little substance to the whole event.

> **RAB S:** I can't even mind who it was, but somebody or other had started it up at Frankie's concert – it might have been the Paks. After that we heard he wanted everyone to hand in their knives. He said if we did, he'd build a community centre. We didn't care about it much, but when Frankie came to the estate we were all there to see it.

Suddenly you had TV people handing you a knife and a couple of bob, and telling us, 'Drop the knife in the bin there...' I went back four or five times. One time a guy asked the cameraman what he was doing, and he said, 'This kid's already handed the knife in – I'm just getting the shot of it.' But he'd given it to me, out a van they'd brought. They were more tooled up than any of us!

MICK SLAVEN: You could tell Frankie Vaughan's heart was in the right place. I think he'd had a hard time when he was young, so he wanted everyone to learn from him. But nobody was really caring. Even the police didn't believe it was really happening.

Nevertheless, records released by the Scottish Office in 2000 under the Thirty Year Rule, prove that the authorities were convinced there had been a 'marked reduction' in violence. Political havers? Maybe.

The Kinks released a live album recorded at the Kelvin Hall the previous April, called *The Kinks Live at Kelvin Hall*; and Status Quo released *Pictures of Matchstick Men*. You notice the Kinks' album loses 'the' from Kelvin Hall, and yet for a long time there was a 'the' ahead of 'Status Quo'? Should it be 'The Marmalade' or just 'Marmalade'? I can never decide, but the tabloid journalist's rule is, if you have two options use the shorter one. On the other hand, if I use the longer one, I'm one step closer to finishing this book and I can be in the pub. I wonder if this paragraph will be cut by my editor.

Anyway, The Status Quo and the Kelvin Hall asides, David Gilmour joined Pink Floyd and soon Syd Barrett was asked to leave. The Incredible String Band, who'd released *Painting Box*, appeared on a BBC2 show with Donovan, who'd released *Jennifer Juniper*. Love Affair admitted that their single *Rainbow Valley* had only featured singer Steve Ellis, while the rest of the band had been replaced by session musicians. They were a big deal at the time, selling more singles that year than any band except those Beatles again. In the resulting melee, the Musicians' Union banned bands from not playing on their own recordings.

As Martin Luther King was assassinated in the US, and the UK welcomed 5p and 10p coins in the move towards decimalisation, a band called Roundabout changed their name to Deep Purple and an outfit called Sweetshop shortened theirs to Sweet. Both acts represented the shape of things to come, but it was Purple's release of *Hush* in May 1968 which announced, loudly – but with maybe just a wee tiny hint of flower-edged hippiness – that heavy rock had arrived.

This time Scotland was, if anything, ahead of the game. Perhaps it's because there was a connection with taking the blues ethic and making it nastier, but there had always been a jagged edge to all but the most poppy Scots exports. More or less everyone but Marmalade could, and often did, sneer with dischord.

One of the first and most successful converts was Tear Gas, consisting of former members of poppers the Bo Weavles. Starting out as a kinda Cream-headed freeform movement, still tinged with lighter deliveries, they quickly became a powerhouse performance, and owned the student circuit in Scotland and areas beyond.

ZAL CLEMINSON, SAHB: The Weavles had been based in soul and funk while Tear Gas was much more progressive, but you could still feel those older styles underneath. 'Progressive' really was the right word, and it was probably very American too. We used to do all these stupid things, dressing up in costumes and pretending to be other bands, like Johnny Rocket and the Zoomers. And the mooning – there was lots of mooning. And we only got Chris Glen into the band because he had a long-wheelbase transit van...

While Tear Gas invented Scottish prog rock, Sweet were on their way to becoming part of what would come

Heroes of the Howff: Brian Young in Northwind, far left; and Beggars Opera posing, above, and in action with sexy white Marshalls, left

afterwards. In the interim, there was another Incredible String Band album, *The Hangman's Beautiful Daughter*. *Nightfall* and *Very Cellular Song* (possibly rhyming slang for 'long', which it is) are top moments in the head trip. People like Robert Plant were massively influenced by the String Band – he's on record as having enjoyed 'being carried away by the whole experience'. Which is what they were after.

Talking about Mr Plant – and here I must own up and admit I used to think his name was Rubber Plant, which I took as a crap joke completely out of kilter with his creative output – it's worth noting that the New Yardbirds became Led Zeppelin months after Deep Purple's debut and weeks before Cream's split (Spilt?). While Clapton and Co. felt they'd taken their music as far as they could, these other two doyens of the hard end were to prove it hadn't even started yet.

Eight-track recording decks arrived in select studios, opening up a new world of potential on tape, while Marmalade had a number thirty hit-ette with *Wait For Me Marianne*. The Beatles' movie *Yellow Submarine* premiered in London and Joe Cocker released his acclaimed version of *With a Little Help from My Friends* – arranged, note well, by a young Scots musician called Tommy Eyre, who was paid £60 for his trouble.

And, wahey, there was time for another Haggis McTartan interlude! You know you love it... As *The White Heather Club* wound to a close after ten years of Hogmanay and weekly broadcasts, presenter Andy Stewart headed for a US tour. Alas, no more would we hear 'Come in, come in, it's nice ti see ye! How's yersel'? Ye'r lookin' grand!' – but now came another chance to hear 'All the lassies shout, "Hello! Donald whaur's yer troosers?"' The thing that made Andy's performance special – bear with me here – was that during the song he'd break into Elvis and Dean Martin impressions. Those wacky kids in the States loved the old Scots pro mimicking their heroes, dressed in a man's skirt the whole time. Wheech, again.

And so, Hogmanay 1968 brought the curtain down on one wally-dugged presentation, and we could only wonder what they'd replace it with. But before that, there came the excitement we'd all been waiting for... After a long long road, gigging high and low, changing their name, risking being dropped by their label and all else, Marmalade became the first Scottish band to have a number one hit.

Amid releases which included Fleetwood Mac's *Albatross* and another strong but non-hitting Poets number, *Alone Am I*, Dean Ford and Co.'s version of the Beatles *Ob-La-Di Ob-La-Da* took five weeks to arrive at the top spot, stayed a week, dropped back for a week then returned again for two. They appeared in pride of place on *Top of the Pops*, dressed in kilts – and even I'll forgive them. Another Scots band, Cartoone, were also on the show, and Marmalade borrowed their gear to do their turn.

With respect to people like the Beatstalkers, incensed they'd never had the option to try making a hit of one of their own songs, it's worth noting that Marmalade had been given that space to create, and the results had been chequered at best. Their *Lovin' Things* was a hit in May 1968, and the band would continue to knock up top ten entries, including *Reflections of My Life*, their only US hit. Let there be no doubt – regular top twenty appearances make you a big deal, regardless of some people's perceptions that it's number one or number none; but the band's sales were inconsistent throughout their career. It demonstrates how tough it is to get it right – right place, right time, right people, right song, right cover, right budget – and helps explain why the Beatstalkers faced the problems they did. True, it was different labels, different bands, different positions; but it's certainly worth arguing about when you're trying to avoid buying your round.

Speaking of the Beatstalkers, it was all over for them. When their van was stolen they faced spending £4000 in 1960s money on a replacement vehicle and gear. But it occurred to them that, perhaps, the situation represented a hint from above.

ALAN MAIR, Beatstalkers**:** The live thing was carrying us on and people were still coming to see us, but it wasn't growing any more. We talked about replacing all the stuff we'd lost – there was no insurance, of course – and I just said, 'You know what, guys? I think it's time to call it a day.' So we did. I've always thought of these moments as the start of something new instead of the end of something old. It was time.

And we recently discovered how it had been stolen... It was a trick that had been pulled on one or two other bands, so we'd suspected it but didn't know for sure. When the van went in for a service, people who worked there took a note of the registration, made spare keys and passed them on to someone else for a fee. That only came up recently – for years some of us thought Ronnie had left the van open when he'd run into the Post Office. He hadn't known that! He was saying, 'What, all these years you thought it was me who'd ended the band?'

Cartoone, meanwhile, were enjoying an explosive start to their career. Not only had they already done *Top of the Pops*, and enjoyed the services of Jimmy Page in their studio sessions, but they wound up touring the States with the Crazy World of Arthur Brown, then doing the same thing again with Led Zep. Their guitarist had decided life on the road wasn't for him, so they'd borrowed Les Harvey from Stone the Crows. It was his second taste of international touring – he'd been out with girlfriend Maggie Bell and some of Bobby Patrick's Big Six on a tour of US air and naval bases in Europe. But this was different. Friends note how the new set of influences changed him deeply – he even changed his dress sense, and persuaded the rest of Stone the Crows to embrace his new vision. As they changed their sound from the bottom up, they moved from their pub residency towards bigger and better things, and were replaced by another act who'd end up following suit. Sadly, Les' return to his own band was the end of Cartoone.

MARTIN GRIFFITHS, Beggars Opera**:** Three years after the Pathfinders showed me how a real band should do it, Beggars Opera got a gruelling debut residency at the Burns Howff in Glasgow. We played every night and twice on Saturdays.

We were taken on by a new agency, Inter City Entertainment, run by Brian Adams and John McGlone. That was where we'd meet all the bands of the day wandering in and out: the Stoics with Frankie Miller, Agatha's Moment, Telephone, Pram, Staircase... We were the sort of progressive rock lot, I suppose, against the established pop bands of the Mac Agency. They had groups like House of Lords, the Poets and Chris McClure. But there weren't so many categories back then. You played your music and it was either rock, pop, blues, jazz or folk. We'd find ourselves on the same bill as the Bay City Rollers, String Driven Thing, Jimmy Saville or Rory Gallagher's Taste.

Your band was like your family and there was no such thing as guesting with other bands. That meant continuity, and the fans knew where they stood, and knew everything about the band they were following. A split in the group was just as painful as divorce. There was fierce competition between bands and the objective was always to blow everyone else off the stage. But it was positive competition – it made you want to be the best.

Lulu celebrated Eurovision success with *Boom Bang-a-Bang*, in a vocal delivery that really did seem incredibly global. John married Yoko and Paul married Linda, while George Harrison and his wife Patti were fined for possession of marijuana. Brian Jones quit the Rolling Stones and was found dead in his swimming pool weeks later, while Judy Garland was found dead in her London flat. The USA took the lead in the space race when Armstong, Aldrin and the other one went to the moon. Allegedly. No really, don't start me.

Hi Fi Combo: Dick and Andy Sneddon, Kenny Murno, Tommy Gray and Eddie Johnstone in the Star Palast Club, Germany

One thing we can prove without doubt happened – *or can we?* – is the Woodstock Music and Art Fair, from 15 to 18 August 1969. It didn't actually take place at Woodstock, because the location there wasn't big enough in the end; it took place forty miles away on a farm in Bethel, New York. Joan Baez, Santana, Janis Joplin, Canned Heat, Joe Cocker, the Grateful Dead, Crosby, Stills, Nash and Young and Jimi Hendrix were just some of the performers who played to an estimated half million people. During the Who's set, Abbie Hoffman rushed the stage to protest about drugs arrests, and Pete Townsend sent him flying to much applause.

Our very own Incredible String Band were there, and played *Sleepers Awaken, Catty Come, This Moment Is Different* and *When You Find Out Who You Are* to many more hordes than they'd expected. 'We were told it was a little folk festival,' Mike Heron told *Melody Maker* later. 'We only realised what it was when we flew in by helicopter with Ravi Shankar. It was like landing in the middle of a whole nation.'

BRIAN YOUNG, CaVa Studios: The Power of Music moved to Germany towards the end of 1969. We played around the Frankfurt area, and the whole experience changed us. We were doing six long nights a week in front of a well-sussed and well-stoned audience of GIs and Germans. We ended up changing our name to Northwind and signed a deal with Regal Zonophone.

EDDIE JOHNSTONE, Hi Fi Combo: Our contract stipulated that we play the Star Palast Club in Kiel, just north of Hamburg, each evening from 9 p.m. until 3 a.m. We played one hour on, one hour off, along with another band, Tommy Bishop and the Ricochets, I think. We never ever mixed with them as we always had plenty to keep us occupied. We were allocated some cold damp rooms under the club, which was actually an old converted cinema. It was owned by a guy called Manfred, who also promoted his own dancing girls called the Amstel Dancers. Now, whether it was because we were a great band – which we were – or whether it was the lure of the dancing girls, I don't know... but that club was packed every night with customers.

The main reason, I suspect, was the US Navy's housing quarters at the Todendorf base. During off-duty time these guys certainly knew how to drink, party and fight in equal measure. And they did just that – occasionally with each other, but primarily with the local guys. I mean, what else was there to do? But the nights usually went well.

One special memory I have from back then was when we were playing our instrumental version of *Summertime*. It was a slow bluesy number on the B side of *You Send Me* by Sam Cooke. Suddenly a black serviceman grabbed a mic and began singing a version we'd never heard, but managed to follow. That was a great moment. Davy Jones – are you out there?

On our return to the digs under the Club at 3 a.m., our road manager Danny had our supper ready – five small glasses of milk and five jam sandwiches. That was all we could afford until payday. At other times we'd get a hot meal from a local pub, made up of leftovers scrambled together in a pan. Thankfully I can't remember the delicacy's name... But I vividly remember you could buy anything and everything – including cream cakes – from vending machines, if you had marks.

Incidentally, the Beatles didn't invent horseplay and pranks on stage. Speak to any group who toured Germany, British or American, and they'll tell you the same. We were all involved in crazy behaviour, just to combat the boredom and strain of the long hours.

NASA's lunar lunacy inspired the Bonzos' *Urban Spaceman* and Bowie's *Space Oddity* (which wouldn't reach number one until its re-release in 1973). BBC1 and ITV began broadcasting in colour, at long last, and the year closed with Marmalade's *Reflections of My Life* making it to number three. Post-Cream, Jack Bruce released his *Songs for a Tailor* album to major applause. High points of a great set include *Theme for an Imaginary Western* and the single *Never Tell Your Mother She's Out of Tune*.

Back home in McBlighty, blues forces, mainly in the guise of heavy rock, were well and truly eclipsing all the other popular styles. Tours were getting bigger and more ambitious – try, for example, the triple-staged extravaganza that was the Jimi Hendrix Experience, The Move, Pink Floyd, Amen Corner and The Nice. Best seats in the house? Fifteen bob or 75p.

The thorny problem of violence at gigs was still far from being resolved, though. Edinburgh outfit Writing on the Wall, who were just about to follow the road to London, had embraced the situation by setting up fights as part of their set. Naturally enough, some folk felt this was a bit much; but as the era of peace, love and the Vietnam war drew to a close, Writing on the Wall did pose the question in a difficult-to-ignore stylee... Where was it all going to end?

PETE AGNEW, Nazareth: When Manny Charlton joined the band that was our classic line-up, with me, Dan McCafferty and Darrell Sweet. We'd been getting into bands like Spooky Tooth, Purple and Zeppelin, and the name 'Shadettes' was way overdue for a change. It had been cool earlier on but now it sounded like the name for some girlie backing vocal outfit... It was only at that point we thought, hey, we might get to record one day.

We did it in Trident Studios, which was pretty ahead of the game. We'd never been in a real studio until then, and when we saw all the gear we thought it looked like it could send us to the moon.

Soon after that we played our worst gig ever. It was also our first gig ever outside the UK, in the Stadthalle in Nuremberg, Germany, supporting Rory Gallagher. His fans were all togged out in the denim gear but we were dressed like Kensington Market Christmas trees, with the spangly gear and platform shoes. We were late getting on too... When we heard the crowd whistling we thought, 'Hey, they're really getting up for the show!' But then we were told whistling is bad news in Germany.

We discovered how bad when we hit the stage. They booed every number and threw what we thought were paper cups – but when we came off we discovered they'd been throwing steel knuckle joints for scaffolding! The only good thing was, they'd all had lousy aims... Funnily enough, Nuremberg is now one of our favourite towns to play, and has been for years.

Stone the Crows released their third album, *Teenage Licks*, which featured a new lineup (minus Jimmy Dewar and John McGinnis, plus Steve Thompson and Ronnie Leahy) with old hands Maggie Bell, Les Harvey and Colin Allen. The record was a gradual movement away from their debut and its follow-up *Ode to John Law*, as the band attempted to capture their live vibe better. Lulu guested on several tracks as 'Wee Marie' – she later revealed that she and Maggie had recorded a song with Jack Cream Bruce, John Zeppelin Bonham and her then-husband Maurice BeeGee Gibb. Imagine that one, if you please...

Tear Gas had also changed line-ups, and now featured drummer Ted McKenna. They were promised big things as Stones manager Tony Calder backed them and they experienced the pleasure of a sixteen-track studio. It wasn't all plain sailing, though.

TED McKENNA, SAHB: The studio was a dead room, terrible for ambient drums, and it made me overplay. I was so tense and nervous I remember thinking, 'I can't play any more.'

DAVE BATCHELOR, Tear Gas: I'd just become a singer – we needed one, someone had to do it, so it was me. But it just freaked me hearing my own voice back and I couldn't relax. I was blown away by the big business connection – the cover art was done by Hipgnosis, who did Floyd's stuff. I can listen to it now and find a lot of pluses, but not then.

ZAL CLEMINSON, SAHB: *Woman for Sale* is still a great song to play, and on the album it winds up with the kind of energetic thing we'd do at gigs. And the middle-eight of *I'm Glad* shows how good a singer Dave was – when he could hear himself properly...

TED McKENNA, SAHB: It ended up quite an interesting album – it's still worth a listen.

As Lennon put the finishing touches on *Imagine*, and McCartney began putting Wings together, Jim Morrison was found dead at the age of twenty seven in his Paris flat. Sweet released *Co-Co* and Slade released *Get Down and Get With It*, while T.Rex were back at number one with *Get It On* and the Who's

Won't Get Fooled Again made number nine. Movies to see included *A Clockwork Orange* (if you could see it), *The French Connection* and *Fiddler on the Roof*. The Upper Clyde shipyards closed and unemployment began climbing across Scotland. Floppy discs were invented and direct transatlantic dialling was introduced. And the fate of Little Baby Don's mama and papa, who'd gone far, far away, was immortalised in Middle of the Road's *Chirpy Chirpy Cheep Cheep*.

KEN ANDREW, Middle of the Road: The extremely severe criticism we suffered from the British music press always comes to mind, but on the whole it passed us by – we were too busy working outside the UK to notice it much. The culprit, of course, was that inflammatory song, *Chirpy Chirpy Cheep Cheep*. It's been loved, hated, ridiculed, praised but mostly blamed for bringing European pop music into ill repute. As if it needed it, by the way!

The responsibility, however, must be laid at the feet of the music business and the record-buying public in the early 70s. Thanks to them, the group's career was blighted by this feathered musical parasite which feeds off the weaker elements that make up musical taste.

The truth is, apart from Sally, we had to be plied with a considerable volume of alcohol before being persuaded to perform it. When we completed the recording we had no idea where we were, never mind that it would prove to be so popular.

We did try to reduce the impact of *Chirpy* by quickly releasing other recordings with more intelligent lyrics: *Soley Soley*, *Sacramento*, *Tweedle Dee Twee* — oh, perhaps not... But they just enhanced *Chirpy's* popularity.

So, I would just like to say how saddened I am that a Scottish pop band has been cruelly labelled as responsible for foisting such a song on the unsuspecting public. But, a word of consolation: thirty-five years on, we're still being forced to sing the bloody thing on a regular basis.

Mind you, as I sit here, with a wee dram and my copy of *Saga Magazine*, what's that I hear from the radio next door? 'Where's your mama gone? Far far away...' You know, listening to it through a foot-thick wall, it almost sounds – well, ethereal... Nurse! Nurse! The bed pan, please...

Ah yes... I call it the *Delilah* syndrome. I'm sure in my time I've caught most of the SAHB crew, including myself, staring at a setlist gaffered to a monitor or a cymbal stand or the stage floor, seeing nothing but that one-word title and thinking, 'Aaaaaaaaaw fuck!' But, hey, you pay us, we're here for you. And it *is* a terribly good dance, isn't it?

The lighter end of Scots music was getting a fair airing, and in the coming months it was to enjoy even more; but when an Edinburgh band released its first single and made it to number nine, no one could have foreseen where it was going to take them. The word 'mania' was about to be bandied about again as the Bay City Rollers debuted with *Keep on Dancin'*.

Middle of the Road came back with *Tweedle Dee Tweedle Dum*, rather incredibly a song about clan warfare; and Marmalade visited number six again with *Cousin Norman*. Just around this time, Beggars Opera had the pleasure of experiencing the nastier side of competition between bands.

MARTIN GRIFFITHS, Beggars Opera: It was our first big open-air show, in Germany with people like Rod Stewart, Family, Rory Gallagher, Deep Purple and Stone the Crows. We were sandwiched between Fleetwood Mac and Black Sabbath. Mac were going through a bad time and were about to change personnel and have huge success with *Rumours* – they didn't go down well with the punters that evening. We were nervous about following them, but the time was just right. It was turning dusk and the stage lights were just coming on. I must say we rose to the occasion – they loved us. *Time Machine*, from our second album, *Waters of Change*, had been played a lot on Radio and TV. That was a big help and we went down a bomb!

Black Sabbath followed us, and they had a hard time, but we didn't think much about it and left for the second part of the concert in Vienna. Apart from having to make an emergency landing at Frankfurt, where apparently I turned a delicate shade of green, we arrived fresh and raring to go. But while we were in the dressing room we were told that certain management from a certain band – let's call them Darkest Sunday – didn't want us to play that night. Our manager went to sort it out, and came back a bit shaken. He told us a loaded pistol had been laid on the table... so, we didn't play!

I spent the evening full of Austrian beer hidden behind Rory Gallagher's Vox AC30. He was just a complete gem – I met him again years later, when he wasn't well and I was on what turned out to be my last single. But we had a laugh about that night in Vienna.

As the Average White Band formed from the ashes of the Vikings, Gene Vincent died at the age of thirty-six of a burst ulcer. Slade got to number one with *Coz I Luv You*, and Rod Stewart had a double whammy of number ones on both sides of the Atlantic with the single *Maggie May* (which he could never understand) and the album *Every Picture Tells a Story* (which he could).

The year closed as the Montreux Casino in Switzerland burned down during a Zappa concert. Watching the drama unfold after they'd made their own escape, Deep Purple recorded the event in the song *Smoke on the Water*. So at least it didn't burn down in vain.

In January 1972 T.Rex took the chart's top spot again with *Telegram Sam*. Other top ten hits included Slade's *Look What You Dun* and Sweet's *Poppa Joe*. Both the compact disc and the video disc were unveiled and Jethro Tull spread a story about their new album, *Thick as a Brick*, being based on the poetry of an eight-year-old boy who'd won a competition but been disqualified for using a four-letter word, 'g—r', on TV. All shite, of course – Ian Anderson's sense of humour has always been underestimated. Midge Ure's first band, Salvation, started up, and Frankie Miller's first solo album, *Once in a Blue Moon*, came out.

ROLLIN' JOE: Now, if you want to hear a real rock'n'roll band, try Shakin' Stevens and the Sunsets. That's the real rock'n'roll underground. I was in them for a few months. They were playing in the John Street Tech in Glasgow but they didn't have a piano player that night, and I knew they normally had Ace Skudder. So I said, 'Look, I can play a bit, let me try out...' I remember it was a Sunday morning and the whole band, Shaky and the Sunsets, all trooped round my house to hear me play! So I gave it a bit and they said, 'Yeah, you're in.' It was great – what an experience!

So then I was down in Wales working away with them, and it was so good to be in a genuine band again. But I had to jack it in – I just couldn't afford it. I never managed to get a band that good together. I tried for years, but either people couldn't play well enough, or they could but didn't want to.

SHAKIN' STEVENS: That was a long time ago! I do remember Joe, though – he was a really hot piano player, as well as a really nice guy. I don't know what his neighbours must have thought about us all turning up – but we needed to be sure! And it worked out fine. It was great having a Scot in the band – helped make those great Scottish gigs even better. We always went down a storm, especially in the colleges and universities.

I met Gordon Campbell when we played Stirling Uni. I say met, but it was more found – he was lying on the dressing room floor, a bit worse for wear, so we looked after him until we left the campus. Gordon ended up writing *Because I Love You* for me years later, and we still keep in touch to this day! And he co-wrote *Radio* with another Scot, Bob Heatlie. Bob also wrote *Cry Just a Little Bit*, *Breaking Up My Heart* and the classic *Merry Christmas Everyone*. Scotland's still a great place to visit and play gigs!

While Marmalade were back with *Radancer*, a surprise Scottish single went all the way to number one, even keeping Elton's *Rocket Man* off the top spot, and doing the same thing to Alice Cooper's *School's Out*, even though it was his label's biggest-selling single ever. But *Amazing Grace*, played by the Pipes and Drums and Military Band of the Royal Scots Dragoon Guards, was the best-selling single of the year.

PETER KERR: When I was young I was in a pipe band, marching up and down the streets of East Lothian, collecting money to keep the band going. I remember playing for the Queen's coronation – seven in the morning through until God knows what time, and it was utter purgatory. People don't realise you're doing all these agricultural shows, garden parties and so on for nothing – it's a real labour of love.

After the Clyde Valley Stompers ended I got into producing albums through the Waverley label. I didn't know anything aside from what I'd seen George Martin do when he'd produced us. What I *had* learned was, you don't interfere. If the musicians are good and well prepared, let them get on with it and keep your ears open for things they don't catch because they're too busy playing. There's no need to be a dictator – but if people do turn up and aren't taking it seriously or can't do the job, they're out on their ear. I think that's a good way to work.

All the American companies were setting up in the UK, instead of having licensing deals, so they were serious about building up their own catalogues, including the military stuff. They wanted it fast – they wanted a dozen or so British ethnic albums quick. In those days you had to do an album in a day.

So I was told they wanted a pipe band – and there were none available. But I'd heard the Royal Scots Greys were heading home after a stint in Germany. They were stationed there with their tanks because we still had the threat from behind the iron curtain. So I said, 'How would you like to record for RCA Records?' And they said, 'We'd like to record for anybody!' Fortunately the military band and the pipe band were both good, so we did one of each.

The regiment was to be amalgamated, it was becoming the Royal Scots Dragoon Guards, and the commanding officer wanted to do a *Farewell to the Greys* album, but RCA said no. I went back and they said, 'Okay, if you can guarantee the regiment will take the first two thousand copies, and you can produce the album on a budget that those two thousand sales will cover, okay.' So basically I was working for nothing.

We went into the barracks with a portable studio, with just one day to record, and at the end we were a few minutes short. They said, 'We've been messing about with this Judy Collins hit.' So I said, 'Okay, go!' and they played *Amazing Grace*. We put it in the can in one take. When I sent the tapes to RCA I said, 'Take a listen to that last track – everyone here got a buzz from it.' They phoned and said, 'Have you gone mad up there, asking us to release a single with fucking bagpipes on it?'

Then the DJ Keith Fordyce played *Amazing Grace* on his military spot, and the BBC got so many

RICKY GARDINER   COLIN FAIRLEY   LINNIE PATERSON   ALAN PARK   GORDON SELLAR

BEGGARS' OPERA

Beggars Opera: Far left, Ricky Gardiner with the Strat he used when he later worked with Bowie and Iggy Pop; above, the Linnie line-up; left, the Waters of Change line-up featuring Virginia Scott

calls and letters and passed them all on to RCA. Then they said, 'Maybe you've got something there, Pete...' Oh, really! The demand was so great that every plant in Europe was involved in pressing those singles. The last figures I saw, including compilations, was thirteen million copies! It shows you how much record executives know about anything...

In May, Stone the Crows' Les Harvey was killed on stage when he touched a live microphone. Right at the beginning of the band's set he went to explain to the audience at Swansea University's Coming Out Ball that there was a small technical hitch; but as soon as he made contact with the mic stand he was thrown into the air. He landed with his guitar touching the live connection, and bandmates and crew all received shocks as they tried to save him.

His elder brother, Alex, was to spend the rest of his career wary of electrics. And his career was about to enter its most successful period, as he formed the Sensational Alex Harvey Band with Tear Gas.

TED McKENNA, SAHB: Not much was said about Les – no one really knew what to say. It didn't really come up until we played in Swansea ourselves. It was one of the first nights everything had come together for us, and I went into the dressing room and Alex started to cry. It was all very emotional – he didn't normally let out like he did that night.

CHRIS GLEN, SAHB: I thought it was very brave to call us 'sensational', especially since we weren't – not until after the first album anyway... But Alex's point was, if we call ourselves that, then that's what we've got to be. So we were always trying to think of things that made us bigger and better. It worked.

Slade's Noddy Holder got into trouble with the law when he was arrested for allegedly using a couple of fruity phrases on stage in Glasgow. It seems the naughtiness in question had been uttered not by Noddy, but by a member of their support act, Status Quo (changed days indeed). Quite a rivalry existed between the bands at the time, but Noddy was a good sort who didn't grass. Later, his management acknowledged that he'd been known to use unacceptable language, including lines like 'Are you all pissed?' and 'Have a good feel of each other'. Straight to hell, Holder...

The drama can only have helped *Take Me Back 'Ome* make it to number one. Sweet got to number four with *Little Willy* (who's being rude now?) and Bowie's *Ziggy Stardust* album turned heads everywhere. It seems that every time Slade released a single, Sweet did too – and it continued when the former had a number one with *Mama, Weer All Crazee Now* and the latter a number four with *Wig-Wam Bam*.

The Watergate scandal began to unfold as five men were arrested trying to bug the Democratic National Committee HQ in Washington, the first-ever email was sent (it was an advert for an 'online pharmacy'), and a Scotsman, Bryan Malloy, invented the antidepressant Prozac. *Singalongamax* records arrived, as did the rollercoaster three-album re-release whammy from David Bowie: *Hunky Dory, Space Oddity* and *The Man Who Sold The World*, all of which charted high. Maggie Bell was voted fourth best singer in the world in a poll, sharing the position with Jagger (Lennon won). And the Royal Scots Dragoon Guards were back with a top-twenty version of *Little Drummer Boy* to wind the year up.

MARTIN GRIFFITHS, Beggars Opera: I left the band in 1972 – the family had broken down. It seemed like we were always on the road, but we were making very little money. Management was paid, roadies were paid and repair bills for equipment and vans were paid... and after that there wasn't much left. I remember a European tour where the drummer, Ray, and I lived off tins of mince and beans we cooked ourselves at the side of the road with a primus stove, just to save money. We hadn't yet discovered the joys of Currywurst... Our management should have jumped on these problems, but they were too involved with their other groups. It was too late.

I'd planned to give up performing but I ended up back onstage, this time in a tux, singing swing in cabaret clubs in Manchester. It had always been an ambition of mine – I remember a journalist writing 'Beggar man influenced by Sinatra' when I was still with the band.

Then I moved to Germany. I hadn't realised how popular we'd been there. I sang in a Bavarian cafe and someone said, 'Hey – you sound just like Martin from Beggars Opera!' So I decided to take advantage of the situation, and started supporting groups on tour including Osibisa, Vinegar Joe, Brian Auger, Exception, Golden Earring and the Scorpions.

I auditioned for the German group Can, who were into total improvisation. I must say I was lost for something to contribute, so as a joke I started singing *Somewhere Over the Rainbow*. They thought it was great – but I'd already decided it wasn't for me. I found it difficult to sing for other bands after leaving Beggars. I did disco for a while, and I'm still singing now.

ROCKY GARDINER, Beggars Opera: We lived Beggars Opera twenty-four-seven in 1969 and John Waterson of the Burns Howff gave us real support. The crowd were Saturday-morning happy and just lifted us with their great vibes. A man in a white suit got us a deal, and off to London we went to record our stage performance Act One. It was all over in two days and there was lots of talk about big money – where did it all go?

Glasgow Art School took us to their hearts. We loved the Picasso, the Paisley Watermill and up north from Tain to Sanquar. Parkie used to sleep on his organ pedals in the keyboards van, and Virginia slept on top of the mellotron. It gave us a bigger classical sound, and that's when you could hear something new was starting to happen. The possibilities seemed endless – the *Waters of Change* album was birthed on it. We had an incredible arrangement of Ravel's *Bolero* which was never recorded but used to get the crowd very spaced. Travelling with a mellotron wasn't easy – we had a techie with us who used to have to rebuild it nearly every night.

After the blond singer abdicated, we were blessed with the magic voice of Pete Scott. With classical training and an amazing facility to improvise blues, he was the best of all our singers – he'd a magical presence and a long snake which he used to drape round his neck, and he made a home brew that induced legendary hangovers.

Linnie Paterson was our only Scottish singer. He was a great performer – but he was to pass away from an illness related to working in an asbestos factory. He had a good heart and was a real Aries – fiery, energetic and full of life. He could really rock and stylistically he was on his own.

Listening through to all our MP3s, what have we got? Melody and riff, buffoonery and opera, and the supernatural all recur. Music just being itself. It's all in keeping with the psychopathology of the life we led and lead. What's happening, what you're hearing, what you're seeing, becomes *you* and is then absorbed and recreated. The music is just what happens.

The serial number of my Strat is between the serial numbers of Jimmy Hendrix's two favourite Strats. As well as all the Beggars Opera albums, I used it on Bowie's *Low* and Iggy's *Lust for Life* when I was beamed up to their world. I wrote *Passenger* on it.

Progress of prog: Top, Tear Gas version one (Batchelor, Campbell, Munro, Cleminson, Glen); right, version two (McKenna, Cleminson, Glen, Batchelor) opposite page, SAHB's early promo shots (McKenna, McKenna, Cleminson, Harvey, Glen and McKenna, Cleminson, Harvey, Glen, McKenna). Now say it ten times fast.

7 ROCKIN'... AND ROLLIN'

Giants. Despite the huge range of Scots talent across the years and genres, it's not all that often we've had giants. Big stompy musical muscle-machines that stride the globe and turn everything tartan... sometimes quite literally. The mid seventies was to be Scotland's first era of giants.

To start 1973, Sweet jammed out a single when Slade didn't, and finally got to number one with *Blockbuster*. Singer Brian Connolly – cousin of Mark McManus who would later star as Tough Glasgow Cop Taggart – was officially one of the bosses of Glamworld. After having lived through too much of the traditional label control, they'd crow-barred their bubblegum output into a harder-edged wrapper, squeezing and squeezing until they achieved the number-one vibe they knew they'd always had. The band's Andy Scott later claimed their extreme fashion sense had only come about so they could chat up legendary *Top of the Pops* dance group Pan's People in the make-up room.

NEIL KING: Andrea, Babs, Ruth, Louise, Dee Dee and Flick... What can you say? We all learned about the birds and the bees off them. You watched the show for them. You listened to a lot of guff because Pan's People were dancing to it – you even put up with those DJs acting like that uncle everyone wants to ignore at parties... These days you have music videos that cost millions to make. But it would be better if Pan's People – well, okay, Pan's People's Granddaughters – were dancing. They were so sexy, but they had that innocence too. All those pop princesses or whatever they call them... they don't have that. It'd be better if they did.

Meanwhile, some of Eric Clapton's superstar friends had got together to bring him out of his drug-induced semi-retirement. At a triumphant comeback at the Rainbow in London, he pulled himself up and pulled all the stops out, and got himself back together. His support act for the evening was the Average White Band, and it was an important night for them too.

ALAN WILTON: The Whites were great that night. There was a funny vibe in the audience because everyone knew Clapton had been clapped-out. We were all wondering what we'd get. I wasn't really interested in a support band, and I don't think anyone else was. But they rose to that challenge and really got the audience going, and the applause they got was genuine. That got them enough attention to head off to America, get a good record deal and eventually make it really big. After that tough night opening for Clapton, they deserved it all.

Elvis's *Aloha from Hawaii* concert was broadcast by satellite – around one billion people tuned in. That's, like, a quarter of the world's population, thank y'very much, ma'am. Thin Lizzy's *Whiskey in the Jar* was a big hit – a fine early achievement, but nothing compared to what was to come later. The US finally announced its complete withdrawal from Vietnam, and on being told mid concert, Neil Young stopped the show to announce, 'Peace has come' – which was slightly wishful thinking, sadly.

Pink Floyd's *Dark Side of the Moon* began a long stay in the album charts, while single-buyers handed over wodges for slices of sonic pleasure including Slade's *Cum On Feel the Noize*, T Rex's *20th Century Boy* and even *Duelling Banjos* from the movie *Deliverance*. Amid the cacophony, Stone the Crows bowed to the inevitable and split up – they'd replaced Les Harvey with Jimmy McCulloch, but of course the dynamic had been altered and things just weren't the same any more. It must have been a tough time for Maggie Bell, balancing the pressures of missing her man, wanting to keep the dream alive and having her own ambitions. She finally announced she was going solo to begin work on her album, *Queen of the Night*, and that was the end of the band.

Alex and his Sensational Alex Harvey Band, on the other hand, were entering their most glorious era. While still at work on their second LP, *Next*, they took a break to appear as the opening act at the Reading Festival, and took the opportunity to unveil one of their new songs.

TIM MARNIE: Just around the time Tear Gas started working with Alex, I was heading down south to start as a professional roadie. We were having a big send-off in the pub the night before – one of the things we were talking about was, will Tear Gas work out with this new singer? Nobody knew much about him, but I was a wee bit older than the rest of the lads, so I'd seen him back in the day. I could see that it might work.

So I'd started hearing these stories about SAHB, although we all still thought of them as Tear Gas with a new singer. I was working at Reading and that was the first time I saw them. First thing was Zal in the make-up – I just thought, 'Och, for fuck's sake!' But then you saw how he was bouncing off Alex, and it was adding a new level to the show. Then you saw Chris in the spacesuit, and you just went, 'Yeah...'

CHRIS GLEN, SAHB: They had a poll on Radio One recently and I was voted the wearer of the third-best codpiece in rock! The guy from Cameo and Ian Anderson from Tull were ahead of me. Fair do's! But the thing is, the codpiece didn't come about by chance. That big Fender bass is a heavy fucker, and the way I played it I kept bouncing it off my 'nads. It was either come up with something to protect me, or goodbye family jewels...

TIM MARNIE: I've read Zal's comments about the magic moment when they started playing *The Faith Healer* for the first time. Well, I was there, and it really was magic. Alex was at the front of the stage shouting, 'Let me put my hands on you!' Then there was this spooky keyboard sound. Chris and Zal were standing right behind him like his henchmen. You could have heard a pin drop. Then it just built up into a bigger and bigger vibe.

I've been round the world a couple of times since then but I've never seen a moment like that – when a whole festival became just one big unit. Every one of those punters must have gone out and bought *Next* when it came out.

Said album killed off the doubt which lingered from SAHB's first release. While *Framed* had mainly been a collection of Harvey standards, many of which had been in his set since the fifties, the new offering was very much a modern rock album. *Faith Healer* and the title track both indulged the band's penchant for theatrics, and there was still time for a tribute to Alex's early days in the form of *Giddy Up A Ding Dong*, which was originally a hit for the first rock'n'roll band to play Glasgow, Freddie Bell and the Bellboys.

Hard rock news continued with Nazareth's first top-ten hit, *Broken Down Angel*, from the breakthrough album *Razamanaz*. They had two other hits that year, *Bad Bad Boy* and *This Flight Tonight*; and despite a wide variety of ups and downs, never looked back.

PETE AGNEW, Nazareth: We'd been told that our next album had to do it or it was all over with the record company. We were okay, though – we knew we had the goods. But we had no idea how big *Razamanaz* would become. There's a mixture of feelings – elation and relief. And of course we went from playing clubs to sold-out concert tours. All the equipment manufacturers suddenly wanted to give us things free that we could now afford anyway...

One of our last club shows was in Paris. We'd done a song on the big French station, Europe 1, and ran into Jerry Lee Lewis, so we asked him along to the show. When we finished he invited us to his table with his wife – what was it, number fourteen or fifteen? And there were three monster guys who didn't say a word.

The drunker he got, the nastier he became, until he eventually tried to hit our drummer, Darrell. We all jumped up – and immediately felt a pain in our shoulders. It was the no-speak guys – they had us clamped and told us quietly and calmly that, yes, Mr Lewis was an asshole, but it was their job to protect him, so why didn't we just leave with no fuss? Anything to stop the agony in our shoulders!

As we were going up the stairs, Eddie Tobin, our manager, in true Glaswegian style, turned back and pointed at Jerry Lee. 'See you! Ah know you – ah'll get you!' We all cracked up. 'Eddie, he's Jerry Lee Lewis. *Everybody* knows him!'

Junior Campbell hadn't liked the taste Marmalade left in his mouth. (I know how he feels – it's just wrong, like crunchy peanut butter or orange juice with bits in.) When he'd quit, he more or less thought it was the end of his pop career, but he was wrong. He'd been writing, arranging and producing for other people; but when he wrote *Hallelujah Freedom* he realised he didn't want anyone else to record it. Same went for *Sweet Illusion*, which made number fifteen in the summer of 1973.

The defining moment in the history of Stealer's Wheel came with the hit *Stuck in the Middle With You*, which made number eight in the UK and number two in the States – and of course enjoyed a lot more chart action when it featured in *Reservoir Dogs* a little later on. Main operator Gerry Rafferty had quit the band, but came back when the single did so well. He'd previously been half of folk duo the Humblebums with Billy Connolly, but he was never really a folkie – and, as it turned out, Connolly was never really a musician. Staff at Unicorn, his management company, recall the conversation where it was agreed – 'The stuff Billy does between songs is better than what he does during the songs.' They told him so, but he didn't go for it and soon left the entertainment industry. An'at, know?

Talking of Unicorn Leisure... You remember how the average home only has seven books in it? Well, here's another argument for extending your shelf: *Apollo Memories*, by authoritative and definitive writer Martin Kielty. It's great, and probably needs a slightly bigger pedestal than *SAHB Story*, available in lots of good bookshops, some crap ones and from a dodgy online outfit split between Camden and Dundee who nicked a couple of boxloads from a tour bus in 2004. (That was my wages, lads, so thanks.)

Unicorn had been in charge of the Mayfair, then the Electric Garden, then expanded into agency and artist management, and were looking for the next punty-up. Under the direction of boss Frank Lynch, they bought the lease on Green's Playhouse and took just over three months to turn it into Scotland's most important rock'n'roll venue. They renamed it the Apollo after the famous Harlem venue; or they renamed it the Apollo after the space missions; or they renamed it the Apollo because the sign cost £250 a letter and it was the shortest decent name they could come up with. Anyway... over the next thirteen years it became the place to play – not just in Scotland or the UK, but damn near everywhere.

RICK WAKEMAN, Yes**:** Scotland was pretty badly served by the rock industry. Scottish venues were often where you just went to do warm-ups before a tour officially started. The Apollo put a new spin on that – the audiences got a better deal than anyone else, because they'd hear and see a much longer set than the one that would end up on tour. Plus they would hear it first. It was good for the band too because the Apollo audiences were so honest – they told you what they thought of the show.

The venue was to host everyone who was anyone in its time. Alphabetically the bill ranged from ABBA to Zappa, chronologically it started with Johnny Cash and wound up with the Style Council. Some people always called the place Green's – the owners' slogan could still be seen in the dyed carpet – while others called it the Purple Palace, after the gaudy glittery paint which stuck itself all over you for days after a visit. It was also famed for its ripe smell and poor backstage decor; but it was the audience, the Glasgow Choir, that brought the bands back again and again. Despite how music fashion ebbed and flowed, and regardless of album sales, live audiences in Scotland seemed to entrench themselves in blues-based rock. The Apollo era stretched well into the 1980s, and all that time the most popular draws were Status Quo, AC/DC, Uriah Heep and SAHB, with most of them etching up over a dozen appearances and Quo in particular topping two dozen. It's all in the book and on the website, www.apollomemories.com. And I'd like to take this opportunity to apologise to Robert Fields and Scott McArthur for keeping hold of their photos for so long. I'm not as bad as Russell Leadbetter, I hear...

On the wider Scottish scene, something of a supergroup appeared, although the phrase was out of fashion by the mid seventies. They were called Blue, and they featured a bitter ex-Marmalade soldier, a Poet who'd lost his muse and a Pathfinder who'd found the road to London paved with shite. Blue's intentions were to lose the cabaret vibe enforced by London labels and put good songwriting back into the mix. By the time the line-up had settled round Hugh Nicholson and Ian McMillan, they were doing just that. *I Wish I Could Fly*, from their first self-titled album, is a spiffing piece of work, and has bog-all to do with Orville the duck.

The year closed with hits including *Ballroom Blitz* (Sweet), *Radar Love* (Golden Earring), the drum-tastic *Dance With the Devil* (Cozy Powell) and the ever, ever, ever bloody everlasting *Merry Xmas Everybody* (Slade). And on the stroke of Hogmanay, in Sydney, Australia, an Oz band with more than a touch of Scottish influence called AC/DC played their first show.

Come 1974, the miners' strike was biting hard across the UK. The speed limit was reduced to 50 mph, street-lighting was dimmed and there were restrictions on using heating in workplaces. The government enforced a three-day week, leading to 885,000 people registering as temporarily unemployed. By the end of January 1.5 million people had had to sign on. Naturally there was a knock-on effect in the music business, including a number of cancelled tours by foreign acts. The tapes kept rolling at Abbey Road Studios, though, because it had its own generator.

Classic Nazareth line-up:
Pete Agnew, Manny Charlton,
Dan McCafferty, Darrell Sweet

Left: SAHB promo material; above: Brian Young in CaVa version one; below: Brian in CaVa version two

The first number one of the year was also the best-selling single of the year – Mud's *Tiger Feet*. Runners-up in the January charts were Sweet's *Teenage Rampage*, Lulu's *Man Who Sold the World* and the Wombles' *Wombling Song*. The Loch Ness Monster was photographed, allegedly, and Peter Benchley's novel *Jaws* was published. (If you know someone who pronounces 'novel' like 'nuvvil', destroy them now.)

Meanwhile, the Average White Band's career wasn't quite working out as they'd hoped – a trip to the States had resulted in average sales for their debut album, and their label suddenly dropped them. They decided that, instead of heading home, they should take a gamble on New York and see what happened. One quick meeting with Atlantic Records later, they had a new deal. See? Sometimes it *does* work like the songs say.

John Martyn enjoyed his finest hour to date with his sixth album, *Solid Air*. As well as showcasing his unique vocal it was a package stuffed with rare emotion, including *May You Never* (later covered by Clapton) and the title track, which was an ode to his friend Nick Drake, who, sadly, would succumb to a depression-related death before the year was out. In an interview at the time Martyn explained how his music career had come about completely by accident – he'd been sixteen and only been playing for three months when he was coerced into filling a half-hour support slot for Hamish Imlach. Hamish just kept having him back.

Lena Zavaroni's rise to stardom was slightly more arranged – she was groomed for it after being discovered singing with her family at a club in Rothesay. At ten years and a hundred and forty-six days old, she's still the youngest person to have a top-ten album, and the youngest star to do *Top of the Pops*. Lena went on to great things, including her own TV show in 1980; but she was to die as a result of anorexic complications, aged just thirty-five, in 1999.

Sonny and Cher began divorce proceedings, Mel Brooks' *Blazing Saddles* lit up cinema screens, and the last Japanese soldier surrendered twenty-nine years after the end of World War Two. Mariner 10 sent photos back from Mercury – but there was a completely different Mercury on everyone's mind by March – the Freddie one. Queen's *Seven Seas of Rhye* thundered into the top ten and announced the arrival of one of the UK's biggest and best musical exports. One ex-Beatstalker was very relieved.

ALAN MAIR: When the Beatstalkers finished we were all twenty-one or so, and even then you were thinking, rock'n'roll is a game for the kids. I had a wife and a son, a couple of the others guys were married... You really do think it's time to get a proper job.

I wound up running a stall in Kensington Market, making leather boots. It did very well – at one point everyone was wearing them. There's photos on album sleeves with the whole band wearing my boots! And I remember sitting in a wee cafe in Amsterdam, a wee place with a clothes workshop, and I overheard someone saying the zip had gone on one of his boots. I realised it was a pair of mine, so I said, 'I'm Alan Mair, give me the boot and I'll fix it for you!' I used the wee workshop in the cafe and it was no problem. It turned out the guy was the bass player from Golden Earring, so that was me hanging about with them...

I had Freddie Mercury working in the stall with me for a couple of years. He used to tell everyone he had a band going, and it wouldn't be long before he turned professional. A lot of the folks from the market went to see their first show – and they were terrible!

People remember Freddie for his moments like Live Aid – but back in the beginning he was a very awkward performer, and he had a tendency to sing sharp. I've always been very critical of live gigs anyway, but it was a bad show. He'd been telling everyone, 'I'm going professional soon, I won't be working with Alan for long...' and here was Queen, just not very good at all! The conversation at the pub afterwards was, how are we going to tell him? But in the end we just couldn't bring him down. I really thought that was that, until one day I was listening to the radio in the van and thought, 'What a great song...' I couldn't believe it when the DJ said, 'That's a new band, Queen, with *Seven Seas of Rhye*.' I arrived at the market and told Freddie, 'That's it, you'll definitely be turning professional soon.'

Years later when they headlined the Rainbow I told him what I'd thought about that first show. He was shocked: 'Whaaat?' 'Yeah, it was pretty dire...' 'Oh well – I'm glad you didn't say then!'

The stall gave me the best camera moment of my life, although I didn't have a camera on me. I'd known David Bowie since the Beatstalkers did his song *Silver Tree Top School for Boys*. We used to go to gigs together. Just after *Space Oddity* was a hit he came to the stall, and I thought maybe he was looking for a pair of boots. 'No,' he said, 'I just came to say hello – I haven't got any money!'

'You haven't got any money? You've just had a hit record! Och, just have a pair – I'll treat you. Here, Freddie will fit them on for you.' What a photo that would have been!

Nazareth made number thirteen with their *Rampant* album and the Scottish World Cup squad released *Easy, Easy*, making number twenty. Now *that* wouldn't happen today, would it? But the big buzz was another mania, this time of the Rolling kind. As the summer went on, more and more kids – well, okay, girls – succumbed to the outbreak. Within an eight-week period Les McKeown and the band went from half-full clubs to sold-out halls, twenty-foot protective barriers, crowd crushes and helicopter escapes. It seems strange to relate the insanity to a reasonably sedate figure of just four top ten hits during 1974, although the album *Rollin'* got stuck in the charts for over a year; but it's a demonstration of how well all those events were manipulated by the band's management.

SUSAN CLEARMONT: I had *everything* – the singles, the stickers, the posters that said they were 'kissable size'. I fell out with my best friend because she fancied Woody too. Sorry, Helen,

wherever you are! We all went to see them on their first big tour – we were still talking then – and on the night I noticed that, if you fainted, you got taken backstage. So I decided... I'm going to faint! I fought my way up to the first few rows and made sure one of the security men was watching, then just fell over. I was terrified – as soon as I was pretending to be unconscious, I had to keep my eyes closed, and I had to let the crowd drag me around. I nearly fainted for real!

Then I felt myself being lifted up and out, and I could tell I was over the barrier. I really wanted to open my eyes and try to get on the stage – Woody was only a few feet away from me by now – but I knew I'd be in trouble, so I kept on play-acting.

Next thing I knew I could feel fresh air. They weren't letting you backstage at all – they were taking you out of the hall! Soon I was standing in a small crowd of crying girls, who'd obviously all had the same idea. They let us back in at the back of the hall but there was no chance of getting near the group again. Asides from the kissable posters, that's the nearest I ever got to Woody...

STEVIE HUNTER: I thought the Rollers were great, but you couldn't really say that, could you? I saw Les McKeown when he was in Threshold and I thought he was good then, so I was into the Rollers before the girls were. Come on – what's wrong with *Bye Bye, Baby*? Perfect pop music, and it took them round the world, so you can't just write them off.

MARIE BRYSON: People talk about the Rollers all the time, but they forget Slik – they were all the rage too back at the start. I remember seeing both of them on the same night. That was a young Scots girl's dream come true. And Midge Ure looks better than Les these days...

DAVID PATON, Pilot: I didn't leave the Rollers on the brink of success without thinking it through. I came to realise I didn't want to be a Roller – no matter how successful they'd become. There was no Les, Woody or Eric in the band when I'd been there, but I still saw the way it was going. I didn't want any part of it. I did find Rollermania quite amusing, though! I got on well with Alan and Derek and they were always very confident it was going to happen for them. When it did, I knew how happy they were and how much dedication it had taken.

The Rollers had always made a point of avoiding the heavier and harder Glasgow circuit, correctly viewing it as incompatible with their pop aims. That's not and never to say they couldn't have done the do amid the long-haired rockers, no matter how challenging it might have been. But the long-hairs were having their own problems, because Glasgow promoters were trying to shunt them in the direction of Les and the lads.

BRIAN YOUNG, CaVa Studios: Northwind's album sold twenty thousand copies in 1972, but due to the usual poor management control we made nothing financially. We'd gained a lot musically, though, and we had some great support gigs including Yes, Free, and Fleetwood Mac at the Green's Playhouse before it became the Apollo. We headlined a concert at Wolverhampton Civic Hall when Deep Purple couldn't make it. But the fun came to an end when Glasgow promoters started insisting that everyone should play disco. Some bands kept going, but only by giving up Scotland. Sad...

After that I'd started a band called CaVa with singer and drummer Kim Beacon, who ended up going to London with the new String Driven Thing. CaVa Studios began in my basement – I had a Revox two-track tape recorder and I borrowed a second one. It was initially set up to record my own music, but word got around, and I ended up with a business recording other people's music.

President Nixon resigned under the weight of Watergate, the Moody Blues opened the first quadraphonic studio in the UK, Lord Lucan did a runner, Muhammad Ali defeated George Foreman in the Rumble in the Jungle, the Beatles were finally legally split up and *Monty Python's Flying Circus* wound down.

Meantime, the Sensational Alex Harvey Band released their third album, *The Impossible Dream* – although it was actually their fourth. Phil Wainman, the man who'd given Slade their sound, had produced *Next*, but he wasn't available for the next project and so the management had brought in Shel Tamby, who'd given the Who their early sound. To say the relationship was a disaster would be to say the Scottish Parliament went a wee bit over budget. The job was nearly finished by the time everyone realised it would have to be binned.

CHRIS GLEN, SAHB: Shel Tamby just didn't work out. When we were energetic, he was laid back and, when we were happy with something, he wanted one more take. He was definitely on the way down as well – all his best work was behind him. It just couldn't be saved, and the management finally agreed. The thing is, Hugh Padgam was the tea-boy on those sessions, and now he's one of the world's most famous producers. We should have given him a shot! After that disaster we got Davie Batchelor in. He'd produced other albums and he did our live sound, plus he'd been in Tear Gas with us – who better? We should have thought of that in the first place...

The year ended with a flurry of Christmas singles – inspired, no doubt, by Slade's success the previous year.

While Mud had the top spot with the Elvis-esque spoof *Lonely This Christmas*, would-be festive frolics were released by the Wombles (*Wombling Merry Christmas*), the Goodies (*Father Christmas Do Not Touch Me*) and Gilbert O'Sullivan (*Christmas Song*). And have another Bygraves album on me – *Singalongamaxmas*. No really, you shouldn't have. It's worth mentioning the Faces' last offering of 1974, since it's the longest-titled single of all time – *You Can Make Me Dance, Sing Or Anything (Even Take The Dog For A Walk, Mend A Fuse, Fold Away the Ironing Board or Any Other Domestic Shortcomings)*. Try selling that on eBay.

Come 1975, January started with *January*. The Pilot song, I mean. Yes, I've used that line before in at least one book and several magazine articles, but it really is incredibly satisfying. The band featured David 88 and fellow ex-Roller Billy Lyall, and while it also featured a very catchy line in multiple-part harmonies, Pilot's construction had a beauty worthy of being called classical music. They'd already hit with *Magic*, but the LP *From The Album of the Same Name* failed to do so well. Oh, oh, oh, it's tragic... Some bands are cursed with being thought of as album bands, while the opposing curse can be just as bad.

> **DAVID PATON,** Pilot: The Rollers would never have been a long-term commitment for me. I saw it as part of my apprenticeship. Tam Paton, their manager – no relation! – had his dream and he was definitely pulling the strings. It wasn't my dream... I achieved that with Pilot. Writing a worldwide number one is surely the goal of every composer.
>
> Billy Lyall was the sound engineer at Craighall studios in Edinburgh and he asked me to play bass and guitar on his songs, and in return he'd play piano for me. We were very lucky to have plenty of studio time to develop our recording skills. We did the first album as a three-piece with Stuart Tosh on drums. The demos had the same ideas and similar sound to the finished work we did with EMI. *Magic* was always a hit song, even as a demo. I'm a Beatles fan and always have been, so I suppose Lennon and McCartney had a big influence on my writing, thinking, and ideas for my songs.

While Steve Harley and Cockney Rebel hit with *Make Me Smile (Come Up and See Me)* and Telly Savalas did the same with *If*, the Average White Band made number six with *Pick Up the Pieces*, which also did well in the USA, and led to their self-titled album reaching the same height in the album charts a few weeks later. The Whites were noted for having achieved a grip of soul that was almost suspiciously good for their ethnic background; but now they went further still, developing a feel for the funk-fuelled phenomenon that led to the ABBA-powered disco era.

The Bay City Rollers finally had their number one, *Bye Bye, Baby*, marking the height of Rollermania – in the UK at least. Say what you like about the Rollers – go on – but there's something very pleasing about easy rhythms and smooth harmonies which, if you can't love, you really shouldn't pretend to hate. They did indeed wear a bit of tartan, but made it cool enough for the coming punks to adopt too, and got us a good bit away from the legacy of Harry Lauder and chums.

> **DAVID PATON,** Pilot: *Bye Bye, Baby* is a really good song and there was no stopping them once that took off. My attitude might have been different if I hadn't had success on my own, but I'd written *Magic* by then and had every confidence in my future. I hated the limelight – I was a lot happier working in the background with mainstream artists, like when I played bass for Elton John. I wanted to be a successful musician but I could live without the fame.

David runs his own studio in Edinburgh and he's still in demand as a singer, songwriter, producer and bass player. Look out for a soon-to-be released CD of Pilot demos – info at www.davidpaton.com.

The middle of the year was the dawn of the summer of SAHB. They were on the road in the USA when two things happened: the mafia stole their guitars and a release they hadn't known about made the top ten, requiring them to belt home for *Top of the Pops*.

CHRIS GLEN, SAHB: We woke up and the truck was gone – simple as that. Turned out it was a pretty standard trick with some family people, if you know what I mean. Then we got the telegram: 'Single's in the top ten, you need to come back quick.' Hold on – what single?

The whole story came out. We'd asked to have our show at the Hammersmith Odeon recorded because we had some new systems in and we wanted to have a listen. Our manager, Bill Fehilly, had heard the tape and said, 'Get that out there as an album, and get *Delilah* out as a single.' They needed a hit – they'd tried everything including having people like Errol Brown writing songs for us. You should have heard that shite...

But we knew there'd be a problem – as soon as you have one hit the label needs another one, and you're on a conveyor belt until you fall off, or you're pushed. We only ever did *Delilah* because we wanted something we could do a stupid dance to. The fans loved the dance we did with *Runaway* and *Delilah* was meant to replace that. End of story.

So they had to fly us first class for once, which cost £1200 a ticket. I woke up on the plane, still pished, and opened my shutter to see this beautiful sunrise. Suddenly a trolley-dolly leaned over and shut it again, but I was like, 'For £1200 I'll have my fucking sunrise, thank you...' She said, 'No, you can't, sir, the Indian Ambassador (or whoever) wants to sleep.' But he's paying the same as me! So in the end they let me have the run of the upstairs bar, just to get me out the way.

TED McKENNA, SAHB: I was recently talking to someone I'd known thirty years ago. She was saying, 'I couldn't remember why I didn't like your band, then I heard *Delilah* on the radio and then I remembered – I don't like comedy bands.' So that was us, a comedy band. I don't think we ever shook that off with some people.

Och, it's not all that bad, of course. You can't not play a song the fans want to hear – ask the Who to drop *My Generation* and they'll be first to say 'Eff off'. In any case, it's completely in context live, with all the drama and humour elements in the right place.

The release of the top-twenty *Live* album helped set the scene a little better – although it's worth noting that bootlegs of the entire concert show how experimental the sound system was that night. Even people in the industry were originally confused about the band's intentions, though; Les Reed and Barry Mason, who'd written the song for Tom Jones, sent SAHB their next effort as if they were now in the market for cabaret-esque material...

SAHB, of course, are a live band. You don't get the half of it when you don't stand in the room with them. During 1975 and 1976 they were the biggest-grossing live act in the UK, and if you wanted to know why, you should have been at the legendary Christmas Shows at the Glasgow Apollo. I've written enough about those nights in other places, but let me assure you I, and the hundreds of people I've spoken to about it, don't use the word 'legendary' without pause for thought.

COLIN McBURNIE: I attended all the legendary Christmas shows at the Apollo, but I only tried going down the lane to meet them once. Alex came out the stage door leaning heavily on a walking stick, and he was being supported by a blondish female, who I presumed to be his wife. I went up to them for autograph but she said, 'Alex isn't feeling very well'. He didn't look it either, so I turned my attention to the rest of SAHB as they came out and piled into a long white limo – the first I'd ever seen in real life. I got Zal's monicker on the back of my concert ticket, to go along with Billy Connolly, who'd been sitting in front of me on the balcony. As the limo pulled away, Zal leaned out the window and screamed, 'Tongs, ya bass!' Nice, eh?

Rod Stewart's *Sailing* cleared the decks, while silly season starred Jasper Carrott's *Funky Moped* along with Windsor Davies and Don Estelle's *Whispering Grass*. Naz enjoyed another couple of hit singles, *My White Bicycle* (fourteen) and *Holy Roller* (thirty-six), while SAHB squeezed in a cheeky wee number thirty-eight with *Gamblin' Bar-Room Blues*. US President Ford survived two assassination attempts and Malcolm Fraser became Prime Minister of Australia – leading to the Scots rhyming slang 'malky' for 'razor'. Charlie Chaplin was knighted, NASA's Viking 1 headed for Mars, Pol Pot took over in Cambodia, North Sea oil began to flow through the pipelines and Maggie Thatcher began flexing her muscles as the new Tory leader.

Billy Connolly's spoof of Tammy Wynette's *D.I.V.O R.C.E.* became his only number one, backed up by strong albums *Cop Yer Whack of This* and *Get Right Intae Him*. Lennon's *Imagine* and Hot Chocolate's *You Sexy Thing* hit, along with another bumper crock of Christmas crap: *Gonna Be a Cold Christmas* by Dana, *Christmas in Dreadland* fae Judge Dread, *Make a Daft Noise for Christmas* out of the Goodies, *Santa Claus Is Coming to Town* via the Carpenters, who really should have known better, and *Let's Womble at the Party Tonight* courtesy of Mike Batt's lovable fluffy monsters.

BILLY RANKIN: Mike Batt wrote *Bright Eyes*. I told him it would never be a hit.

The Only Ones

Left and above: the Only Ones featuring Alain Mair on bass; below, the Jolt early promo material

WISHAW'S New Wave group, The Jolt, have just released their second single on the Polydor label.

The group — Iain Shedden (drums), Robert Collins (lead guitar and vocals), and Jim Doak (bass and vocals) — have

"What'cha Gonna Do About It?"

The Jolt have just completed an extensive series of dates with Generation X and now have embarked on a major tour with the Motors which should encourage interest in their debut

group had a successful gig at Queen Margaret's Union in Glasgow and they are working their way back south until the tour finishes on May 27.

TAPPING

deserves. Like many records, you may have to listen to it several times before it starts your feet tapping.

The Jolt have been doing well in the south and this single could revive the following they have in Scotland.

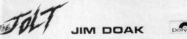

JIM DOAK

8 PUNK

The revolution *nearly* came in 1919. The Russian civil war was in full swing and the Soviet Union was about to be created, and all over the world governments were nervous. When striking Clydeside shipbuilders raised the red flag in George Square, the authorities' response was heavy-handed in the extreme: overnight, Glasgow became a city under siege by English troops, tanks and machine gun posts. No one trusted Scottish soldiers not to side with the strikers, and chances would not be taken.

Perhaps you don't know much about all that. The tale of the tanks in George Square isn't much of a chunk of anyone's education these days, even though it should be. Now that the bravery of the men shot for cowardice in the trenches has been recognised, it's probably time the Red Clydesider era was re-addressed...

Anyway, my point is that modern Britain has always managed to stamp down any attempted revolution, during four centuries of everyone else getting away with them. It's been said that the underlying reason is the force of middle-class politics; back in 1707, the English government was able to buy Scottish nobles' votes to push through the union of parliaments because, secretly, everyone has their price.

Or maybe that's just shite. There's no doubt that punk – the real actual what-we-all-call 'punk' punk – *was* a revolution, and it did sweep quite a lot of rock'n'roll away. Like the skiffle and beat revolutions before it, punk told a bored young population: you can do this; it's for *you*.

This revolution came in mid 1976. I know I said I wouldn't do that tsunami thing again, but the music beach was quiet – *too* quiet – as the sea rolled away and waited for something to happen. Early chart-toppers that year include Slik's *Forever and Ever*, Marmalade's *Falling Apart at the Seams*, Tina Charles' *I Love to Love*, Brotherhood of Man's Eurovision *Save all your Kisses for Me*, the Wurzels' *Combine Harvester* and the Real Thing's *You to Me are Everything*. But none of that was the news – by this time the music press was buzzing about the Sex Pistols. It was a buzz that, certainly in the beginning, didn't mean all that much up north. There was a certain Englishness about the whole thing that meant its take-off in Scotland faltered. But once we'd worked out our own angle on the new and very good idea, we ran with it – although, at brass-tacks level, we were all being Jock Tamson's bairns.

ALEX OGG, writer: The myth that a lack of musical ability was a barrier to participation was taken to heart. But, being Scotland, there was a natural resistance to swallowing the London phenomenon wholesale. When the Valves sang *Ain't no Surf in Portobello*, they weren't talking about West London, but their local sewage treatment works. The concept of tackling regional issues was also embraced –

take Exile's ferocious assault on local 'Fascist DJ' Tom Perrie for his refusal to play any punk or new wave records.

Many, notably the Prats, Scotland's take on Eater, were schoolkids having a go. Some Scottish artists headed south to London – Midge Ure almost becoming a Sex Pistol, Alex Fergusson joining ATV and John McGeoch, arguably the most innovative guitarist of the period, are three such examples. Others never got out of the bedroom.

Looking from the outside, Scotland's punk revolution by and large mirrored the key elements of its southern incarnation. The DIY and anti-authority ethics of records by the Pistols and Damned were snapped up by eager teenage hands. Others were already loaded up on Ramones and New York Dolls imports. And just as in London and elsewhere, there were working bands who saw the chance to break out from the confines of the pub scene. Examples include the Zones, Zips and Exile in Glasgow, while the Edinburgh scene was split between more arty bands like the Scars and Freeze. The east-coast prole punk threat was based around Blair Street's squat scene, whence came the Axidents, Badweeks and, eventually, and tragically for all concerned, the Exploited.

ROBIN SAUNDERS: If the Edinburgh punk scene could be said to have a heart, it would have to be the Blair Street practice rooms. Not a healthy heart by any means – its arteries clogged with the grime of centuries and the accumulated sinking damp of the city's spectacular rainfall. To spend time there was to guarantee a respiratory complaint and, for the hypochondriacs among us, fear of bubonic plague.

Think about it: you're the leaseholder of the last building on the left of South Bridge, where planning regulations forbid any kind of structural alterations, where only a couple of measly windows admit any daylight and where most of your floor space is sited underground. What do you do with it? You rent it out for band practice space, fill the place with scruffy rockers unlikely to raise any objections to the conditions, grateful for somewhere – anywhere – to crank it up without any neighbours to annoy. Then along comes punk and suddenly every kid and his dog wants to be in a band. You find yourself sitting on a goldmine, and you milk it for all it's worth.

The Rezillos undoubtedly headed up the early punk movement in Scotland. From very early on, there was a general but more-or-less secret ban on punk in the Glasgow area, overseen by people we now just know as politicians, but in those days called themselves the City Fathers. Doesn't that phrase make you want to hit something? (I just lost the '~' key from my keyboard with an angry thump but it's okay ~ I never use it.)

They'd banned the Pistols, of course, but the first whisper of a wider policy was when a Glasgow councillor tried to have the Ramones' *Now I Wanna Sniff Some Glue* suppressed. In later years the Tubes and the Stranglers would be banned from performing, with top penpusher statements like: 'Glasgow doesn't want anything to do with these sex people.' Still, acts like Johnny and the Self-Abusers, the Jolt and the Zones made it out of the west to join a burgeoning scene which wasn't any worse than anything that went before.

The difference this time was everyone seemed to feel something was happening. When skiffle came along there had been an impromptu and honest burst of passion: 'Oh *yeah*, I like that!' When beat moved in it turned heads from people who hadn't been expecting it: 'Wow, that's better than this!' When heavy rock arrived it clicked into place in seconds: 'Okay, that's where I wanna go next.' But punk came about the other way round – folk were already queuing up: 'Will someone please bring us the next thing? *Aah* – thank you! Been waiting for that... Let's go!'

Another difference was that this one really did scare the olds. The kids said, 'We don't know what we want but we know how to get it.' and the adults believed them. Like the Teddy boys of the late fifties, probably just four per cent of the punterage was really looking for a fight but, because of They All Look The Same To Me (a deep-seated attitude that decades of political correctness just won't crush), it made sense to send the tanks back into George Square – or at least send a memo round *from* George Square.

As Alex Ogg points out, though, many punk musicians had already been in other types of bands. Alex Harvey himself was once known as the world's oldest punk, and was generally credited with having predicted its arrival. Back in 1972 he'd said, 'Some young guy is going to come out with something and freak everybody out. Someone's got to come along and say, "Fuck you! All your ideas are a load of wank. *This* is where it is!"'

ALAN MAIR, The Only Ones: Eventually I had to go back to music. My wife at the time couldn't understand it. I think a lot of people's partners can't understand when you realised you have to go back. Especially since my business was doing so well – everyone was like, 'Why are you quitting?' I had to – I just had to.

Mind you, it was right in the middle of the dinosaur rock thing. I remember going to see a supergroup and thinking, 'Yeah, it's good, but it's so old hat.' I tried out with the Streetwalkers but I very quickly fell in with the Only Ones. The sound, Peter's voice, the songs – I just liked the whole package, but it didn't occur to me it was ahead of its time.

But people *really* didn't like us at first. It took them a while to make sense of it. Then I remember going to see the Pistols – a lot of people say they were there, but I actually was. It was exactly what we'd been needing. And I realised we were on top of that.

The winners always get to name the battles and write the history books, but we all know there was more going on than just punk. Disco, rock and good old classic pop music were still buzzing away, filling the charts week in, week out – and there were no punk singles on sale anyway.

Donna Summer had *Love to Love You, Baby*, Robin Trower released a live album, the Bay City Rollers had *Love Me Like I Love You*, Brian Ferry had *Let's Stick Together*, T.Rex had *I Love to Boogie*, Billy Connolly had *No Chance* and Elton John visited number one for the first time with *Don't Go Breaking My Heart*, duetting with Kiki Dee. One hundred and three hostages were rescued from a plane in Uganda, Paul Kossoff and Agatha Christie died, and there was a heatwave across the UK.

MARTIN GRIFFITHS: I met Ralph Siegel of Jupiter Records in Munich with a bunch of songs I'd written and an idea for a cowboy musical. I came away with a recording contract – not for my songs, but for a new life as a disco performer! Ralph was riding high with a US number one, Silver Convention's *Fly, Robin, Fly*, and Frank Farian was recording Boney M just down the road. There were new discos opening by the hour all over Germany. It even had its own disco and DJ organisation – playing their annual gala was a must.

I recorded disco versions of *Dock of the Bay* and *Israelites*, but the recording company let me write the B-sides. *Israelites* was a hit, so I was invited to play the gala after Grace Jones. She rushed in with two body guards, sang *La Vie En Rose* then rushed out again to tremendous applause – not an easy act to follow!

My disco career lasted a couple of years. It was great but I realised how plastic and pointless it all was when I was asked to sing *Israelites* in a film made about the pleasures of the Ibiza disco scene.

Brian 'Robbo' Robertson

I was flown out to Ibiza along with four guys from the film crew and a hundred of the loveliest Playboy Discogirls. Things started to go wrong as soon as we arrived. Sponsors had failed to come up with the readies and what was to be a kind of advertising documentary had to be changed to a musical extravaganza. Luckily I had copies of my other singles and my guitar, so they ended up featuring all I had – plus a song I'd composed on the way called *Oh Ibiza* – which was my last single. I continued to compose and perform – now I mix singing with my son's band Alias Eye and singing with the JOB Big Band, complete with evening suit and bow tie.

Benny Gallagher and Graham Lyle, who'd left McGuinness Flint some time previously, enjoyed a successful run with their album *Breakaway*, and two hit singles, *I Wanna Stay with You* and *Heart on my Sleeve*. Spookily, all three offerings made number six in their respective charts. It was promoted with a white label EP bearing the hand-written inscription: *For producers only... The folks at Irving/Almo Music consider Paul Simon the greatest composer of contemporary songs in the twentieth century. For the past fifteen years his consistency and genius is unparalleled. We believe he has some competition now. If you'll take fifteen minutes and listen to these songs by Gallagher and Lyle we think you'll agree with us. Need we say more?*

Phil Lynott's Thin Lizzy had been in the wars line-up-wise, but the band broke through at last, bringing with it the twin-guitar sound which was to inspire the new wave of British heavy metal a few years later on. And guess what? Like all the best tricks, it came about by accident, part-engineered by Scots six-stringer Brian Robertson.

BRIAN ROBERTSON, Thin Lizzy**:** I joined the band soon after I'd been fired from a music shop for nicking records and guitar strings. The guy's wages were crap, so I thought, 'I'll pay myself!'

I met Lizzy when they were a three-piece, although I didn't meet Eric Bell that time. They were staying at a hotel just down the road from my house. My best mate, Big Charlie, was roadying for them, so I went into the hotel bar after I finished a gig. I ended up sitting down with Phil and Brian Downey and we had a lot to drink. I went to Downey's room and we went through lots of blues stuff – he was hitting the bed with sticks and I was playing my guitar without an amp.

When Eric Bell left they started holding auditions, and Charlie said, 'Remember that mate of mine from Glasgow?' So I got a train down to London and ended up staying in a squat with the roadies for about a month. I got the last audition – Phil was going to call it a day. Downey remembered me straight away from the night in the hotel, and we just took it from there.

I think Phil wanted to keep it a three-piece but Downey and I wanted another guitarist. Being honest, I don't think I was good enough to carry it as a three-piece! I didn't have the equipment either. I think if it came round again I'd have kept it as a three-piece – you have the equipment for it these days.

I'm a very lazy player, as you know – I can't be bothered playing chords and stuff, so I'd always be looking out for hook-lines and melodies to play, because they're much easier to do and more difficult to fuck up. So the thing is, if you have a nice strong melody, it's natural to add a harmony to it. And that's really how it came about. After that we just kept saying, 'Remember what we did on that song? Let's try it on this song now.'

But it does have a very Gaelic, Celtic thing about it. Phil's writing was very warm and personal so it's not a surprise the playing went that way too. I mean, I can't speak for Gorham, being a Septic, but for us Scots and Irish it was true...

'Septic tank' = 'Yank', in case anyone's in any doubt. Lizzy enjoyed their top moments in the punk era, with hits including *Jailbreak* (thirty one), *Don't Believe a Word* (twelve) and, their crowning moment, *The Boys Are Back in Town* (eight in the UK, twelve in the US). The track has been listed as the 499th of *Rolling Stone's* 500 best rock songs of all time, fact-fans.

As has been noted, a lot of by now traditional concepts failed to survive the punk era. Glam died on its arse and for a short time even the Beatles couldn't get a look-in. Lizzy made it through, though, being treated as gods among the young pretenders, as did SAHB – who, sadly, managed to destroy themselves instead.

Their greatest chart moment came with *Boston Tea Party*, a track which celebrated the USA's bicentennial, and did so with controlled fury and a kicking rhythm. The story goes that even DJ Tony Blackburn felt the wrath of Harvey by daring to shorten the band's name. While recording for *Top of the Pops*, complete with a plastic teapot and cup, Blackburn announced, 'The Alex Harvey Band.' And Alex bellowed back, 'Haw, Tony, it's the *Sensational* Alex Harvey Band!' as take two was prepared.

The summer of 1976 proved to be their greatest time. Despite having just completed their own UK tour, they were added to the Who's four-date stadium tour to top up ticket sales. Normally promoters wouldn't touch a band who've just been out, because only a small percentage of fans will want to see them again so soon – not with SAHB. The jury's still out on whether they or the Who were the best band on the nights.

DAVID BOYES: When they played Parkhead, it was the first time a lot of Rangers fans had ever shown faces there – you have to remember things still ran deep back then. Alex was telling all the bands they'd better not be shite because he had four hundred cousins in the audience. Then, just as SAHB started, a big cloud of smoke wafted across the pitch, and some bluenose shouted, 'That's it, Alex – burn the fuckin' place down!'

CHRIS GLEN, SAHB**:** This is one of my favourite stories, which I tell even more often than the other ones... Harvey Goldsmith was promoting, and he'd arranged for 30,000 salads to be on sale at the show. I told him, this is Glasgow – put on pies and Bovril! But he went with the salads, and had 26,000 sitting at the end of the day. He left them in Celtic's boot room – can you imagine what it must have been like when they went in at the start of the season?

Soon afterwards, SAHB's manager Bill Fehilly died in a plane crash. He'd been a fixture in rock'n'roll for decades, and was credited as being the only man who could control his protegé. Alex, having lost his brother in 1972 and now his closest friend (as painfully recited in the lyrics of *No Complaints Department*), started dipping badly and never recovered. SAHB's final album, *Rock Drill*, could have gone down in history as a superb rock-punk crossover moment, but by the time it was released the band had already split up.

The Damned won the race to be the first punk act on vinyl, with *New Rose* released in November 1976. The Sex Pistols made number thirty-eight with the definitive *Anarchy in the UK* a month later. David Soul's *Don't Give Up on Us*, Julie Covington's *Don't Cry for Me Argentina* and Leo Sayer's *When I Need You* passed through the number one spot at the same time, surrounded by Smokie's *Living Next Door to Alice* (who the fuck is Alice?), Johnny Mathis's *When A Child Is Born*, Boston's *More Than a Feeling* and ABBA's *Knowing Me Knowing You* (Aha!). Hit albums included the Bay City Rollers' *Dedication*, Thin Lizzy's *Johnny the Fox*, Billy Connolly's *Atlantic Bridge*, Gallagher and Lyle's *Love on the Airwaves* and Queen's *A Day at the Races*.

Glen Matlock was replaced in the Pistols by Sid Vicious, while the band lived through being signed, dropped, signed, dropped and signed again, and their planned UK tour collapsed through multiple cancellations. The Queen's silver jubilee year gave them the chance to cut *God Save the Queen*, which made it to number two. At the same time Rollermania exploded in the USA, Fleetwood Mac's *Rumours* made platinum in a month, Alice Cooper's snake died, *Star Wars* arrived and an air collision killed five hundred and thirty eight in Tenerife. Todd Rundgren told the *NME* that his new album was called *Ra* after he heard a big booming voice through his radio. As of now, I want a radio show so I can tell the Pussycat Dolls to call their next album *We're Shite – Don't Buy This*.

In Scotland, the Rezillos' *I Can't Stand My Baby* was an anthem, as was Johnny and the Self-Abusers' *Saints and Sinners*. In a massive punk stylee they split up the day it was released, but singer Jim Kerr and guitarist Charlie Burchill were soon back with Simple Minds. In Dunfermline the Skids got together and further east the Scars came into their own.

BRIAN HOGG, writer: I remember going to see Simple Minds supporting Generation X in Edinburgh, just after they'd changed their name from the Self-Abusers. I'd worked for Bruce Finlay in Bruce's Records, and now he had his label, Zoom – he had the Minds' demo but hadn't thought much about it either way.

I phoned him and said, 'You really have to see this band live.' The next day he caught them at the Mars Bar in Glasgow, and signed them. I ended up working for the band for eighteen months, but I couldn't get into working as a publicist – it wasn't really me. Plus, I saw them developing into an almost Joy Division type heavy guitar noise, but they changed to something quite different, and it just wasn't to my taste. Then again, they went on to become one of the biggest bands on the planet, so what do I know?

IAIN SHEDDEN, the Jolt: Our first pub gig was at the Crown Hotel in Wishaw and we played to exactly zero people. Now and again one of the long-hairs from the pool room next door would stick his head round the corner to check out where the almighty din of two-minute punk delights such as *You're Cold* and *Responsibilities* was coming from. Then he'd shake his shaggy mane and bugger off back to his game and the Eagles on the jukebox. It was bad enough having our passion, commitment, frenzied delivery and rage against conformity ignored – suffering it to the occasional strain of *Hotel California* was a bitter pill to swallow. Still, within weeks they were queuing around the block. A little victory, but an important one.

We weren't daft boys exactly, but we were incredibly naïve and signed to Polydor, who immediately set about cloning us in the manner of their success story, the Jam. We did three British tours with them, dressed in similar suits, copping it from the press for being Jam wannabes. In truth we were a different kind of band, but we allowed ourselves to be moulded into something we weren't, and that was ultimately our undoing.

Bitter? Bollocks. The pointy end of those early days in Glasgow, vying for position with the likes of Johnny and the Self-Abusers and playing with the likes of the Jam, XTC and the Saints was life-affirming stuff. Clubs dripping with condensation and passion and raw energy and sex and you at the centre of it, living the dream and imagining it going on forever.

I remember the Jolt being banned from the Burns Howff when we'd only done a handful of gigs, after the *Evening Times* ran a story about us being a threat to civilisation. I also remember schoolboy Edwyn Collins coming up to us at the door afterwards to tell us how disappointed he was we couldn't play. Then there was the thrill of every record company in the country trying to sign us; me sitting on the stairs of my mum and dad's house talking to record producers and A&R men with *Coronation Street* going on in the background... My mum offering a selection of biscuits and cups of tea to punters who turned up at the door in binliners.

Punk was mainstream – except, of course, in Glasgow, despite a very successful Stranglers show. The ban had spread to Hugh Cornwell and Co. after a disastrous show at the City Halls; but the Apollo management had argued that was due to bad planning and asked for another chance. The City Fathers (argh) agreed, on condition that some of them attended.

BILL AITKEN, MSP: I will long remember the Stranglers concert. The City Fathers arrived at the Apollo to find an enormous queue of youngsters awaiting entry. Clearly there had been a lot of publicity surrounding the granting of the permission to hold the event – along with the stern warnings about the consequences of any bad behaviour. The kids were extremely pleasant and there was quite a lot of enjoyable banter.

We entered the theatre and were taken to a room in which there was enough drink to float a battle-ship. I got the impression the promoters wanted us to have an enjoyable evening – and wouldn't have been too concerned if we never left that room! Adopting my usual Cromwellian approach, however, I think I had a beer, then took the members out to watch the performance.

When the Stranglers came onstage they played one number, then said, 'Before we go on any further, where's Mr Aitken and his mates?' We stood up, and there was considerable applause, punctuated by some good-natured booing. The concert then proceeded and there was absolutely no trouble in the hall at all. It was partly to do with people having to stand at their seats, whereas in the City Hall they could mill around and get themselves into possible conflict situations.

At the end of the concert we went into the dressing room, and we had much good-natured banter with the Stranglers – who were much smarter than they would have you think. We parted good friends. I told them that they could come back any time, but that they wouldn't be allowed to perform in any hall where the layout was not conducive to good order. The Apollo was, in fact, an ideal venue.

As we left there were still hundreds of kids milling around, again behaving themselves just as kids do, with absolutely no hassle. They were genuinely very appreciative that we'd come to the concert and had been prepared to allow the Stranglers another chance.

Believe it or not this is a great example of how city government should operate – and it's provided a host of laughs ever since!

Did you get that? 'The Apollo was an ideal venue'. Bill Aitken (Con.) (really) and his concern for making sure pop music was accessible to the people of Glasgow is a matter of record. He frequently used to point out how football fans were allowed to get away with murder, and how the smallest misdemeanour from someone with a guitar led to all manner of over-reaction.

The Jam, the Stranglers, Eddie and the Hotrods, the Boomtown Rats and many others began entering the charts, although biggest-sellers continued to include Rod Stewart, ABBA, Queen, the Bee Gees and, em, Baccara. And in a remarkable, tragic illustration of the changing times, Elvis Presley and Marc Bolan both died.

Edinburgh's Fast Product label, founded by Rezillos manager Bob Last in December 1977, was an icon of the

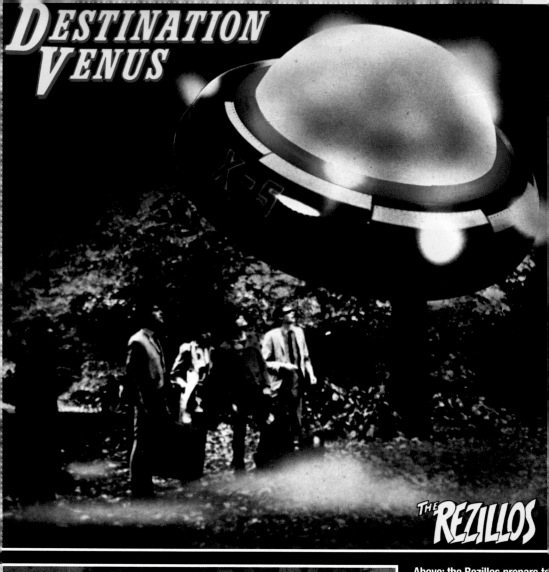

DESTINATION VENUS

THE REZILLOS

Above: the Rezillos prepare to do what NASA can't; left and right, the Axidents in the Edinburgh Dungeon where the punks thrived

era. In fact, an icon was all it was – a title, a slogan, which only later on became a record label. For the next two years Fast Product would knock up thirteen releases, not all of which were to be records. Along with singles by the Human League, the Scars, Mekons and Gang of Four, there were also three 'ear comics', compilation discs designed to display 'hundreds of new stars for EMI and Virgin to spend their money on', as the handwritten press ads stated.

Having a deal with Fast Product was not the same as having a record deal, although Last is remembered for actively encouraging acts to move up from his personal art project. Eccentricities included releasing a Human League flexidisc which carried only a conversation between Last and the band about what to put on it, and inviting fans to mail in blank tapes, on which the company would record Fast product and post it back. Fast was wound down when Last felt it was getting too big. He went on to form the Pop-Aural label.

ROBIN SAUNDERS: Everything quickly divided into warring cliques. You had the pub rockers trying to play R&B fast enough to keep up, the thug rockers playing at being fascists, then lumpen punks like me, destined to become short-haired hippies. Biggest of all was the art college crowd, like the Rezillos. But the Scars... now they were different. They broke most of the punk rules.

Most people would have heard of them when they released *Adultery/Horrorshow* on Fast Product. They had stage gear, and maybe a bit of make-up, and their hairdos didn't conform. They could actually play, and not just in the Ramones' style. While you had the rule that 1977 was Year Zero, the Scars paid tribute to folk like Mick Ronson and Steve Harley. They were inspired by poetry and film noir. Their gigs were theatrical too – actually worth watching. During *Crash*, Rab the singer would roll about on stage, acting like he was being tortured.

Paul the guitarist even improvised on stage, which was a big no-no. For me there's only Hendrix, James Williamson the Stooge, Steve the Pistol and Geordie from Killing Joke. Paul from the Scars really was in that league.

I'm biased, of course, but the bands in our little scene at Blair Street were a lot more interesting than most of the stuff around. Almost all of the rest of it, Scars and Freeze excepted, was, frankly, crap!

While another Elvis – Costello – entered the big time, Wings' *Mull of Kintyre* was the big song on the scene, accompanied by Sweet's last top-tenner, *Love Is Like Oxygen*, Terry Wogan's *Floral Dance* and Althia and Donna's pre-ska *Uptown Top Ranking*. Hit albums included AC/DC's *Let There Be Rock*, the Stranglers' *No More Heroes* and the Pistols' number-one moment, *Never Mind the Bollocks... Here's the Sex Pistols*. Then, perfectly, they split up.

Gerry Rafferty's album *City to City*, which made number six in February 1978, was yet another landmark moment in what had already been an incredible career. Naturally enough, the whole LP is dominated by the powerful sax riff on *Baker Street*, but there's not a poor track on the disc, and it's been noted that the release gave him the clout to do whatever he wanted for the rest of his career – a luxury we'd all pay through the nose for, wouldn't we?

ALAN MAIR, The Only Ones: *Another Girl, Another Planet* was my baby. We recorded the demo in a little country studio with an eight-track, and it was all spontaneous. Then we got the record deal and we were recording in a big studio, but I said, It's just not as good as the demo – and I played it, and everyone agreed. So we went back to the eight-track, and even had to borrow the original recorder because the tape wouldn't play on another machine. We couldn't get separation on the drum track, so Kelly said, 'I'll just play another kit on it...' No one thought he could do it, all the same fills and things. But he said, 'I don't just play music, I paint pictures.' In two takes he got it spot-on. By that time, all the people who hadn't liked us at first were fans – there was enough going on around us for them to get it.

Meat Loaf's *Bat Out of Hell* arrived, and *Hazell* was the single out of Maggie Bell. Andy Cameron hit with *Ally's Tartan Army*, making number six in the UK chart, ahead of the Blockheads' *What a Waste* and behind the Bee Gees' *Night Fever* and Boney M's *Rivers of Babylon*. Rod Stewart made number four with the Scottish World Cup squad and *Ole Ola*, while Travolta and Newton-John's *You're the One that I Want* was the biggest seller. Meanwhile, eco-aware Sweden became the first nation to ban aerosols, Bob Marley helped end warfare in Jamaica with his One Love Peace Concert, the first test-tube baby and first cellular phone arrived, John Lydon formed PiL and Charlie Chaplin's coffin was stolen from its resting place in Switzerland (it was found ten days later).

The death-knell was being sounded for the Glasgow Apollo, as the management were unable to reach an agreement with the owners. Strapped for cash, the landlords agreed an offer from Mecca to turn the venue into a bingo hall. A petition gathered nearly a hundred thousand signatures in support of keeping music live – that's one in six of the population of the Greater Glasgow area – but the City Fathers refused to help; and the Scottish Arts Council said they weren't allowed to.

I've gone on about this before but I think it's worth saying again, despite the impending demise of the Arts Council... Their remit was to support artistic endeavours which couldn't make money. It was possible for the Apollo to make money because people wanted to see the bands, and therefore the Arts Council couldn't help. The same month, they managed to help an American artist put on an exhibition of blank canvasses – an event which didn't stand a chance of being profitable because no one could possibly want to see it. That's our money they were spending, folks. It must have annoyed the hell out of anyone in the Arts Council who really gave one about contemporary culture, and I'd hope that was them all – in fact, I hope it *still* annoys those of the council who are still around today. There... all done now.

Asides from a rather disappointing gala night, where no big-name act in the world was available, the last show in the Apollo was the Clash. A recipe for intrigue, to be sure, which results in a nice big riot and several arrests, including the band's Joe Strummer and Paul Simonon. The story goes that the infamous Apollo bouncers were looking for an opportunity for one last big barney before they had to find other employment, and the arrival of several thousand pinned and padlocked punks had them all acting like that boy Begbie from *Trainspotting*.

JIM WYPER: The atmosphere that night was very bitter. The bouncers have to answer for that. I remember the unnecessary provocation they were giving us as we went in. They told me to take off the chain and padlock I had round my neck, but I didn't have the key and the chain wouldn't fit over my head. They told me I wasn't getting in because it was an offensive weapon – how could it be when I couldn't get it off? Soon there were about fifty of us in the same boat, but there was a decent big bouncer and he managed to open our padlocks with a wee penknife.

You could feel the tension as soon as you went into the hall. The bouncers were just out to give us a hard time. Anarchy in the UK came over the tannoy and punks were jumping around as if a shock current had gone through their seats. It was brilliant! But the bouncers took it as a cue to start flinging everyone out. It was a shame, because most people were just having fun. After that they didn't let up

Scottish Screen

The Glasgow Apollo lived up to its nickname, the 'Purple Palace'

all night – taunts and comments. Even during the show Joe Strummer kept asking the bouncers to leave people alone. They really earned their reputation that night. A lot of them should never have been there.

HUGH REED: I was waiting for them at the wee lane at the side after the gig, and I saw them being bundled into the meatwagon – as a rock'n'roll way to exit a gig, this takes some beating...

COLIN MILLEN: I wasn't there, but I worked with a guy who'll die happy because he got the jail with the Clash that night!

A few months later, as Keith Moon died, Carl Bridgewater was murdered and Sid Vicious was accused of the murder of Nancy Spungen, the Apollo re-opened under new management. The bingo deal had fallen through amid arguments over repairs and after not a little obscure political behaviour had been discovered. It was to remain the rock'n'roll heart and soul of the west of Scotland for another seven years.

Mike Scott first appeared on the scene in Another Pretty Face, whose debut *All the Boys Love Carrie* was an instant success, and even made *NME*'s single of the week on release.

MIKE SCOTT, Waterboys**:** My first band was called Karma and we played in my living room every Saturday afternoon for six months – we never played a gig. We did covers of Bowie and Stones songs. Our favourite was *Moonage Daydream* and we'd play fifteen minute versions of it with our lead guitar player Davy Flynn doing Hendrix-esque solos. My first band to play a real gig was a three-piece called Triton, who played a lunchtime show at Ayr Academy, where the other two members of the band were still at school. We played *Sympathy for the Devil, Eyesight to the Blind* and three originals. I was on bass and vocals.

I'd also been doing my fanzine, *Jungleland* – we did nine editions. The first four were done in Ayr, all in 1977, copied on the Social Work Department photocopier, where I worked for a year. They were full of record and gig reviews and retrospectives on Patti Smith, John Lennon, Bowie and others. Issues five to eight, which were late 1977 to early 1978, were done in Edinburgh, printed at a place called Ronde's on Queen St, and written by me and my mates. They featured interviews with Richard Hell, Tom Robinson, Bob Geldof and others – basically whoever was playing shows in Edinburgh that week. The last issue, number nine, was done two years later and was completely different, with poetry and image collages. Every copy was individually paint-splattered, Jackson Pollock style.

When we got Another Pretty Face together, our manager Edward Bell – usually known as Z – put up the money. So New Pleasures was his label, named after a very fine Richard Hell song. Everyone was starting labels back then – it was fun, designing the sleeve and logos, often with Letraset. It was real back-of-the-car stuff, pulling up at Rough Trade or other shops in London, asking them how many copies they'd take, then driving away with a little white sale-or-return slip or, if we were very lucky... a cheque!

I don't know what we expected of *All the Boys Love Carrie* – but it was the first record of mine I ever heard on the radio, which was a thrill. It got very good reviews, which led us, in our naïvety, to expect the same for our next record, *Whatever Happened to the West* – but it got bad reviews.

ROBIN SAUNDERS: I wound up playing bass in Badweeks, sentenced to several evenings a week in a Blair Street cell. In the *Lord of the Rings* trilogy we're never shown the dwelling-places of the Orcs – but I have a bank of mental images to draw on for that.

Our next-door neighbour was Mike Scott, then there was the Freeze, responsible for a couple of classic early punk singles of the kind which now fetch funny money on eBay from deranged Japanese collectors. Singer Gordon Sharp's haunting voice would later grace the first This Mortal Coil album, preceding his rise to international subcultural celebrity of sorts under the name Cindytalk, sadly still without honour in his own country. Late arrivals on the scene were an outfit by the name of Blak Flag – note the missing 'C', so nothing to do with Henry Rollins' hardcore heroes. You'd recognise the guitarist and drummer as those bespectacled twins who went on to unlikely stardom as the Proclaimers.

On band nights I was usually the first to arrive. Solitary in the cell, munching chips on top of my bass combo, listening to the latest tractor production figures from Minsk on Radio Moscow, which the amp seemed to pick up very well... The room had shared occupancy in the evenings between Badweeks and Twisted Nerve, and during the day with a good-natured rat. I often saw his tail disappearing as I switched on the light.

Electricity was metered, so maintaining a continuous supply required careful forward planning. We were regularly plunged into darkness and silence, then by a fumble for coins with cigarette-lighter torches. When the coins ran out you could always repair to a communal area where there was a drinks machine supplying water – not quite hot enough to soften a PotNoodle, but we ate them anyway. There was also a jukebox, surprisingly lacking in punk records and on which we often took great delight in pissing off the serious types – Joy Division fans, mostly – by playing Captain Beaky over and over again.

There was a less-friendly rodent population too. After a night on the town, too drunk or too lazy to struggle home, you could spend the night in Blair Street – if you were feeling brave. Try to claim the pool table – they can't climb up the legs, can they? Try to drift off to sleep accompanied by the patter of tiny feet...

In August of 1978, the Rezillos' *Top of the Pops* saw them appearing on the selfsame TV show, after which they split up, leaving their album, *Can't Stand the Rezillo* , as the only evidence of what could have been. 10cc were at number one with *Dreadlock Holiday*, followed by *Summer Nights* from the Grease brigade, and the Boomtown Rats' *Rat Trap*. Surrounded by the Buzzcocks, PiL, Undertones, Queen, Blondie and the Village People (who were later sued by the YMCA), Frankie Miller entered the top ten with *Darlin'*.

DAVY ARTHUR: Frankie had done loads by then already. Things really took off when he'd done his solo album *Once in a Blue Moon*. Ray Charles recorded a version of *I Can't Change It*, which was more or less the ultimate compliment for Frankie. Then Allen Toussaint took him to New Orleans and they did the *Highlife* album, which really let his soul leanings come out.

He didn't have a band for a while after that, but he worked with Phil Lynott on *Still in Love with You*, and of course that became a big part of Thin Lizzy's live set right till the end. Later on he did a couple of songs with Procul Harum and all the reviews said he'd woken up a band that seemed to be half asleep. That show at the Rainbow was one of his top moments.

After that he did *The Rock*, recorded within sight of Alcatraz prison. Frankie always said he'd have wound up in jail if he hadn't discovered music, so he dedicated the title track to prisoners everywhere. Then *Double Trouble* took shape, with Steven Tyler from Aerosmith guesting. *Darlin'* came off the *Falling in Love* album – it took a long time for Frankie to get his top ten, but that says more about the record-buying public than him!

GERRY TURNER: First time I heard *Darlin'* I thought it was Rod Stewart come of age. The voice was all there but there was more depth to it than Rod's usual stuff. Then I heard it was this guy, Frankie Miller, and that was me a fan. Later on Rod himself said Frankie was a better singer than him. Sorry, Rod, but I have to agree!

The United Nations declared 1979 the year of the child, although they didn't say which one, right enough. Blondie's *Heart of Glass* was the first number one of the year, companion hits including Elvis Costello's *Oliver's Army*, the Blockheads' *Hit Me with Your Rhythm Stick* and the Bee Gees' *Tragedy*. Nazareth made number twenty-two with *May the Sun Shine*, and the accompanying album, *No Mean City*, made number thirty-four. Sid Vicious was dead, as was TV horse Mr Ed, and it snowed in the Sahara for half an hour.

The Skids' *Into the Valley* was their first hit, making number ten. It's always been difficult to work out just exactly what Richard Jobson meant with his lyrics, but it's been suggested the song was about a notorious Dunfermline backwater where gangs met to fight. *Scared to Dance* was the band's first album on Virgin, and it dripped with promise and potential. But even back then guitar hero Stuart Adamson's delicate dynamic was evident – he did a runner midway through the sessions, and had to be coaxed from his Dunfermline home back to London to finish the job(son). Which he did, thankfully.

Simple Minds also cut their first LP, *Life in a Day*, which owed more to their punk roots than the stadium rock they'd end up mastering. The Clash's anthem *London Calling*, I dare suggest, wouldn't have found itself entirely out of place on the Minds' LP, although it arrived some months later.

Scots music was displaying all manner of tendencies, with another Average White Band album, *Feel No Fret*, charting at fifteen, the Rezillos' bow-out *Mission Accomplished...* making thirty and Gerry Rafferty's *Night Owl* making number nine.

But if anyone had any fears about running out of things to write about, the whole fabric of our nation was about to change – Thatcherism arrived. Now, it's not within the scope of this book to get bogged down in politics, but there can be no doubt that Scotland was changed fundamentally in the Thatcher era, in a way it hadn't been since the Highland clearances. It wasn't just financial, it was social to the point of painful awareness. Let me just say I admire Lady Thatcher as a hard-working moralist who believed she was right, and that I'd like to first-foot her one Hogmanay with the traditional piece of coal, saying, 'There ye go, hen, that's the last o'it.' And we'll say nothing – *nothing*, mind – about the home-rule referendum.

The bonnie bonnie banks played host to the first Loch Lomond Rock Festival in May 1979, which starred the Stranglers, the Boomtown Rats, Dr Feelgood, the Skids, the Average White Band, Buzzcocks and Underhand Jones. This first attempt at staging a full-sized outdoor event in Scotland was also my first encounter with rock'n'roll, when a lanky, beardy hippy dood wandered up our street, handing out festival stickers. That was my first, 'Mum, is that a boy or a girl?' moment – and, on realising I could be like that, previous ambitions of being a road workman or a binman went out the window. (I achieved the hair and beard but never the lankiness – I maintain I have the physical presence of a short fat hippy in order to warn people that's exactly what I am.)

On the slightly less bonnie bonnie banks of the Clyde, at Glasgow's Customs Quay House, there can still be found the remains of a bandstand. The wood-slatted seats are all rotted and you'd get a nail up your bracket if you tried to sit there; and the stage roof is long gone. But back at the end of the seventies, it was a hotbed of young musical activity, and just about the only place you got away with playing punk in the city.

JOHN McNEILL, the Zips: We did two singles, the *Zips EP* in 1979 then *Radioactivity* the next year – that was the first release on our own label, Tenement Toons. They both got good airplay from Brian Ford on Radio Clyde and John Peel on Radio One. We played everywhere, especially the Mars Bar in Glasgow and the Bungalow Bar in Paisley.

But we wanted to reach the under-eighteen audience, so we started doing Saturday lunchtime gigs at the Customs Quay House bandstand. We let new bands support us, using our equipment. The city council still hated punk, so I used to tell them we were just a wee pop group.

It was the place to be seen, mainly because Brian plugged the shows heavily on his *Streetsounds* programme. People would write in every week and give him reviews of the last show. One name in particular, Teabag, used to crop up all the time. Everyone thought it was me just trying to plug the Zips, but it wasn't... He used to put a used teabag in the envelope, hence the name – good thing he wasn't called Condom! I often wonder who he was and whether he's still around.

I Don't Like Mondays, said the Boomtown Rats. *We Don't Talk Any More*, said Cliff. *Get It Right Next Time*, said Gerry Rafferty. *Bang Bang*, said BA Robertson, *Cars*, said Gary Numan (well, it wuzznae going to work for ever, wuzzit?). Several of Iggy Pop's UK tour dates were cancelled because Glen Matlock was in his band;

Chuck Berry was jailed for tax evasion; and Dire Straits, Joy Division, the Specials and digital recording were the new buzzwords. And Billy Connolly was *In the Brownies*.

Annie Lennox and Dave Stewart's Tourists were next up, scoring a number four with *I Only Want to Be with You*, and promising the world never-before-seen live experiences on tour. Simple Minds released *Real to Real Cacophony* and Dougie MacLean released his *Caledonia* album. Dougie, who recounts warmly how many Americans think he's singing 'California' – and maybe he is – remains a master of the cottage industry, having built up Dunkeld Records to the status of tourist attraction in the town, and I don't mean Annie and Dave recorded there – although maybe they did.

Like Alex Harvey before her, a young lass called Sheena Easton won fame and fortune in the public eye when a TV talent search called *The Big Time* followed her attempts to become a star. She signed to EMI and within months had three singles in the charts at the same time: *9 to 5*, *Modern Girl* and *One Man Woman*.

The Sugar Hill Gang's *Rapper's Delight* suggested the direction a goodly proportion of the USA were heading in; and it's fair to say that the UK punk thang really hadn't worked for them at all. But as the post-punk sound began to be heard, the Damned, the Clash and dead Sid Vicious albums all made heavy dents on the charts, scrawling a menshy on behalf on the suddenly older guard. Great new things were expected – even if Pink Floyd's *The Wall* was to become the most marked LP of 1979.

IAIN SHEDDEN, the Jolt: When we got to London we were beside ourselves, really – playing all of those places – the Marquee, the Hope and Anchor, the Nashville – that we'd romanticised so much in our heads while reading the *NME*, *Sounds* and *Melody Maker* in our bedrooms. That was the most exciting time... seeing the likes of Billy Idol or Chris Bailey or Siouxsie Sioux in the audience, there to see us, or in some cases just to be seen.

We played the Marquee quite a few times and didn't always make it to the end. Spitting was always a problem, of course, made worse when the gob was accompanied by a pint glass. I remember playing with X-Ray Specs there and lasting about fifteen minutes before it turned really nasty. It's best not to return the pint glass to its original user from the stage in these circumstances...

Various band members – including, I'll always remember, Doll By Doll's Jackie Leven – hustled our gear from the stage into the tiny dressing room before it could be destroyed. Same thing happened there with Generation X – and to them.

In a roundabout way my future was determined by the Jolt meeting the guys from the Saints when they first came to Scotland. *I'm Stranded* was a staple on our record players when they turned up at one of our gigs in Edinburgh. We became instant friends, did quite a few gigs together and I ended up joining the Saints for most of their second phase in the 1980s, which in a roundabout fashion is how I've ended up as music writer for *The Australian* newspaper in Sydney.

The most obvious thing about those punk days and the Jolt's role in them is that it was a means of escape. Like football, the armed forces and boxing in the old days, punk came along and offered the three of us a way out of the bleak industrial landscape that was Wishaw – although you can now remove 'industrial' from that description. Not to mention escape from predictable career paths and all the things we were reacting so much against, like people over thirty with long hair.

The Jolt's only album was re-released for the first time on CD a few years ago. I hadn't played it for a while and was surprised at how well the songs stood up after all this time. I can quell the rumours now, however, by saying that the Jolt reunion is not on the agenda. We were three schoolmates and formed our first band just at the right time to catch the punk wave and ride it for all it was worth. And it was bloody great. You can't ask for more than that, can you?

ALEX OGG, writer: The most interesting aspect of Scotland's immersion in punk was the way it allowed so many artists to take their baby steps. The Skids' Jobson is now a filmmaker, the troubled Adamson found global success with Big Country, and the Rezillos are now back as a going concern. But there were many others who were either once part of punk's cause or adept at seizing the opportunities it offered.

Novelist Ian Rankin once performed with long-forgotten punk band the Dancing Pigs. Edwyn Collins was a Nu-Sonic prior to Orange Juice, Roddy Frame laboured in a band entitled Neutral Blue and Davey Henderson was a member of Marxist art punks the Dirty Reds (who also included actor Tam Dean). Alan McGee, the Creation Records founder, also had a bedroom punk band and continues to talk up the impact of the Pistols et al. to this day. Without punk, some of the most important records of the eighties and nineties might never have been made.

Icon: Frankie Miller

Icon: Gerry Rafferty

9 POSTCARD AND POST PUNK

Maggie Thatcher was a punk – with the added advantage of knowing what she wanted and how to get it. When the steelworkers called a strike which was to last from January to April 1980, it was the beginning of the end for anyone who didn't do things her way. Thatcherists did what they liked and everyone else could just fuck off. *That's* anarchy in the UK.

As Kenny Rogers sang about the *Coward of the County*, a four-night fundraiser for Kampuchea (Cambodia) took place in London, Paul McCartney was jailed for ten days in Japan for drug offences, the revamped Radio Caroline sank, Emerson, Lake and Palmer split up, AC/DC's Bon Scott died of drink complications and the New Wave of British Heavy Metal began to gather momentum.

If a huge chunk of Scots musicianship had been holding its breath through the pure punk years, this was its hyperventilation. Scores of bands embraced new technology and new attitudes to move away from the traditional blues influences. Our new wave was inspired by American pop art and post punk, with name-checks for acts like Pere Ubu, Television and Talking Heads who, with David Byrne's Dumbarton roots, feaured that strange wee influencing-the-influence thing that Scotland always seems to have for itself.

The icon of the era was Postcard Records, set up by Alan Horne as an act of defiance against the majors down south. Remembered as a man who liked to say things that would wind folk up, his intentions were similar to those of Fast Product, but his methods couldn't have been more different. The label's first release was *Falling and Laughing* by Edwyn Collins's Orange Juice. Previously known as the Nu-Sonics, their new name refleced the band's puritanical attitude – like several of their contemporaries they didn't drink, didn't do drugs (except maybe a little speed) and didn't do the groupie thing. It also alluded to the first-thing-in-the-morning post-hangover refreshment offered by their brand of jingly-jangly pop.

Another Scots icon appeared in the shape of Billy Mackenzie of the Associates, via the duo's debut album *The Affectionate Punch*. Like most of the best biggest Scots, Mackenzie was nothing but a show-off, with an incredible sense of theatrics which made it hard not to love him, no matter what you thought of his music. The Associates' first single, a cover of Bowie's *Boys Keep Swinging*, led to comparisons – but while there was a certain similarity between the two voices, there was no resemblance between how each artist did what he did. Mackenzie shared that particularly Scottish trait of being able to give you a real emotional grip on what he was talking about, without actually talking about anything much, except whatever it meant to him. *The Affectionate Punch* was well-received, with one review calling it 'a kind of masterpiece'.

While the Police were *So Lonely* and Blondie were *Atomic*, the Tourists scored another top ten with *So Good to Be Back Home Again*. Annie Lennox's classically-trained voice and Dave Stewart's construction ability was already dripping with potential, but the band were experiencing industry difficulties in that they were actually supposed to be employed as songwriters rather than performers. They struggled on, though.

Outfits like the Associates and the Tourists represented the opposite end of the new wave spectrum; they were also trying to move away from Scotland's now traditional influences and embracing something more Eurocentric. Heavier reliance on keyboard sounds and drum machines helped draw a line across the decades. Despite that, there was still a bluesiness to many top Scots' singing voices. Must be in the air.

JUSTIN CURRIE, Del Amitri: When I formed the band at school we were into the Gang of Four, Wire, the Fall, Buzzcocks, the Undertones – pop melody inspired punk, essentially. Our key album was *Dragnet* by the Fall. In our pathetic middle-class punk sensibility, we were pretty antipathetic to the trendy new wave bands on the Glasgow pub circuit.

People like Endgames and Tutonic Veneer, we suspected, were punk pretenders who were actually just seventies careerists desperate for commercial success. Now, commercial success, or at least the abandonment of art to attain commercial success, was total anathema to us. We were sixteen and we'd spent the last three years reading radical punk treatises by Julie Burchill, Nick Kent and Paul Morley in the *NME* – and even Dave McCulloch in *Sounds*.

It was this generation, I think, which went on to form the loose indie-schmindie scene of the early eighties, characterised by a hideous inverted snobbery, a wilfully cute amateurism and an ironic attitude to rock. It reached its apex in the Smiths and can still be heard today in parts of Belle and Sebastian's approach.

Barbara Dickson enjoyed her first top twenty with *January February*, while Dexy's Midnight Runners made number one with *Geno*, a tribute to the beat-scene bandleader and character Geno Washington who more or less everyone on the 1960s circuit ran into. The Jam hit the top with *Going Underground*, followed by Blondie again with *Call Me*, and the Average White Band scored a magnificent return to form with *Let's Go Round Again*.

The Whites' album was called *Shine*. Now, I have to take issue here – how the hell damn many albums do there have to be called *Shine*? I can see why you might want to use it, but that's why everyone else does, *meh*. Another thing that really gets me is the amount of bands who've been called Rise – same issue: the reason why is the reason why not... And the minute Rise release *Shine*, I'm outta here.

BA Robertson's *To Be or Not To Be* made number nine – it's my considered opinion the song was about deciding whether to name a dog Toby. (Does that work in print?) As Midge Ure joined Ultravox, Buggles joined Yes, Mount St Helens erupted, Alfred Hitchcock and Peter Sellers died, and the Pistols' movie *The Great Rock'n'Roll Swindle* was released, there was a second Loch Lomond Rock Festival, starring the Jam, the Tourists, Stiff Little Fingers, Gillan, Bad Manners, Wishbone Ash and Saxon.

STUART McHUGH, writer: I was at the Bear Park – remember that? – for the second Loch Lomond festival. I missed the first one because of exams so I was there bright and early. I actually had ticket number 00001! The Jam, SLF, the Chords and Punishment of Luxury were an unmissable end-of-term bill.

The Chords were a mod band with a new wave sound, so they united the rival tribes, and they even

John Martyn with Brian Young, above, and Midge Ure, below, in CaVa Studios

got a quick encore. Next up were Bad Manners – and in twenty years I've never seen a worse performance. They were downright awful! But because the Chords had encored, the DJ asked, 'Do you want some more Bad Manners?' Together, with one voice, the punks and mods all shouted, 'No – fuck off!'

They came back on anyway, so they got pelted with bottles, cans, rocks and bear shit. Stray missiles started hitting bystanders so it turned into a pitched battle. Fortunately, the Tourists went on, and everyone fell into a coma at the horribly miscast powerpop.

The Jam got everyone back together, though – and I think it was the first time they played *Going Underground* live. Asides from the second day, which was all metal and Runrig, that was the end of Loch Lomond and music.

The Fire Engines were the next newcomers, led by another bit of a performer, Davey Henderson. *Get Up and Use Me* was their first release – a rabid construction which could easily be regarded as pop art rather than pop music. There seemed to be a sense of overt experimentation in what they did, as demonstrated by their mini-album *Lubricate Your Living Room*.

Ultravox' first outing with their new singer was *Sleepwalk*, which made number twenty-nine near the Skids' *Circus Games*, AC/DC's *Whole Lotta Rosie* and Joy Division's *Love Will Tear Us Apart*. *Vienna*, Ultravox's album, made number fourteen while the Skids' *Absolute Game* LP reached number nine.

> **BRIAN YOUNG,** CaVa Studios**:** Midge had come back to us when we went twenty-four track, to produce *Modern Man* for MAM Records. When he'd finished, he left me a cassette of rough mixes from his new band, Ultravox, and the sessions they'd done in Germany. I played it and thought, 'See you in the charts, Midge.'

Simple Minds had reached a crossroads and steered through it with their third album, *Empire And Dance*. Their statement of intent was as grand-sounding as the LP's title; following the Scottish vibe of the moment, Kerr, Burchill and Co. steered towards the European feel, as achieved with *I Travel* – which, of course, they had by then. In *ZigZag*, Lindsay Hutton wrote, 'I have a vision of this band returning after a triumphant tour to the Glasgow Apollo to a packed house. It's all systems go into *Sweetthings* (not to be confused with Bowie's *Diamond Dogs* tune) and Jim'll swagger out à la Lou Reed and the place will go bazooks.' Not too far wrong there, which is why Lindsay's blog, Next Big Thing, is still essential reading.

John Martyn's *Grace and Danger* was, of course, resting comfortably amid the more traditional blues vibe. There was something very grippingly special about it, though. A concept of sorts, the album was a working out of his split from his wife, who'd worked on his previous two releases with him. Everything is laid bare in the delivery of *Baby, Please Come Home*. He explained later that he'd never understood why the split had to happen, although he suspected a lot of it was his fault.

> **BRIAN YOUNG,** CaVa Studios**:** We did six albums with John. I discovered he was Aretha Franklin, one octave lower. Hearing Bonnie Raitt singing along at the back of the control room was an incredible moment.

John Bonham died, as did Steve McQueen and Mae West. JR Ewing was shot (I did it), and as the New Romantics started making an appearance, John Lennon was murdered by Mark Chapman. Unsurprisingly,

Imagine shot to number one all over the world; its companion best-sellers at the end of 1980 were Blondie (*The Tide Is High*), St Winifred's School Choir (*No One Quite Like Grandma*), and ABBA. *Super Trouper* mentions Glasgow, so can we say it's Scottish? Would we want to?

An interesting wee aside came in the shape of the inner sleeve of Sneeky Pete's single. It featured a hand-edited map of central Glasgow, marking out all the music landmarks of the time. Most of them are long gone, sadly – but if you're about to put a CD out, I reckon a similar type of map would be a great idea for where you are now. Whoever writes this book's successor in fifty years time will thank you, particularly if you save it as a layered PSD file.

'*Punk's not dead!*' bellowed the Exploited as 1981 began, and they weren't wrong, and still aren't. Thing is, though, they were never quite a punk band in the way their predecessors were. They embraced the ethic; frontman Wattie Buchan had anger on tap while Big John Duncan, Gary McCormack and Dru Stix provided a noise which was verging on thrash, years before thrash appeared in the States. Several line-ups later, the Exploited are still making headlines – for example, a show in Europe in 2005 resulted in a tear-gas attack which ended the party. Punk, as they say, rock.

From the sublime to the ridiculous, and a quick reminder that music-hall entertainment wasn't dead either. One of the country's most successful exports at the time was the Krankies, the husband-and-wife Tough team, Ian and Janette, who masqueraded as Ian and Wee Jimmy. They presented *Crackerjack*, had their own TV shows and did tours and pantos endlessly. Let no one say it wasn't hard work – particularly when they had to squeeze in the recording of their album, *Fandabidozi*...

PETER KERR: Ian and Janette are a right pair of characters. I had to write most of the tracks on the album because the material just wasn't there; and they were dotting about on summer seasons and all that. We had to put down their vocals then record the backing tracks on later – which is the wrong way round, of course. It was hard for them, no doubt, but they're a pair of troupers.

Janette's got a good set of lugs on her but Ian's a wee bit slower on catching the melody, so we were doing the *Fandabidozi* track and Ian was lagging behind. Janette just said something to try and make things easier, and Ian said, 'Aye, alright, leave me alone...' and she said, 'I'm only trying to fucking help, c**t!'

Wee Jimmy Krankie using language like that! I kept a splice of it for years, in case I could blackmail them about it or something... The funny thing about that album is that it did okay when we released it here – but it made number one in Italy. The Italians went crazy for the Krankies!

Talk about girls been schoolboyish is bad enough, but girls being schoolgirlish could often be worse. So it could have been with bubblegum-poppers Altered Images, starring Clare Grogan's stylised delivery – but backed with some damn-fine solid musical intelligence to save it. The band had some mighty influential friends, not least Steven Severin from the Banshees, who produced half the *Happy Birthday* album. However, the title track, the one that hit, was done by Martin Rushent and it fulfilled all the requirements for a throwaway (in the best sense) pop single.

The problem is, Clare Grogan was gallus in the way Lorraine Kelly is – men who aren't Scottish lap it up, but it has a tendency to make some folks' fists tighten. On the other hand, view her as the Britney Spears who could kick your head in and now we're talking. A talented performer to be sure, but possibly not quite as musically talented as a certain Johnny McElhone from the band, who went on to much bigger and much more global things.

KENNY CHALMERS: I remember seeing them in Dundee, and just staring all night. Actually, not at Clare Grogan – she didn't do anything for me, although I suspect I was the only one of my mates in that boat. I was trying to work out, 'Do I like this?' I thought there was a wee bit of punk going on but I didn't know if they meant it. Clare said, 'Is it anyone here's birthday today? No? Aah – it's nobody's birthday!' And went into the obvious song. That was just pop, right enough, but that thing with the bass kept me thinking. I never did make up my mind – but years and years later, I saw a punk band T-shirt that said, 'It's nobody's birthday' – so that proves Altered Images at least had some kind of punk to them!

The Associates returned with *Fourth Drawer Down*, the album's title based on the place they kept the drugs which brought them back to life after a gruelling twelve-hour studio stint. They'd had a cunning plan, you see – they got a deal to record six singles, then found a way to record the singles much more cheaply than the budget allowed, which meant they had plenty of cash left to live it up a bit. Which, of course, they did. *Tell Me Easter's on Friday* is the choice track from this album, which is the result of their skulduggery.

Bucks Fizz won Eurovision, and the first space shuttle, Columbia, went into space but didn't take the Fizz with it. Sheena Easton sang the *For Your Eyes Only* title song, Charles and Diana were married, the IBM PC went on sale for around £1500, and Bananarama appeared on the scene 'performing with backing tapes'. So, dancing then. As Soft Cell's *Tainted Love* was replaced at number one by Edinburgh lass Aneka's *Japanese Boy*, Ultravox released the *Rage in Eden* album and John Martyn's *Glorious Fool* was Phil Collins' first production job outside his own work.

Josef K, another Postcard act, achieved a fascinating transition from American art-pop to something much more Scottish. There's no doubt vocalist Paul Haig's voice led the way for several later success stories, and their album *The Only Fun in Town* is a showcase of *Fun'n'Frenzy* – one of the track titles. This was actually their second album; both band and label had decided the first effort, *Sorry for Laughing*, was too slick, and went back to the drawing board. The decision cost them six months of lost momentum, and when *Only Fun* was released their media champions hated it. The band realised they'd made a mistake – they called their decision to drown out the vocals 'commercial suicide' – but it was too late, and they split up.

Sorry for Laughing was finally to be released in 1990 where its point is made – it does indeed sound more studio and less live; but that's a problem many Scottish bands failed to resolve, notably rockers like SAHB and Nazareth. But you can still draw a straight line between Josef K and Franz Ferdinand, with plenty of stops in between.

Stuart Adamson had left the Skids and was beginning work on his grand vision – the result of which would be Big Country, of course. Meanwhile, in a similar but different vein of Scottish-oriented rock, Runrig's grandest moment came with their near-concept album, *Recovery*.

DONNIE MUNRO, Runrig: Obviously, we grew up with traditional music, but we pretty much rejected it at the time in favour of rock'n'roll. But when we all went to uni, we grew to appreciate those traditions because we'd been removed from them. So it was an easy decision to try merging those influences.

I suppose people tend to see us as a political band – but I don't think any band really can be. I mean, we were six people who could hardly agree on the bloody set list, far less any major political issues! But in the songs, and particularly on the *Recovery* album, we did focus on things like land issues, language and the right to self-determination within communities.

One of the most significant things for us was a song which translates as 'Twenty Years'. That's how long it had taken us to find out about and understand our own social history. When we were at school there was just no reference at all to the agitation that took place in the late nineteenth century. We didn't know what our grandparents and great-grandparents had been involved in. There was this rage – why did it take me twenty years to find this out?

There's a museum here in Skye that I take my children to. There's an exhibition with a reconstruction of the Napier Commission, which was set up after the last land battle on British soil to look after the rights of the crofters. I discovered by pure chance that the man in the reconstruction, the central figure, was my great-great-great-grandfather! And I'd been going to the museum for so long with my kids, unable to point that fact out because it had been so difficult to discover...

Aztec Camera's debut release was *Just Like Gold*, which featured as the B-side of Orange Juice's *Poor Old Soul*. While Alan Horne had harboured great hopes for these two acts, they both moved on to major labels, and that was the end of Postcard. The label's influence must never be underestimated, though. Many standard tricks, like bonus flexidiscs, multiple versions and formats and sudden title deletions – all designed byHorne as a backlash against the majors – have become mainstays of rock'n'roll promotion.

The year wound to an end with the Polish government struggling to hold back the force of Solidarity and the deaths of eighteen seamen in the Penlee lifeboat disaster off the Cornish coast. The Exploited's *Dead Cities* reached number thirty-one and Altered Images' *I Could Be Happy* made it to number seven. Album entries included the Police's *Ghost in the Machine*, the Human League's *Dare* (now featuring former Rezillo Jo Callis) and *The Pick of Billy Connolly*. Rush released their *Exit Stage Left* live album, a tribute to the Glasgow Apollo. Meantime, Robbo Robertson *hadn't* been in Wild Horses.

BRIAN ROBERTSON I wasn't in that band – they were in it with me. I don't care what anyone says – I paid everyone out of my bank account, because the management would have nothing to do with it. I bought the equipment, I did the work. It was my band, although that's not the way I treated it at the time. When I get into a studio I want it done the way I want it done, but I wasn't Richie Blackmore or anything like that.

The first album worked out for me, and that was when I was in total control. I was accused of treating the first album as a solo album. Of course I did! I didn't really *want* to – I wanted a band, but it was going to take a couple of years to work up. I'm not just going to walk in and hand a quarter share to everyone, especially when I'm paying for everything.

Jimmy Bain didn't like it, but he was on heroin, and so was Kit, and they started just doing silly things. They'd told me no one would be in the studio because something had broken down, and I caught them out – they were there. That's when I took the equipment and fucked off.

The second album's a heap of shit. I don't have a copy and I don't want one. The only good thing about it was the cover . When you see the photos on the cover, you notice no one's looking at each other. Fin Costello took the shots and he later told me it was one of the hardest shoots he'd ever done. He was sure someone was going to punch someone's head in. And he was right as well...

It's bad enough when you've got a long-term plan and no one understands that – what really hurts is when you trust your mates and you get fucked. But when heroin's involved, trust goes out the window. We all did things wrong, but that drug is the wrongest thing you can possibly do.

Donnie Munro

Alex Harvey, Reading, 1977: In his last SAHB show he performed Framed as Jesus and dropped the cross on Fluff Freeman

The 1981/2 festive season passed with one of the coldest temperatures on record: −27.2°C near Braemar. The Human League's *Don't You Want Me* was at number one. A spate of Christmas singles by Holly and the Ivys, Lennon and Slade – guess which two of those were re-releases – didn't scratch their way above number twenty-eight.

As *Don't You Want Me* became the first UK platinum-seller in four years, Mark Thatcher was lost and found in the Sahara, Randy Rhoades and John Belushi died, and the Associates' *Party Fears Two* became a top-ten hit. It was taken from their third album, *Sulk*, which was voted album of the year in several industry polls. By all definitions it was an unusual hit – despite a cheery synth riff it really doesn't have a hook, especially a vocal one, making it one of the least accessible songs in chart history, but all the more enjoyable for it.

In an interview at the time, Alan Rankine noted how success changed the flamboyant Billy MacKenzie. 'He'd go to Monte Carlo for a night and blow £5000, or book into Claridges for a week. He had a fleet of cars even though he couldn't drive! He could vomit at will as well – that became legendary on a tour with Siouxsie and the Banshees. We were getting gobbed on by the punks, so Billy went off, downed four shorts, then came back and projectile-vomited over the first four rows. They loved it – they cheered us after that!'

Alex Harvey had just completed a European tour with his new band, the Electric Cowboys, when he died of a heart attack in February 1982. It's difficult to gauge his input to Scottish culture, especially since he was out of the limelight when he died, but there are a very small number of musicians who achieved success in every era of rock'n'roll over twenty-five years and he was one of them. Skiffle, jazz, beat, folk rock, heavy rock, punk and post-punk – he'd been there, done that. In his obituary piece Charles Shaar Murray wrote, 'I've lost my sergeant... I never met anyone like Harvey and I never will again.' His final album, *The Soldier on the Wall*, was released posthumously.

CHRIS GLEN, SAHB: When he died, I was living with Michael Schenker and we were in MSG together. Cozy Powell raced round to the flat as soon as he heard, because he didn't want me finding out on the radio or something. I just got drunk and don't remember the next few days. He'd asked me to join his last band and I'd said no, then he'd asked me to manage him, and I had to say no to that too. I've got no doubts at all we'd have got back together eventually.

JACK McDOUGALL: I'll never forget meeting Alex. I was around fourteen and I was being taught bass by my neighbour, Charlie Casware, who'd been a regular on the big band scene. I'd discovered SAHB and told Charlie about how *Swampsnake* had blown me away. Charlie said, 'That's my mate – he's coming up from London soon and will probably visit me. Do you want to meet him?' I probably cartwheeled across to my house that night.

That first meeting, for a starstruck teenager, was absolutely nerve-racking. From the minute I got in from school, I watched voyeur-like from my ma's bedroom window – until, a couple of hours later, the man himself jumped out of a taxi in the stage jeans and belt he always wore, black T-shirt and a massively-checked jacket Arthur Montford would've been chuffed with.

I was phoned over, introduced and sat listening to his great stories. He'd occasionally say, 'D'ye know what ah mean, Jack?' as he talked. I probably sat open-mouthed and said, 'Aye...' like a stupid daft boy.

They went to the pub – the Cochrane House Hotel in Johnstone – and came back later. Alex, I remember, had coaxed the manager to sell him vodka. It was a Sunday and you weren't supposed to get cairry-oots. It had cost him plenty because he'd had to buy it by the measure. By that time I was less nervous, they were half-pissed, and the stories went on. The singing started, and I remember *Goodnight, Irene*, because that was Charlie's wife's name.

I felt he was genuinely pleased to see a teenager being so into his music, and being able to join in on some songs – albeit on the bass strings of an acoustic. I was to meet Alex several times. He sent me photos, albums and the like, in return for letters to London of what I thought of the albums, shows, and how my bass playing was coming along. Not many folks get to meet or know their heroes. Harvey was daunting – scary, even. A wee guy, but larger than life. I'm glad I met and knew him.

In moving to Polydor, Orange Juice started towards a rather more commercial sound than the material they'd done previously – which was to be expected, of course. *You Can't Hide Your Love Forever* made it to number twenty-one in the album charts in March. Almost immediately after that the ubiquitous musical differences came to a head and the band line-up changed significantly. The band felt it was an aftermath of leaving Postcard – towards the end they'd felt Horne's claims that they were a pure pop act had hurt their standing and offended them personally. Dave McClymont said, 'He told everyone we were going to be a pop group with huge hits – but I thought we were like Pere Ubu. That's why I'd joined.'

Back north of the border the pub scene was strong enough for the BBC to take notice, and announce a new TV show, *Street Buzz*, which would feature unsigned acts by way of showcasing the nation's talent. One show featured Shoot the Moon, who'd already grabbed attention by coming third in a UK-wide battle of the bands.

RONNIE DAVIDSON, Shoot the Moon: One of the things that made bands like us so good was that in some places you were playing to a room full of other bands. The best you'd get was, 'Aye, you were okay.' so you were always under pressure to be better. That helped us win the Glasgow heat of the battle, then we made it to the final in London.

The judges were John Entwistle, Paul Gambaccini, Mike Read and Noddy Holder. We didn't know anything about the voting – we were waiting in our dressing room and someone came in and told us, 'You came third!' We went to a club later and I spent half the night talking to Noddy about music.

After we'd been on TV, with the battle and with *Street Buzz*, you really did get noticed around the place. I was having a tyre changed one day and the guy recognised me – weird moments! But it goes to show how much telly could do for you.

As opposed, I have to say, how much battles of the bands can do for you. For a start, anyone who reckons there's outright war between bands is already off on the wrong foot. Sure, one or two personality clashes take place, but there's no competition the way there is between athletes and politicians. There's no underlying personal focus.

I've had to play in the bastards, I've managed bands who had to play in the bastards and I've even judged the bastards too and my considered opinion is this: if you must get involved in a battle – and these days there's almost always a better way to get attention – make sure you're getting as much or more out of it than the people who are running it. Hardly ever happens, I'm afraid...

Paul McCartney and Stevie Wonder were at the top of the charts with *Ebony and Ivory* when the Falkands 'police action' War broke out. Simple Minds hit with *Promised You a Miracle*, showcasing their new, clean, powerful sound, polished almost to less-is-more perfection, which would shine out of the *New Gold Dream* LP. Meanwhile, Jim Diamond's PhD, featuring ex-Jeff Beck Band members, hit number three with *I Won't Let You Down*. By the time the *Belgrano* was sunk (the infamous 'Gotcha!' moment), Altered Images had released *Pinky Blue*, Joe Strummer had done a runner from a Clash tour, the Musicians' Union was trying to 'sack the synth' and the new kids on the block were Haircut 100 and Boy George.

But wait – that's not all. Scotland's proudest World Cup moment came that year, not on the pitch, of course, but in the studio. Who can forget waking in the night with a fever, when the sky was the darkest blue? John Gordon Sinclair, aided and abetted by the national squad, propelled BA Robertson's *We Have a Dream* to number five in the UK charts. It's got to be the best Scotland World Cup song of all time.

BRIAN YOUNG, CaVa Studios: The anthems were recorded at CaVa in 1982, 1986, 1990 and 1994. It was always a great buzz – especially if you're into football. It wouldn't be fair to say which one I think was the best – but we all have a dream... don't we?

Talking of which, get this... England's 1986 effort stalled at number sixty-six in the charts. Can you believe that? Even subconsciously they can't shut their faces about it. (I recall a mate of mine who'd go into shops in London and buy items to the value of the vaunted number. Then when the checkout assistant said, 'Sixty-six...' he'd have a stupendous huff and trounce out. Small victories... you take them where you can find them.)

The later part of the year was an extended season of anthems. In music we had Dexy's' *Come on Eileen*, Survivor's *Eye of the Tiger* and, em, Renee and Renato's *Save Your Love*. On the road we had the Ford Sierra. On the water we had the *Mary Rose* – which nearly didn't rise at all, as *Blue Peter* fans will recall. Squeeze and the Jam split up, as did the Only Ones.

> **ALAN MAIR,** the Only Ones: I had been about to leave a few months earlier. It was just time to go. I was about to make the phone call when the word came through: we're supporting the Who in LA, San Diego and San Francisco. Woo! That was my final payout! And it was great – in the middle of all this real-life Americana there was John Travolta wandering about with a bevy of beauties. I was in my element, and the shows were great.
>
> But I remember one night at the hotel. Some of the band were all hanging around the pool, surrounded by fans – I suppose you'd call them goths now – and the drugs were flowing. Kelly, the drummer, looked at me with this knowing half-smile, and it meant, 'You've had enough, haven't you?' And I half-smiled back, 'Yeah, that's it for me.' So I went to Peter straightaway and said I was going to leave after the tour. He said, 'Well, if you're leaving I'd like to break it up, because I've wanted to leave for the past six months.'
>
> That was a surprise, but it was much better. It's hard to leave something that's still going – you're tied up with thoughts of loyalties and what-ifs. But you've still got to go when it's time – you owe that to yourself and everyone else. Nothing good would have happened if I hadn't said what I'd said.

With the dust settling on the Falkland Islands, Lebanon kicked off instead. Channel Four kicked off too, and Michael Jackson's *Thriller* was released. And remember Orville the Duck? Well, try harder then. The new year opened with the death of Billy Fury at forty-one, the split of Thin Lizzy and the retirement of tennis hero Bjorn Borg. (At this point I must make mention of a mate of mine, who attended a fancy-dress party painted silver with robotic bits of hoover tube stuck out of him, and a tennis racquet in place of one hand. He came as Bjorn Borg – geddit?) The charts of 1983 opened with Men at Work – fronted by Scot Colin Hay – in pole position. Amid a flurry of post-split Jam re-releases, the Eurythmics (I have to bloody retype that three times every time) scored with *Sweet Dreams*, Marillion made their chart debut with *He Knows You Know* and Big Country hit with *Fields of Fire*. Respective frontmen Fish and Stuart Adamson supplied a Scottish take on products which could have otherwise been seen as heavy metal; instead, Fish was noted for interacting with his audiences in a way more suited to a Hollywood crooner – well, okay, the jokes were cruder – while Adamson made sure Big Country's output was pop-oriented, no matter how riff-led.

The eighties vibe was being defined by ideas as diverse as Duran Duran's *Is There Something I Should Know*, New Order's *Blue Monday* and Bowie's *Let's Dance*. Meantime, CD players were introduced at the knock-down price of £450, Karen Carpenter died at the too-young age of thirty-two, Muddy Waters died at the too-young age of sixty-eight and Alan McGee formed Creation Records with a £1000 loan. Robbo, meantime, was winding up a short stint with Motorhead, in which he nearly got everyone killed, allegedly.

> **BRIAN ROBERTSON:** I stepped in to finish their tour because Eddie Clarke had done a runner. How did it go? Scarily – very scarily... We did the Roxy in LA, and the Angels were doing security because they were all Lemmy's mates. We had a bus parked outside and I was going in and out,

because I had to sit on the bus and learn the songs. Coming in new, they all sounded the same to me, so it was a job learning them.

So the Angel on the door had let me pass in and out all day. Eventually I got my ten-minute call and tried to go into the dressing room to tune up. This guy was out of his knickers by now, and he asked for my stage pass, and I said, 'Sorry, it's in the dressing room – but you know me.' He said, 'No – stage pass.' I'm this wee Scotsman with bright red hair and I've been going in and out all day!

I just said, 'No, come on, excuse me,' but he wouldn't move. I've only got ten minutes, so I thought, bollocks, and I nutted him. He just collapsed! Our roadie John had seen everything, and he's saying, 'Fuck's sake, Robbo, what have you done?' I said, 'Look, you deal with it – see you in a minute...'

So I got on with tuning up, then Lemmy comes in. 'What the fuck have you done? We're all going to die – you don't hit Hell's Angels! I'm saying, 'Look, he's not dead or anything...' I didn't even hit him hard... He wouldn't have fallen over if he hadn't been so drunk. If my dog had jumped up on him he'd have fallen unconscious – nobody was more surprised than me!

And that was it... no big deal.

It was a good year for former-Postcardies Orange Juice and Aztec Camera. *Rip It Up* was the Juice's biggest hit, reaching number eight. As well as that smoother, mellower sound, Edwyn Collins' lyrics were decidedly more light-hearted and less political than those which had gone before. Roddy Frame and Co.'s album *High Land, Hard Rain*, showed how they were also exploring a less cynical, jaggy feel. Speaking at the time, Frame said, 'I was sort of bitter in a romantic way – I wasn't the best person to have at your party. But now I can cope much better. I'm more intuitive and a bit more groovy. We're much more humorous and more confident on stage. I enjoy having a good time now – I used to frown on that.'

JOHN McNEILL, Passionate Friends: After the Zips we had a band called Passionate Friends, and we had one great year of nearly being stars. One of the top moments was on 18 June 1983, when we opened the show for Rod Stewart, along with the Jo Boxers and Gary Glitter.

It was a gloriously hot day and the crowd started to fill up the ground quite swiftly when the gates opened. We'd been tutored about how to move around and make grand gestures so the people at the back could see us. A whole different ballgame, if you'll pardon the pun, from our regular Sunday shows at Nightmoves on Sauchiehall Street. The punters were right at your feet there – here they seemed like they were a million miles away. The master plan to run energetically from one side of the stage to the other came to grief – we didn't have radio packs so we were restricted to running the length of our leads! But we were the only local band on the bill and the crowd got right behind us.

The Jo Boxers followed us. They'd had their hit, *Boxer Beat*, and it was the only song anyone knew. They kept themselves to themselves backstage – unlike Mr Glitter, who sashayed along the dressing room corridor, waving regally and lapping up attention from the backstage staff. We were all young boys – luckily we kept our distance...

When Gary took to the stage the audience went berserk. He played all the Glitter hits, and refused to get off at the end, which meant Rod and his band were late on. Not that they were bothered – they only arrived minutes before stage time, in a tour bus which drove up on the pavement outside the main door. They trooped in and went directly to the stage area. When they came off, they headed straight for the bus again. No contact with anyone backstage that I could see. Still, he did give the paying punters what they wanted. It was a great show.

Ian Donaldson's H2O enjoyed a season in the sun with the singles *Dream to Sleep* and *Just Outside of Heaven*. Veterans of the pub scene, they took their hard-earned musicianship down south and managed to make it work for them, even if it was for just a short time. Back in Glasgow, Campbell Forbes of local band the Dolphins proved the point about musical competition being different from other kinds. He wished H2O luck as they escaped the Scottish circuit and argued that it was good for everyone whenever someone was drawing attention up north.

IAN DONALDSON, H2O: Having a hit record is equivalent to climbing Everest or walking to the south pole for anyone making popular music. And in the UK, appearing on *Top of The Pops* was like punching the air when you got to the summit of the mountain, or when you finally stood at the top of the world. All the years of playing every toilet up and down the country, of rehearsing and rehearsing and rehearsing, of listening to the records your heroes made until you knew every inspiring word and every sound they made... all of it was suddenly worthwhile. It's very satisfying to know that, no matter what happens next, no one can rob you of your place in pop history.

CAMPBELL FORBES, the Dolphins: Our best show was at the Kelvingrove Bandstand. We arranged it ourselves and it was a load of work. Even before the technical stuff we needed to deal with the police and the city council. We knew it was going to be a good night, but we didn't expect to sell out – four thousand people! These were people paying to see us, and listen to our songs. Local bands don't get that any more. It was a great night, and we even ended with a fireworks show – very special.

I work with a lot of bands these days. It's a shame so many of them don't know how to work the gear they've got – I'd have killed for the stuff you can have in your bedroom these days. Mind you, we had our own PA, our own sound man, and we knew we could get a good sound every night. There isn't much of a chance to build up a following these days.

IAN DONALDSON, H2O: Now I'm in Fourgoodmen with Bruce Watson from Big Country and Derek Forbes and Mick McNeill from Simple Minds. Being in a band is like being in the SAS. Becoming successful in the music industry is highly unlikely for almost all who try. To do it twice is virtually impossible – but who dares wins. That's us.

Scotland's own oversized rock band, Heavy Pettin', scored a Polydor deal and released the album *Lettin' Loose* – a real Celtic take on the big-haired US sound. With titles like *Love on the Run*, *Rock Me*, *Shout It Out* and *Hell Is Beautiful*... well, you know what you're in for, don't you? And if you can't enjoy it, FOAD, as we used to scrawl on walls.

PUNKY MENDOZA, Heavy Pettin': They laid it on for us – support slots with Kiss and Ozzy. I'd grown up listening to Kiss so it was a dream come true. Gene Simmons and Paul Stanley were really into us – there was talk of them producing and co-managing us. That would have been incredible. And as for Ozzy... that's a book itself! Touring with Motley Crue was just a big long party. It was a pleasure to meet Brian May too – what a nice guy. He gave me a signed copy of the *Starfleet* album. It says, 'To Punky... it's partly thanks to you I committed this to vinyl.' That's yet another story!

10 POP AND POLITICS

Stadium rock. There, I've said it, and it's out there. It's a different kind of entertainment experience, one which, by nature, isn't too Scottish. That's because it involves a kind of generic communication – if you'll allow me to over-simplify, you have to be more concerned with creating music people won't hate rather than music people love. That's by no means an insult; it's just a completely different talent. When you go there, you're effectively saying bye-bye to the possibility of playing those small clubs again. And Scottish music, in general, thrives on the close personal contact those smaller places provide. Mid league, you can only make out the first three or four rows of faces, because of the lights; but when you play to several tens of thousands of people, even the bouncers are too far away to make contact with. And if you need your radio pack changed, you'd better know about it forty seconds in advance, because it'll take your roadie a while to reach you.

The challenge of this new environment came to Simple Minds first of all Scots outfits. The single *Waterfront* sounded as big as its subject, the River Clyde. *Sparkle in the Rain*, the album, was released in February 1984 – and there could be little doubt of its number-one dynamic. The Minds were effing huge.

As *Thriller* passed twenty-five million sales and the miners' strike began, other Scot-edged releases also demonstrated a certain largeness. Big Country's *Wonderland*, the Eurythmics' (I did it!) *Here Comes the Rain Again*, Marillion's *Fugazi* album and Ultravox's *Dancing with Tears in My Eyes* would and could be performed to town-sized audiences.

The Bluebells arrived, and took the sound of Orange Juice and Aztec Camera to its logical pop conclusion – bright, bouncy, angular and fun, as portrayed in the unforgettable *Young at Heart*, which added a pleasing wee element of traditional influence too. Still, imagine how Edwyn Collins would do it... Meanwhile, Jill Bryson and Rose McDowall took the rough-edged bubblegum of Altered Images to *its* logical conclusion with Strawberry Switchblade. Their big hit, *Since Yesterday*, features an Imagesque construction of strong whimsical vocal and leading bass notes – but of course, the most unforgettable thing about them was the polka-dots.

JESS McINTYRE: We all wanted to dress like them. It was outrageous and brilliant. But we didn't want to actually *be* them...

From the convivial to the controversial. The western world's 'greed is good' outlook and the UK's widening poverty gap gave rise to a style of political songwriting that was far more pointed, and arguably more angry, than the perceived rebellion of the punks eight years earlier. At the commercially successful end of that spectrum, there was Jimmy Somerville and Bronski Beat. The video to their single *Smalltown Boy* told the story of a bewildered teenager trying to deal with his homosexuality. The follow-up album, *The Age of Consent*, listed the related legal definitions across the world. Nevertheless, they were eager not to be taken out of context. Jimmy told the press, 'You can't just pounce and say, we're definitely right and you'd better listen. You've got to be subtle – human beings are sensitive.'

The Bronskis went on to world success including that much dreamt-of American tour – while, back in Glasgow, Scheme barely managed to get out of Easterhouse. They were massively politically active, as seen in their involvement in the People's March for Jobs, and vocal support for CND. The song *Bow Out, Maggie* couldn't have been more pointed. But again, despite how the world might view them, they were only doing what you're meant to do – write about what you know.

TOMMY DEVLIN: It's a mystery why they never got a record deal – not even on a minor label. They're the only unsigned band who ever sold out the Apollo. By that time they'd long since outgrown the pub circuit. They're definitely the biggest band never to have made it.

ME: Perhaps another problem was being a flash in the pan – the right kind of music and the right kind of politics and attitude. You always have that risk if you have a political element, where you're judged differently from a band that steers clear. I don't reckon bands supporting things like the current war on poverty are being political – it's just an obvious thing to do. Whereas sticking your neck out and making a point, regardless of its popularity (à la the Dixie Chicks taking a stand on the war in Iraq and seeing their sales plummet) is a brave and dangerous thing to do.

I'm very uncomfortable when musicians start preaching politics. I understand a lot of art has an edge – much of Burns' poetry was designed to keep Jacobitism alive, for instance – but I'm not convinced a medium like mainstream rock'n'roll is the best conduit for a manifesto. (Red Wedge, anyone?)

When you get too close to a particular bone, you generate a situation where only people who like your music *and* your politics will buy your records. You're not making it easy for yourself, which is why people like Bono and Sting don't start preaching until they're millionaires. (And I'm not having a go at Bono or Sting there.)

DWIGHT D EISENHOWER: Why not have a go at Bono and Sting? They're both plonkers. In Sting's defence, though, at least the Police had some good songs. U2 are half a pound of sugar in a ten-pound bag, in my humble opinion...

TOMMY DEVLIN: I totally agree about Scheme's politics, though – and do you know what? So do Scheme. Half of the band didn't really care if they made it big or not. So they were free to sing about anything they wanted. They'd never have allowed themselves to be moulded into a pop band with rules and guidelines. But outside the political stuff they could write some really good pop-rock songs. They created a buzz – but they didn't allow it to go all the way.

On top of all that, pop-rock wasn't exactly in at that time – although that's another argument to suggest that Scheme, by just playing the music they wanted to play, were no more political than anyone else in Scotland who felt disenfranchised in those years. Politics, of course, is meant to be about people, and so is music. The only time you have a clash is when someone wants to make money rather than just express themselves. So, full marks to Scheme for making their point, having fun and having us talk about it years later.

Bloody'ell – almost real journalism there! Best get back to the job in hand...

The Jesus and Mary Chain's debut single exploded into life, and it was a real jawdropper. Released by Creation, *Upside Down* featured a literally astounding experimental feedback effect which blasted through the song. You either loved it or hated it – that one single was a mini-punk revolution.

BRIAN HOGG, writer: The great thing about the Mary Chain is that the base of their songs are classic American teen surfing tunes that have been ripped apart and stuffed with feedback. But once you get through that original noise you realise that they are just fucking great songs. But I have to say, it was the racket that originally attracted me!

GIBBY: I started playing bass late. Part of the problem was that most of my classmates from East Kilbride were highly accomplished musicians... Steven Lironi from Altered Images, who went on to produce Black Grape and, em, Hansen, and session muso Colin Smith, whose finest moment was, perhaps, the instantly recognisable bass line from the original *Grange Hill* theme tune.

My first band was called Satellite after the B-side of the Sex Pistols' *Holidays in the Sun*. Our most memorable gig was our first one at the Village Theatre – me and Jim the guitarist thought it would be a smart idea to smoke some really strong grass before we went on. I spent the whole gig with my back to the audience, thinking, in a fit of paranoia, 'What the fuck are these fuckers staring at?' But we went down a storm – and even got asked for our autographs after the show!

Stardom beckoned... I was approached by Jim and William Reid about the possibility of me joining their band, the Poppy Seeds. The songs they'd recorded on their Tascam Portastudio were good, but they were all acoustic guitar tunes. As a long-haired Van Halen freak, it didn't strike me as the sort of thing I really wanted to do. Along with many others I suggested a guy from our youth club, Douglas Hart, who seemed much more on their wavelength image-wise. He couldn't play! Of course, they went on to become the Jesus and Mary Chain.

CHAS CLARK: I heard it again just there for the first time in years. I'd never noticed before, but the feedback is actually arranged very carefully – it's harmonic, or maybe anti-harmonic or something, but it follows the music. I hadn't even thought of that back then. It was just a breath of fresh air.

CLAIRE SWEENEY: I saw the Mary Chain at the Barrowlands – I was fifteen but I got in anyway. I was waiting in the usual massive queue for the toilets and I got chatting to this older, motherly-type woman in front of me. She seemed a bit out of place, but I'm the talkative type and she was very nice. She asked me how I was enjoying the gig and naturally I went into raptures about how great they were. Then she said, 'They're my boys – come and meet them!' I was off like a shot – me and about three other girls who'd overheard and decided to join the party.

So we get backstage and I'm practically gibbering with nerves – I'm just about to meet Jim and William! Unfortunately for us, someone clocked how young we all were and their mum was taken aside and asked to get rid of us. She made up some story about leaving her handbag in the loo and asked us to help her look for it. We could hardly refuse, and that was that – once we were back outside there was no way we were getting in again.

She must have felt bad, though, because the next thing we know, there's Jim at the backstage door and his mum's going, 'Now, give them a nice kiss on the cheek.' So although I didn't get to hang out with them I did get to meet Jim and even got a wee kiss from him...

Billy Rankin had left Nazareth and tried his luck with a solo release. It worked out – the album *Growin' Up Too Fast* did fine, and he even had a hit in the States with *Baby Come Back*.

BILLY RANKIN: Towards the end of my Naz days we were being sent to more obscure territories, like Russia and Poland. One day, our agent called to offer us a week in Beirut. Nazareth in Beirut? Shurely shome mishtake... Zagreb had been cancelled earlier, because we couldn't get insurance for tank damage... But this? We declined the offer, and then asked, 'Why us?' The answer was, 'Because Boney M won't do it.' I chucked it not long after that.

Among the high points was becoming pals with Alvin Lee. He was one of my heroes – we used to play Ten Years After tunes in my first band, Phase. We were jamming at a promoter's house and I said, 'Gie us *Goin' Home*!' Big Alv pointed out he'd been gie'n us *Goin' Home* since 1968 and would rather french-kiss a skunk. 'Ah'll play it, then,' I said, and I did. And it was going well too, till I got to the second verse and sang, 'I love my babe with a rigorous arm... I love my babe with a rig–'

'With a rigorous *what*?' he said.

'A rigorous arm – y'know... phwaar!' I stuck my arm up like a big boaby.

'It's 'with a red dress on'!' he told me.

Nowadays, when Alvin gies us *Goin' Home*, he alleviates the boredom by singing 'rigorous arm'. Honest, he does!

BRIAN YOUNG, CaVa Studios**:** Recording Billy's album for A&M was our first serious outing with American musicians and an American producer. It's great to know there's a place in Scotland these guys were prepared to work.

BILLY RANKIN: My wife has never been over-impressed with the music business. I remember I came home from the pub and A&M had left a message. I called back to be told, '*Baby, Come Back* has made the top forty in the States.' Brilliant – I shouted to her, 'I'm in the top forty!' She says, 'That's a lot of record sales... Who's buying it? That's the one you wrote in the lavvy, isn't it?'

I used to keep my gold and platinum discs in there till she said they lowered the tone of the room...

At the broadsheet end of our nation's musical output there was the art-tinged material of the Blue Nile and Lloyd Cole and the Commotions. The former's *Walk Across the Rooftops* LP was recorded in complete obscurity, and thus it came out of nowhere to demonstrate a mature and satisfying take on thoughtful construction. The latter's first album, *Rattlesnakes*, was a masterclass in songwriting confidence.

As Madonna arrived with *Like a Virgin*, Virgin Atlantic took to the air and the Tories' Brighton conference was bombed. Jim Diamond's songwriting achieved world acclaim when he was nominated for an Ivor Novello award for *I Should Have Known Better* and he achieved even more acclaim when he asked people to stop buying it in favour of Band Aid's *Do They Know It's Christmas?*.

JIM DIAMOND: *I Should Have Known Better* was an idea I'd had around for a while. I eventually turned it into a song with Graham Lyle, and we knew it was good, and that we'd done the best we could with it. We didn't expect it to go to number one – you don't really think in those terms as a songwriter. You're just trying to do your best.

PhD's *I Won't Let You Down* was number one in Europe, although it was only number three here. Being number one here was a great feeling. But the best thing about it is you can keep on playing the music you love – you've achieved a certain amount of security. Money and plaudits aren't important, but the bills need paid and the kids need fed, and you need to think about that.

I thought Band Aid was a great idea – like a lot of people I'd seen Michael Buerke's reports from Ethiopia, and it seemed obvious to encourage people to buy that single instead of mine. I didn't think much about it – I'd honestly expect anyone in my position to have done that. In fact, I'm surprised more people weren't saying it...

BRIAN SALES: I remember seeing Jim on the telly, saying, 'It's great to be at number one, but next week I don't want anyone to buy it – buy Band Aid instead.' That's in-fucking-credible. Anyone's who's been in a band, spent years trying to make it then finally gets to number one knows what that cost him to say. Your whole life has been spent working your arse off to get there, and as soon as you do, you get out of the way? In-fucking-credible.

You have to remember this was years before compassion fatigue. The government had just said they couldn't make Band Aid VAT-free. People were still talking about whether a charity single was worth doing – it was the yuppie era and a lot of people were thinking, 'Aye, I don't mind helping, but there's no problem with making a few quid myself.'

When you look at it that way, you realise how much folk like Bob Geldof, Midge Ure and Jim Diamond were fighting against. Just by being nice guys...

If Britain had narrowly avoided political revolution through a series of accidental stages, the music scene seemed to have pulled the same trick by the mid eighties. It's easy to see a cyclical pattern of regeneration starting with skiffle – and a turn of the wheel was very badly due in 1985. It didn't come, though.

Perhaps Band Aid had taken away a certain innocence from the mainstream – there was an awareness that stars with loads of cash really should be giving something back, and the realisation was bound to affect people's musical output. It was possibly more to do with people not really knowing how to deal with the situation. Anyway up, no one felt like being overtly pushy enough to introduce a new craze.

While some parts of Scotland, notably industrial areas, enjoyed something of a punk resurgence, the desire to just play away drew focus towards the pub circuit. Now, calling someone a 'pub rock band' wasn't initially an insult. It meant you were on a particular rung of the ladder – one on which you learned your trade, before moving up to club tours, before being experienced enough to start looking for a record deal and, later, a concert-hall tour.

But when Dire Straits were at the top of the charts, you knew there was a problem. They just weren't good enough – competent, enjoyable, with a spark of ingenuity with would certainly allow Mark Knopfler to continue developing his musicianship. But it wasn't music people loved – it was music people didn't hate. That could (and did) work in stadium rock, but it couldn't work in real life. In the same way that SAHB's Ted McKenna has always said, 'The Blues Band was for people who didn't like blues', the mainstream of British music in the mid eighties was, on the whole, for people who didn't like music.

The first half of the year saw Def Leppard's Rick Allen losing his arm in a car crash, the first Vodafone call by Ernie Wise, the phase-out of red phone boxes, the New Coke fiasco and the Bradford City stadium fire in which fifty-six people died. As if to mark the passing of something peculiarly Scottish, the Glasgow Apollo closed its doors in the summer. It was out of time and long past its best, and there wasn't anything like the furore this time – people had known it was coming.

MIDGE URE: That place was my education. Because I was managed by Unicorn I could go in and see everyone who gigged there. You just kept on learning. After the Apollo went there was a big hole in the music scene. There was nowhere for bands to learn any more.

GAVIN DUNN: They wanted us to go to the SEC and act like it was the Apollo. How could you? The SEC didn't stink, it wasn't dark, you could sit on the seats without and danger of them collapsing – and there weren't any bouncers, there were just event stewards. The place had no soul.

I remember walking up Renfield Street night after night as the Apollo was pulled down. I'm not one of the folk who took a brick or a seat, but I wish I had. I did have one of the pink foyer posters somewhere... But even as the place was being wrecked, it still had more soul than the SEC ever could. At least we've still got the Barras – for now...

Graham Lyle won a Grammy for co-writing Tina Turner's *What's Love Got to Do With It?*. Bronski Beat teamed up with Marc Almond to cover *I Feel Love*, while the Associates released their *Perhaps* LP and Marillion came up with the classic *Misplaced Childhood* album.

But of course, 1985 was dominated in every way by Live Aid, representing as it did the battle for what music did and where it went next. Responding to the continuing plight of Africa's famine victims and realising the Band Aid single hadn't done enough, Bob Geldof pulled together nearly everybody who was anybody. The result was a pan-Atlantic gltizfest, taking place at Wembley Stadium, London, and JFK Stadium, Philadelphia, at the same time. Stars included Status Quo, Ultravox, Spandau Ballet, Joan Baez, Run DMC, Sting, Howard Jones, Bryan Ferry, Judas Priest, Crosby, Stills and Nash, Bryan Adams, U2, Simple Minds, Bowie, the Who, Elton, McCartney, Neil Young, Page, Plant and Jones and Duran Duran. Phil Collins appeared at both shows through the cunning use of an 'Aero-Plane' device, and Queen stole the show from everyone. The event is thought to have raised upwards of £150m.

Talking of Simple Minds... 1985 was the year their track *Don't You Forget About Me* was featured in the movie *The Breakfast Club*, representing the pinnacle of their global sound and giving them a US number one and a UK number seven.

The Mary Chain released their *Psychocandy* album, moving on from the *Upside Down* single to explore what happened if you ignored punk and turned surf music paranoid. Now featuring Bobby Gillespie on drums, the band were rapidly building a fanbase, and a reputation for playing fifteen-minute sets.

Jim Reid would later recall, 'That was genius – sometimes we even did nine minutes. To us it was a very important statement – it had much more impact than if you did an hour and bored people. And we only did it when it was 50p or a pound to see us. But people took it the wrong way. Then, when we were doing forty-five minutes, people got pissed off because we hadn't just done fifteen. So they were missing the point the other way!'

Mike Scott, meanwhile, was exploring wide-eyed mythical concepts in a kinda post-psychedelic fashion. The Waterboys' album *This Is the Sea* could be called a bit of a trip-hippy thing, but it could also be called a very fine rock record. The title track is only eclipsed by the single *Whole of the Moon*, a song which manages to say a lot more than one originally thinks.

MIKE SCOTT, the Waterboys**:** When I'm writing, what happens is that a window opens inside, and I get a 'Go!' feeling. Sometimes the whole shape or landscape of a song will be revealed at once, and all I have to do is get it down. That's the best writing experience I know, and it's a rare and beautiful thing. Other times it may be just a line, or a title, or a melody, then the rest comes out gradually.

I've learned over the years that I usually have no idea in advance which songs will catch on with the audience. *Whole Of The Moon* and *Fisherman's Blues*, for example, weren't songs I expected to be hits when I wrote them.

Lloyd Cole and the Commotions released *Easy Pieces*, featuring the top tracks *Lost Weekend* and *Brand New Friend*. Cole's an Englishman, but he was studying literature in Glasgow when he put the band together with a group of Scots from all over. Their first LP, *Rattlesnakes*, wasn't far gone when *Easy Pieces* came out; that probably damaged the second record's impact. Responding to criticisms that his lyrics were designed to show off his literacy, Cole said, 'Next to Billy Idol I look like a literary, intellectual guy – but next to the genuine article I look like a pop singer.'

Greenpeace's *Rainbow Warrior* was sunk while the wreck of the *Titanic* was found. Microsoft's Windows was released and Floyd's *Dark Side of the Moon* spent its six-hundredth week in the US charts. Twelve-inch singles went on general sale as cassettes outsold vinyl albums, and the Mary Chain filled first, second and sixth positions in the *NME's* annual best-of chart.

As the year wound to a close – featuring Aled Jones' *Walking in the Air* from the *Snowman* animated movie, a-ha's *The Sun Always Shines on TV* and a predictable but still very successful re-release of *Do They Know It's Christmas?* – at least two acts of the future were coming together. But the creation of Wet Wet Wet and Deacon Blue caused the destruction of another budding outfit.

GEORGE FUTTER: I used to do a jazz gig in a ruffty-tuffty venue called Broon's Bar in Stirling. It was organised by me and Bill Wells, the only Scottish musician I could truly call a musical genius. He's what you could call a 'band doctor' now – he's called in when you need proper musicality. Did some great work with Belle and Sebastian.

We organised the 'pad', as we jazzers call our repertoire, and some of it was very challenging... Charlie Parker, Zappa, Gil Evans and some original stuff. But we had no problems getting players, and it soon became a firm part of the jazz scene. Calling it 'jazz' is too small, though – sometimes it was out-and-out rock'n'roll. Sometimes there was a five-piece horn section, and there was always a strong element of funk.

We had plenty of major players dropping in – Duncan Findlay, Graham Brierton, Kennedy Aitcheson, Fraser Spiers, Bruce Adams. Guys visiting from London would want a piece of it too. But the main attraction punter-wise – and if I'm honest, personally – was seeing these major players getting their musical arses felt! Especially when it was by me, a violinist, whose instrument is constantly ridiculed in both jazz and rock circles. Those nights made up for some of the kickings I got at school for playing the violin...

We had a couple of young pups from Glasgow in for a while – Graeme Duffin and Ewan Vernal. They got through it pretty well – the boy Duffin, I thought, had the makings of a good player... But one night they both came up to me and said they were leaving the band. Graeme had been rehearsing with a mob from Clydebank called Wet Wet Wet, and Ewan was with another band, Deacon Blue.

'Well,' I said, 'I can't see a band with a name like Wet Wet Wet going far – I mean, what's it all about? They sound like a novelty act or something... And as for Deacon Blue – what level of plagiarism is this? Man, they've even pinched their name from a Steely Dan track!'

Even worse, they were leaving that night, which was well short notice for a gig we were doing at Stirling Uni that Thursday. I wished them luck, but told them to keep their options open, and I hoped they knew what they were doing. And, yes, as they left that night, I shouted after them, 'The money ain't good in this gig, but at least it's steady!' Honest, I was half joking – but I did say it!

Then around twenty-three years passed. I was doing the *Fred MacAulay Show* on Radio Scotland with the Hugh Trowsers Band, promoting our single *Living the Dream*. During the phone-in bit Fred announced, 'We have Graeme Duffin from Wet Wet Wet on the line! To what do we owe the honour?'

Graeme's voice came through, 'I just wanted to say hello to George Futter...'

'How's it going, Graeme? Been a long time,' I said.

'Aye, hiya, George – I just wanted to phone and apologise on behalf of myself and Ewan for leaving you in the lurch for that gig a few years ago...'

'Aye, ye'r awright man,' I said. 'Water under the bridge now.' Fair made my day!

When Altered Images split, Johnny McElhone joined Hipsway that same day, and they were signed in 1986 without recording a note. Their first single was *The Honeythief* and it set them up as a perfect guitar-driven pop outfit – which was really the only current option if you wanted to chart with real instruments. Another track, *Tinder*, found fame in a lager advert; but the band weren't to fulfill their ambitions, suffering musical differences which led to full collapse after their second album.

As Ozzy was accused of driving a fan to kill himself with the song *Suicide Solution*, Phil Lynott died and the RAF admitted they may have shot Glenn Miller's plane down during the war, Goodbye Mr Mackenzie arrived. They set themselves up as something akin to a mix between Dexy's Midnight Runners, SAHB and something even weirder. Nothing they did matched, which made it all the more wonderful. Their first single, *The Rattler*, was starting to show promise of doing quite well – but it was suddenly banned when someone decided they detected suggestive lyrics. Strange – everything about the Mackenzies was suggestive...

Smooth soulsters Love and Money were next out of the bag, with a debut album *All You Need Is Love and Money* showcasing intelligence, style and careful confidence. Remembered for sensitive acoustic guitar and an understatement that belied their attention to detail, singer James Grant and Co. were one of those 'wee bit special' moments that, sadly, didn't make the big time – but could've easily been eggshelled by it anyway.

CLIVE YOUNG: I'm not Scottish – I'm American and I've never even been to Scotland, but in the eighties it seemed like great bands were pouring out of the country... Aztec Camera, Lloyd Cole and the Commotions, Simple Minds, Big Country, Deacon Blue, the Blue Nile, APB, Altered Images – and, in particular, Love and Money. They all made Glasgow sound so exotic – they sang about rain and drinking. We had that here, only our city's musicians just got hooked on cocaine and killed themselves.

I was in university, and I'd become a writer for the campus newspaper. I saw in *Village Voice* that the band was going to play the Palladium in Greenwich Village. That was awesome! Then I saw the bad news – the concert was scheduled for the night before three final exams. If I went, I wouldn't get back to campus until at least two in the morning. Worse, I was already scheduled to work from four until eight in the morning on exam day. Going to see Love and Money would be nothing short of academic suicide. Naturally, I went!

The room held maybe two hundred people tops. There were a lot of industry folks there, mainly because Mercury hadn't bothered to promote the band – so the label workers had to show up at the gig to make it look like people came to the show. The opening act was a ragged garage band called Too Much Joy – they were great. They were a horrible match for Love and Money, but for me, they were fantastic. Their only problem was their parents were in the audience and really standing out – so to hide their embarrassment the band had all been drinking. Before long they were ruining songs and making jokes that came across very badly. They were still a good band, though.

Then I spotted Lloyd Cole at the bar. Damn! I mean, *the* Lloyd Cole, one of my all-time favorites, here, in New York! I went over to bother him. It turned out he'd come to see the show and hang with Bobby Paterson, Love and Money's bassist. He offered to buy me a drink. I was in awe – my hero wanted to buy me a beer. But with three finals the next day and still being under twenty-one, I turned him down. I still kick myself about that...

I asked him what he'd thought of Too Much Joy, and he said, 'Ha – the world's got a Replacements... we don't need another one!' Two things happened then. I realised your heroes weren't always right about everything, and a friend of the band overheard the conversation and must have told them something like, 'Lloyd Cole's in tonight and he says you suck!'

I noticed a little later that some of the band were standing round Lloyd, and they were having an intense chat. I thought, good, they're getting some pointers from a professional – what a nice guy for doing that. But when I spoke to one of them later, he said, 'We heard he was talking shit at the bar, so we went and had some words...' Great! Trying to hang with a hero and I'd started a fight instead...

Love and Money finally came on, and James Grant greeted the cheers by saying, 'This is a very special night for us on this tour of America. That's because there's people in the audience.' The crowd had reached its peak of maybe eighty people in the place, so it was easy to walk up to the stage, where I watched in awe for the rest of the show. When it was all over, I was happy, exhausted and satisfied. It may have been cliché, but I had indeed been rocked. I got in as expected around two, slept for two hours, got up, went to work, then hit my three finals – which I passed with flying colors, much to my amazement.

As it turned out, Love and Money never played New York City again. If I'd skipped the show, I'd never have had the chance, the honour, the luxury of seeing them live. Lloyd Cole moved to the US permanently, becoming a fixture on the New York scene for a decade before moving to Boston. During his time in New York, if you knew which late-night club to stumble in to, you could find him jamming away with Brilliantine – a band that included the bassist from Too Much Joy.

To a background of the Chernobyl and Challenger disasters, Edinburgh's Shop Assistants released a self-titled album, which was to be their only LP, while the Big Dish released *The Swimmer*. Jimmy Somerville moved on from Bronski Beat because he felt the need to be slightly more political, and landed in the Communards. Sigue Sigue Sputnik attempted to sell ad space between their album tracks, then cancelled their UK tour; Metallica's tour bus crashed in Sweden, killing bassist Cliff Burton; bus deregulation arrived to make us all feel safer and better-served, Cary Grant died and MTV arrived in Britain.

Grangemouth's Cocteau Twins, usually a three-piece, released their fourth album, *Victorialand*. It was almost entirely acoustic, featuring Robin Guthrie's guitar and Elizabeth Fraser's vocals; but it was the vocals which always attracted most attention. At times completely incomprehensible, Fraser's delivery was still loaded with meaning – the word is 'ethereal'. They noted how the lack of connection with either the Glasgow or the Edinburgh scene, along with only a passing interaction with London, allowed them to stay unique.

GIBBY: I had a miserable time in London. I'd managed to join Mick Ransome's band by turning up the day before two hundred other hopefuls, and sharing a huge carry-out with them. It worked, and that was me in a band called Texas – stupid name, I thought. There *were* highlights – playing the Marquee, and having my song *Lies in Your Eyes* recorded in Trident Studios. I'd been in Sirrocco Studios in Kilmarnock, but this was the real deal.

Trident wasn't cheap, though, so I had no money to live on, and I nearly starved to death! Only the intervention of my dad, who'd just got a job in London and found me living in a dump in Braintree, saved me. I'm not kidding – I really was nearly dead...

I realised Mick really didn't give a fuck about anyone and quit the band. Mick went on to form the Tattooed Love Boys, who did okay. Back in East Kilbride, a dismal failure instead of the returning hero, I gave up playing altogether. Fortunately my mates Kenny and Cummy wanted me to join their band, the Ligament Blub Brothers. The idea was to celebrate ten years since punk – and since the songs were so fantastically out there, especially the outrageous lyrics, I was in.

We set up our own label, Scrundleplatch, and released the single *Big Shoe Boy*. It was distributed by the cartel, which meant it was available throughout Europe. For a while we were outselling the Mary Chain in France – we went top ten in their indie chart. John Peel kept playing it, along with both tracks on the B-side. Anne Nightingale, Andy Kershaw and Radio Clyde's Mark Goodier were all on our side too. *Sounds* wrote, 'A band so beautifully named, a band so fantastically East Kilbridey, what could possibly go wrong here? They could start singing, that's what...'

We loved it – because the thing is, while everyone thought *Big Shoe Boy* was an anti-fascist rant, it was actually about a barber we knew who had orthopaedic footwear. He stood corrected, get it? So did the DJs when we told them!

We did a live radio interview with our cocks hanging out, and the DJ didn't notice. We did the Arran Aid festival and went down a storm even though we were totally drunk. We did a gig in Blackfriars in Glasgow, where we thought it would get us some good press if a couple of mates sort of threw glasses at us. We made a mistake there – firstly, our mates got plastered and so we really did get glassed... secondly, we forgot to invite anyone from the press... and thirdly, why did we ever think 'Glasses Thrown in Glasgow Pub' could ever be a headline?

We started attracting major label interest, and Kenny and Cummy decided the punk thing to do was split up. So we did – much to my dismay, I must admit. Still, we had a good laugh. We've got a mention in the *Great Scots Musicography*, a book which fails to mention a lot of better-known bands than us. And I found a website that called us 'legendary' and revealed that an Ayrshire band had released a cover of *Big Shoe Boy*. I don't know how it went, but it can't have done worse than ours...

11 THESE PEOPLE AREN'T LIKE US

It was 1987 and the revolution still hadn't come, so Stock, Aitken and Waterman staged one. The only other way to look at it is to accept their movement as the natural progression. Blundering flip – *how* did we let that happen? If the folk who'd slammed rock'n'roll in the late fifties had seen this guff, they'd never have said a word against Elvis, Gene Vincent and those guys.

I must make an admission here – for a short, *short* while I was involved in the management of similar such manufactured pop products. Not for long, and not deeply, I insist – in fact, just long enough to notice the trend for Evian water meant the backstage beer supplies were being abandoned every night. I managed *that* situation, to be sure.

The rule was you picked up some good looking kids, you taught them a few dance moves, you found a song for them to just about sing and you put them on the treadmill, relying on their desperate desire to be famous and their youthful energy to carry them through. It was a packaging and sales job, and you told them: bank every penny, because you've got two years tops before nobody gives a flying one about you. Witness the earliest pap-pop poster boy, Rick Astley, who actually could sing but got the hell out of the Hit Factory because he completely and utterly hated it.

It didn't take long to work out the new movement had bollox-all to do with music – this was a discipline of the entertainments industry completely devoid of artistic merit. The sessions musos were great, as usual, but you knew that, if someone could find a way of marketing a group without having to do the music bit, they'd be all over it.

ANDY McEWAN: A lot of the road-crew work at my level had dried up. Blondie's tour had been cancelled because of poor ticket sales – I remember them saying it was the Rolling Stones' fault for charging £30 a ticket, back in the eighties... It took money out of other tours because people couldn't go to both. But some of the labels thought, 'That's it, our bands aren't doing Britain.' and that was it.

So I wound up working on a Stock, Aitken and Waterman tour – I won't say who it was. There I was, do-de-doo, do-de-doo around the stage.... Hold on, there's not a lot of inputs up here, is there? I've got seven mic stands, seven mics and one channel. Eh? One of the old hands must have recognised my expression – he just smiled and patted me on the back.

Come showtime, I just couldn't believe it! Everyone was miming – *everyone*! The only reason they had one mic open was so the guy could talk between songs. Sometimes I thought he was singing but the old hand said they'd never let him – if the show sounded any different from the record, there'd be trouble.

I'd spent years slagging off bands I worked with, the way that you do. But at least they worked. I remember one Hit Factory act, who should have known better, getting caught miming because they stopped singing to say, 'Come on, crowd, let me hear you!' and her lead vocal kept going behind her...

In the resulting desperation, any real music at all was good music. Chart entries early that year included U2's *With or Without You*, the Pogues and Dubliners' *Irish Rover*, Freddie Mercury's *Great Pretender* and Alison Moyet's *Weak in the Presence of Beauty*. (If you hear that last one on the radio, try singing 'I go *beep* in the presence of beauty' – 'tis a chuckle.)

Wet Wet Wet finally made a move in the charts, after two years of fighting with their label. The bosses wanted one thing but the Wets, under manager Elliott Davies, were sticking to their guns. *Wishing I Was Lucky* was an overdubbed demo rather than the squeaky-clean label version, and it made number six, followed by *Sweet Little Mystery* making number five. Their *Popped In Souled Out* album was a triumph of supercharged poppy R&B, and as it soared into number one even a record label exec might have been thinking about admitting he'd been wrong. Aye, right.

Coatbridge had spawned cousins Ted and Hugh McKenna in the sixties, who became part of SAHB; and in the eighties the same town spawned the Kane brothers, Pat and Greg, who became Hue & Cry. They found themselves in a similar situation to the Wets, but dealt with it differently, accepting the challenge of making their musical ambitions match their label's requirements. *Labour of Love* ably demonstrated their R&B leanings, making number six and immediately putting the onus on them to do better next time.

Pat Kane told the *NME*, 'The label's been completely honest with us – they told us we'd be presented as two desirable young males, and our masculinity was to be as important as the music. I thought, "Great – we can re-examine homoerotic imagery." But they said, "No, you're gonna be juicy boys the wee lassies fancy!" Still, *Labour of Love* started out as an anti-Thatcherite song...'

JIM BRADY, Barky! Barky: It's hard starting a band in a place like Cumbernauld – you're pretty far removed from any sort of scene. We were playing places where the audience were expecting cover songs like *Twisting the Night Away* – and there we were with a drum machine, singing songs about Thatcher and nuclear power.

We decided we had to put a single out, so my brother Johnny sold his motorbike, and I sold my record collection, and we brought out this single called *Animals*. It didn't matter if it didn't sell as long as it raised our profile – sure enough, we came to the attention of Craig Tannock, who went on to open the 13th Note, and we started to play places like the Shelter, and got to know a lot of Glasgow bands. We always did well in Edinburgh for some reason, and I think the Glasgow bands were impressed with that, plus the fact that we had a single out – even though it didn't sell in the end.

We got some decent support slots with people like the Shamen, and the Young Gods – they were a revelation. We realised we were like the yin and yang of each other – we were both playing kind of electro-metal grunge stuff, but with different instrumentation. We became really pally with them and they even namechecked us on some of their records. Record companies started phoning us because they'd heard the name, but then they didn't like the material. I remember the head of A&R at Chrysalis phoned up, and said he was interested. I said, 'Have you seen the band?'

'No!'

'Have you heard our music?'

'No – but we've seen the name about.'

So I reeled off a list of bands on his roster and said, 'We're not like any of them.' He still wanted to hear us, and I'm like, 'Look, we made the record on a shoestring, I'm on the dole, and you expect me to send you a copy when you could have gone into a shop and bought it yourself?' I was really trying to put the him off in a nice way, but he kept insisting. I said, 'You probably won't even listen to it – we know how it is, but – okay.'

Five weeks went by and I heard nothing, so I sent the guy a really irate letter saying, 'If I'd asked you for a free record, you wouldn't have given me it, so you owe me a fiver for that single and the postage...' Lo and behold, he sent me a cheque for a fiver – no letter, mind you! The best thing about that, other than pissing an A&R guy off, was that in every press release afterwards we were able to say we'd had our single paid for by Chrysalis. I didn't cash the cheque – I've still got it...

C86 was a compilation cassette cover-mounted with the *NME*. As the title hints, it had been put out in 1986, and it carried contributions from some of the bands thought to be pioneering the future. Primal Scream's *Velocity Girl*, the Soup Dragons' *Pleasantly Surprised*, the Shop Assistants' *It's Up to You* and the Pastels' *Breaking Lines* all appeared. Soon afterwards, these Scottish bands and several English ones too became known as the C86 movement. And along with the BMX Bandits and Teenage Fanclub, the Dragons were also part of the Bellshill scene.

SUSHIL K DADE, the Soup Dragons**:** The attitude, certainly in our circle of bands, was to help each other out as much as we could. Borrowing equipment, and even musicians, was par for the course. I remember one night, at the Hattonrig Hotel in Bellshill, our drummer, Ross, played for us, the Bandits and Gods for All Occasions and I think our guitarist Jim played more than two sets as well!

For me it had to be the bass. I was tuning into John Peel most nights and the dub reggae tracks with the low moving bass lines were great. Strangely, at our early rehearsals, I decided to take off all the bass on the amp and turn the treble up full. Back then I was mostly playing chords and melodies – that was until we did our first Peel Session, which was produced by Mott the Hoople's Dale Griffin. He added flange to my bass, which was truly hideous – not sure if I've recovered yet, but at least it helped me rediscover what the bass was for...

JOHN MARTIN: I masqueraded under the name Martin St John and I was the resident tambourine man in Primal Scream until 1987. At the time we were a jingly-jangly sixties-influenced pop group with a manic edge. We nearly died before it all got going, though. We were to play the Boardwalk in Manchester, and just outside the city the driver decided we were going the wrong way. Next thing we know, we're upside-down on a dual carriageway, skidding in slow motion... When we finally stopped moving we all staggered out, and some sick fuck stops his car, takes a photo then drives away! What a cheek! Bobby Gillespie and I were worst hit, but we got stitched up and did the show anyway. The crowd had heard what happened to us so they were on our side all night.

Next night, we were doing the Splash One Club. All I remember is dropping a tab of acid before I went on – we were all blitzed, so Bob G decided it couldn't get any worse and we stormed into a demented version of *Belsen Was a Gas*... I was tripping out my tree as I came off, and I got lost in the mirrored backdrop – I finally managed to get offstage by climbing into the crowd...

The Mary Chain's *Darklands* album caused a certain amount of uproar amongst fans, not just because the band were moving towards more melodic songs. The pop-terrorist concepts were starting to be skimmed off, leaving a band who knew how to apply passion and drama – and now, easy-access melody too. Tracks like *On The Wall* and *Happy When It Rains* were the way ahead now.

Roddy Frame brought Aztec Camera back with the *Love* LP, three years after his last outing with *Knife*. It featured the lovely pop piece *Somewhere in My Heart*, complete with the bubblegummy chime bell run which I absolutely insist everyone air-plays along with me, unless we're at a funeral.

It was the end of the road for Lloyd Cole and the Commotions, whose album *Mainstream* was to be their last. It's a perfect title – it sums up the conclusion of their recording career perfectly, and tracks like *Mr Malcontent* show how a confident, poppy maturity had replaced their earlier confident clever wordplay and noteplay. The band continued performing until 1989, and the split, I'm pleased to say, was amicable – it was a natural end.

One hundred and eighty people died in the Zebrugge ferry disaster as televangelist Jim Bakker's career collapsed and eventually led him to prison, followed by a prodigal-son reinvention of his career. Mathias Rust landed his plane in Moscow's Red Square, Simple Minds were praised by Amnesty for their human rights work, Volkswagen badges went missing as the Beastie Boys arrived, Thatcher won her third term and sex-pixie Kylie's version of *The Locomotion* was her first hit. Meanwhile, Runrig became a stadium band as their album *The Cutter and the Clan* took them to global success with the likes of U2.

DONNIE MUNRO, Runrig: We'd formed our own label, Ridge Records, purely because no one was interested in what we were doing. But we already had a substantial live following and that worked in our favour when it came to approaching bank managers. There was still a huge element of risk involved – there's something very daunting about hiring a huge ballroom, using your own money, and wondering if anyone will turn up...

The only bad time we had was the first time we tried signing to another label. They were called Simple Record and they couldn't have been more complex – in fact, 'dodgy' is the right word. They ended up flooring most of the bands they'd signed, and they'd have floored us too if we hadn't had that incredible live following.

When we signed to Chrysalis and re-released *Cutter and the Clan*, we were at last with a company that cared. The experience of running our own label helped enormously – we knew things like how much the pressing cost, and how much to budget for artwork and so on. I remember first time we went down, they sent a limo to pick us up at the airport. A lot of bands would have been impressed, you know, 'Wow, we've arrived!' But we knew we were the ones paying for the car!

Former Blak Flag punksters the Proclaimers followed Donnie and Co. to Chrysalis Records, and were an instant hit when they performed *Letter to America* on *The Tube*. Craig and Charlie Reid were the Beatles to Runrig's Stones; both acts featured strong, deep songwriting far apart from their proud Celtic delivery.

Deacon Blue presented another facet of the Scottish pop-rock onslaught. *Raintown* was also something of a concept album, dealing with growing up in Glasgow, and expressing those not-quite-but-nearly Schemesque feelings in an altogether more commercial vibe. *Dignity* – nuff said.

Ex-Fire Engine Davey Henderson's new band, Win, took those early-eighty sounds and pushed them in a powerpop direction. The album *Uh! Tears Baby (A Trash Icon)* is most remembered for the single *You've Got the Power*, which featured in that famous McEwan's Lager ad with the guys shoving the stone balls around. Interestingly enough for a Scottish company to support, the lyrics were ever-so-slightly anti-Tory: 'You've got the power to censor what's real/You've got the power to generate fear'. Strike! Well, no, you couldn't any more.

JIM BRADY, Barky! Barky: We did a gig at Barlinnie Prison once. It had been arranged that a couple of members of the very captive audience would get up and sing with us. I say 'arranged' and I mean it – the governor and a social worker woman had pre-approved the acts.

The first guy came up to do his own song on an acoustic. He got to the mic and said, 'I was going to sing a particular song but I've decided to do a different one...' You could see the governor starting to look a bit worried. The one he'd had approved was all about how prison had made him a better person. But the one he sang was about the lack of women in jail: – 'Shagging's great, I love fannies...' It was jaw-droppingly rude by any standards – every part of the female anatomy was discussed. There were even a few German moments in there! We were trying to back him but kept having to stop with laughter... Everyone was killing themselves, guards, the social worker, other prisoners – everyone except the governor, whose face was like thunder.

The next guy who got up was built like a brick shithouse. He said he wanted to sing Leo Sayer's *When I Need You*, and we weren't about to argue. I'll never forget it – he had the sweetest voice imaginable. He was built like a pit bull but his voice almost moved me to tears.

Afterwards, we were invited into the governor's office for tea, and I said that I hoped the first guy wasn't going to get into trouble for his song. After all, he wasn't encouraging anyone to get violent or escape or anything. But the governor said rules were rules, and the guy had to be disciplined. Then he leaned in and said, 'These people aren't like us...' My hackles fuckin' shot up and the claws were ready to come out when Stu Who crossed the thirty-foot room in about two seconds and wheeled me out of it. I think he thought I was going to pop the guy and we'd get to stay in Barlinnie overnight!

Labels, artists and the MU were steeped in arguments over the idea of sampling. Paul Hardcastle's *Nineteen* had started the ball rolling, introducing the twin notions of recycling as an art form and the DJ as artist. A massive great hurricane wrecked a million greenhouses in southern England, Black Monday's stock market crash wrecked a million yuppie ambitions and Lester Piggot's jail sentence for tax evasion wrecked a million betting slips. Work began on the Channel Tunnel, Enniskillen was bombed and thirty-one people died in the King's Cross underground fire.

Musically, there was a backlash taking place. You had that awful stuff made by rich folk with computers who could afford cute young wannabes to front the results – Bros, Tiffany, Vanessa Paradis and all that. Then you had George Michael's *Faith* and George Harrison's *Got My Mind Set on You* (great video) which proved that even teeny heroes in the old days had required some kind of talent. It was songwriters versus song performers, and as 1988 kicked off, Scots were in the thick of the fighting.

Deacon Blue celebrate the fruits of their labour in CaVa Studios

Early hits included Aztec Camera's *How Men Are*, the Communards' *For a Friend*, the Wets' *Temptation* and Danny Wilson's *Mary's Prayer*. As the first major anti-Communist campaigns began to roll in the USSR, there was a remarkable anomaly in the singles charts – three number ones in a row were Scottish. First came Fairground Attraction's *Perfect*, next was the Wets' *With a Little Help from My Friends*, and finally the Timelords' *Doctorin' the Tardis*. The Timelords were actually KLF's Jimmy Cauty and Scot Bill Drummond, now of soup-making fame.

> **ROSS SKIVINGTON:** I was working for a music PR company at the time, drawing up a list of target clients. I suddenly realised – there's around two hundred big-name acts on the major label rosters, and nearly forty of them are Scottish!

Hue & Cry's second album was to shift four hundred thousand copies and generate two top-twenty hits, *Looking for Linda* and *Violently*. The Wets' success that year came via the *Memphis Sessions* LP. Remember what I said about record execs never learning anything? Well, they'd been at it again, refusing to release the album until the band insisted upon insistence... and it made number three. Nyah labels.

The Jesus and Mary Chain's *Sidewalking* stalled at number thirty, suggesting a change of direction might be in order if they wanted continued success. It was at this point they began messing about with yet another new sound, bringing in hip-hop influences. It was one of those times when you kept hearing rumours – 'Wait till you get a load of what the Mary Chain are up to...' Deacon Blue's *When Will You Make My Telephone*

Ring had also fared badly in chartworld – and what they did next was difficult to keep a lid on.

BRIAN YOUNG, CaVa Studios: You don't always get a feel for how good something's going to be. But when they came to do *Real Gone Kid*, everyone in the room just knew from day one. The arrangement was right, the song was right – everything was right place, right time. That was a buzz.

Big Country and the Proclaimers entered the charts, sandwiching Guns'n'Roses *Sweet Child of Mine* with the former's *King of Emotion* and the latter's *I'm Gonna Be*. The Reid brothers' single was to explode a few years later when it was used in the soundtrack for the movie *Benny and Joon*, and like Simple Minds before them, made them overnight stars in the States. The accompanying album, *Sunshine on Leith*, is their crowning achievement and still sells well.

The Soup Dragons joined the ranks of the bands who'd made it to the big league, signing with Sire Records and releasing their debut album, *This is Our Art*.

SUSHIL K DADE, the Soup Dragons: Our first gig was supporting Primal Scream at the legendary psychedelic Splash One club. It was my birthday too, I think, so around lunchtime I had a vodka and fresh orange, although I stayed off the drink for the rest of the day. After the gig, the Pastels, Brian Superstar and a couple of mates piled into my dad's van and, within minutes, I was pulled over by the police. They asked if I'd been drinking, and I said, 'Yes, sir, I've had some vodka...' I had to do the breathalyser but the crystal colours were on my side. I got a fright, though.

It's funny to think, years later, I'm now a qualified driving instructor, and I've ended up teaching everyone from the Pastels to the Fanclub! I remember one day I was waiting in Glasgow to do a lesson with John from National Park, and I saw someone who looked a lot like John Peel. Sure enough, it was – he'd been playing some tracks from my *Galaxy of Sound* LP, so I stopped him and we had a wee chat. The other John joined us, and for around a hundred and eighty seconds the three of us bonded in perfect pop. It was a real thrill when John Peel played a track I'd been doing with John Park the next night. What a generous, sweet guy he was.

The Soup Dragons' first release was done with the help of Stephen Pastel, and it was a flexidisc that went out with my fanzine *Pure Popcorn*. It must have been the longest fanzine ever – me, Stephen Donnelly and Paul Woods used to sellotape the pages together so it opened in a big concertina.

The flexidisc very quickly became the *NME*'s single of the week – before we knew it we were playing in London, sleeping on Dan Treacy's floor (from the Television Personalities), and taking our entire backline on the underground with our superstar roadie Norman Blake, who went on to become the wonderful vocalist and songwriter with Teenage Fanclub. It was all too beautiful!

It was a turbulent year in the headlines – as the acid house movement began, the Piper Alpha platform exploded and killed one hundred and sixty seven. Iron Maiden fans died at Donington's oversubscribed Monsters of Rock Festival, and even those nice Deacon Blue folk were bottled off at Reading. 'Terminal Man' Sir, Alfred Merhan (the comma is part of his name) began an eight-year stay at France's Charles de Gaulle Airport. Midge Ure left Ultravox and Fish left Marillion. Jean Michele Jarre's super-pompous giant megashow at London's Docklands went off alright, as did the one and only flight of the Soviet Union's space shuttle. The Netherlands, those forward-looking souls, became the second country to connect to the Internet, after the USA, of course.

Hue & Cry in CaVa

Goodbye Mr Mackenzie signed to Capitol and re-recorded *The Rattler*, this time featuring the furious guitar of Big John Duncan, but still those lyrics which halted its progress at number thirty-seven. In a later incarnation as a member of the Gin Goblins, Big John explained how he'd never quite fitted the band.

BIG JOHN DUNCAN: I went out in the middle of a song and started handing out biscuits to the crowd. I think they were Abernethies. The band stopped the song! They stopped the song, and they were like, 'What do you think you're doing?' 'Handing out biscuits – what does it look like? I nearly left the band after their attitude with the biscuits incident. They really weren't rockers, the Mackenzies. Oh, no, they weren't. Oh, yeah, the Blood Uncles ruled!

DAVID MILLER, Finitribe: Edinburgh seemed so grey in the eighties. The only colour came from JJ's, Valentinos, Nite Club and the fantastic Hoochie Hoochie Coochie Club. I think I went there Thursdays, Fridays, Saturdays and Sundays – every week. All these colourful people would appear, people who were really into music. It really was a great time to be part of that.

We were booked to support a band called Sian – featuring Marc Bolan's wife – at the club above the Edinburgh Playhouse. I can't remember anything about the music we played but I do remember the presence of Big John – he was and still is larger than life...

I remember seeing him come up to the front of the stage, then he started shouting and screaming at us. He was legendary for his heckling, and he was livid – he *hated* us, calling us fucking faggots... He started gobbing at us, and one of the gobs flew straight into Chris' mouth. He was immediately sick all over the stage. John was laughing his head off... Everyone was terrified of him, but a few years later we became friends and he's one of the loveliest guys I'd ever met. Punk's no deid!

In December, one of Scotland's biggest modern-day tragedies took place – and it was also the world's worst terrorist attack until 9/11. On the longest night of the year, PanAm flight 103 fireballed into Lockerbie and killed two hundred and seventy people. That same month, thirty-five died in the Clapham Junction rail crash, and Roy Orbison passed away.

January 1989 saw the release of the Waterboys' *Fisherman's Blues*. Mike Scott had reformed the band and moved it to Ireland, and the resulting LP was far more Celtic in feel than previous works. Between *Whole of the Moon* and the new album's title track, Scott was on record as a prolific and resourceful songwriter.

MIKE SCOTT, the Waterboys: I don't feel obliged to play *Whole of the Moon* – or any of my songs for that matter... Actually, I should say that *Moon* isn't the main one people expect to hear – that honour rests with *Fisherman's Blues*. But I love playing *Moon*. If I didn't, it just wouldn't get played, old curmudgeon that I am... I'm in my element playing my music, that undefinable, unclassifiable thing that is Waterboys/Mike Scott music.

Johnny McElhone, that lucky character, was allowed a third bite at the cherry. He'd hit with Altered Images and Hipsway, and now enjoyed his biggest and best success with his new band, Texas. It was a team effort from himself and Sharleen Spiteri; they set out their stall with the number-eight hit *I Don't Want a Lover*, and they've been selling ever since.

KEVIN MORGAN: I'd always been a fan of anything Johnny did, but I read about Texas before I heard them. Female vocal – good, reminded me of Altered Images... but the name was a bit dodgy to me. I thought, 'Oh, right, they're pretending to be American.' You know that way in the sixties when space-age superheroes were called things like Captain Laserblast and shit? That's what I thought of their name. Then I read the album was going to be called *Southside*, and I thought, 'Oh, no, now they're being Glasgow parochial.' To be honest, I was sick of Glasgow bands.

It just shows you not to judge books by covers. I heard them do a half-hour set in London and it all made sense – everything Johnny had been trying to do the whole time. I just got it. And don't be fooled by the heavy studio work – this is a rock band.

While Poison simpered *Every Rose Has its Thorn* and the Reynolds girls cackled *I'd Rather Jack*, Simple Minds had their first number-one single with *Belfast Child*. It's an anthem of galactic proportions which, quite simply, is awe-inspiring. If someone introduced a law that said bands could only be remembered for one moment, it has to be this for the Minds. It was pop, it was rock, it was of its moment and it crossed all manner of boundaries. If you ever wonder about whether a band could be said to be 'important', *Belfast Child* is a portable definition for you.

Jim Kerr spoke a little later about how, after finally having taken some time off, the band felt invigourated and had enjoyed every second of their 1989 world tour. 'There's a lot of perks to this life,' he said, 'and I'd hate to look back and think I didn't enjoy it. For instance, I know we played Live Aid – I've seen the video – but I don't remember anything about it. I didn't want that to happen again, so I decided to take time out to enjoy things, see the Van Gogh Museum in Amsterdam, watch AC Milan at the San Siro Stadium. This life we have is pretty remarkable.' Isn't that incredibly refreshing? It is for me – I spend far too much time surrounded by road crew, who even whine about not having anything to whine about...

Deacon Blue were doing a touch of complaining – creating their album *When the World Knows Your Name* had been a generally unpleasant experience for the band, despite the success of *Real Gone Kid* and the LP's subsequent number-one placing. It was the classic pressures of success routine – no one wanted to take any risks, and as a result the product was a horse designed by a committee. 'The playing was compromised by this overwhelming desire to impress,' Ricky Ross observed. 'People kept talking about the sound instead of the songs. We had multiple producers then multiple studios. They took us to LA to record in the sun – we hated it.' As we all know, you can't have great music without risks; so it's a tribute to the band and their talent that this set of songs achieved longevity.

Meanwhile, Sharleen Spiteri's cousin Mark Rankin arrived with his band, Gun, who filled a gaping hole in Scotland's output by being a straight-out no nonsense rock band. The debut single *Better Days* was a modest success, but the album, *Taking on the World*, left no doubt as to what the band could achieve.

> **GIBBY:** I was a huge fan of Gun – went to see them loads of times. Baby Stafford was a great showman as well as a great guitarist, and so was his replacement, Alex Dickson. Their manager, Rab Andrew, used to give our band a lot of good advice. We went through to see him one day and we spotted Gun's drummer, Scott Shields, who was obviously going there too, so we gave him a lift. He turned out to be completely off his face – so there wasn't much conversation during the journey! When we got to the studio, Rab took one look at Scott and said, 'Where's your suitcase? And don't tell me you've forgotten your passport as well...' Turns out the band were leaving for an American tour that day, and Scott was so far gone he'd forgotten all about it. Rock'n'roll – don't ye just love it?

Sadly, the nation's other great white hope of rock, Heavy Pettin', reached the end of the line and split.

> **PUNKY MENDOZA,** Heavy Pettin': I just think the label just lost interest – we weren't in the wrong

place at the wrong time or anything. We needed consistent input if we were to survive as a business – and we had to be business. We didn't get that from Polydor. In four years we had four A&R guys, and each time we had to start building the relationship from scratch.

Our last album, *The Big Bang*, was a terrible disappointment. Some of the things we wanted to do didn't turn out. Polydor wanted to turn the band into something it wasn't. The technology got in the way of the music. Our songwriting was a bit vague too – a bit old influences, a bit new influences. Even the packaging was pathetic.

GIBBY: You hear the word 'underrated' a lot, but it definitely applied to Heavy Pettin'. They were not only outstanding live – they made great records too. I think what killed them was doing the heats of the Eurovision Song Contest. They did *Romeo* and it flopped – it was a very ill-advised decision...

Their bass player, Brian Waugh, went on to design album sleeves. He did the Time Frequency's stuff. I used to meet him from time to time and he always said he had no regrets. They toured with Kiss and Motley Crue – for a bunch of young guys it's fairytale time, isn't it?

Scotland gave the world two more classic pop albums that year: the Blue Nile's *Hats* and Danny Wilson's *Be Bop Mop Top*. The Nile's Paul Buchanan was never in better voice, with arrangements and lyrics that allowed you to almost be there in a very touching way. *Saturday Night* is the album's top moment. Danny Wilson's second LP was a pleasantly smooth jazzy collection, which would have led to greater things if they hadn't split the following year.

GIBBY: After the Ligament Blub Brothers I'd stopped playing again, until me and a few mates recorded a one-off song, *The Party*. Unbelievably we got some major attention, until they realised it was our only song, and left us to it.

Then I joined a solid rock band, Fastlayne – the audition was a nightmare because I hadn't played in three years, but they must have heard something they liked because I was in. We entered a Tennent's Live battle of the bands, and even though Brian the singer lost his voice halfway through the set, we won! The prize was having a demo recorded at Riverside Studios in Busby, but drink and other substances were playing havoc with our drummer so in the end I had to program the drums on a keyboard. Not very rock'n'roll... It seems AC/DC's Vanda and Young liked the tape, but Brian, who was in charge at the time, didn't follow up on it for some reason.

I was working with Robert Traish at the time, and he was singing with the popular thrash band Drunken State, of *Kilt By Death* fame. I went to see one of the shows – it was sold out and they went down a storm, but they didn't impress me at all. Robert's vocals blew me away though, and I told him our band was much better and he should join us. Drunken State were telling him not to jump around on stage so much, while I knew it would be brilliant with Fastlayne. Eventually, Robert agreed. He made his debut with us at the Loft in East Kilbride. He was wearing these enormous furry slippers with a telephone attached to each and he kept interrupting the gig to take imaginary calls from various people – great stuff!

We ended up managing things ourself, after a succession of managers kept fucking it up. The most memorable would have to be rich kid Grant Curry, who ran Idol Merchandise and carried a mobile phone the size of a small bungalow. He once took us backstage to meet the Red Hot Chili Peppers, to discuss us supporting the band, and spent the night boring them to tears about why they should sign up with his company for their T-shirts!

Heavy Pettin'

Colin Millen

The eighties was a tough decade for the music industry. Pressures had included loss of interest, loss of relevance, the rise of music-free variety acts, charity events and compilation albums. Scotland had done itself proud, though, by having honestly and deeply examined itself, passed its MOT and led the way through much of the period. As the nineties approached there was a greater sense of purpose in a variety of synth and guitar based acts. The secret, all along, had been songwriting.

Danny Wilson's Gary Clark observed during an interview: 'I don't like to be lumped in with all the other Scottish bands – but I'll admit that one thing most of us have in common is an emphasis on songs, and I'm sure that's partly because we're all so removed from the fashionable club scene in London.'

The more things change and all that.

Oh, aye – and Andy Stewart's *Donald Whaur's Yer Troosers?* came round again. Ach, he can have that one on me. It really didn't seem all that bad in the face of Stock, Aitken and Waterman. For a ten-minute writing session in the cludgie, that song did the old trooper affy well, didn't it?

12 STEAMIN' AND GREETIN'

By my calculations, it seems to take around eighteen years for nostalgia to kick in, and odd-numbered years have to wait until the year after it becomes cool. Hence, 1988 recently officially became fondly remembered, while 1989 will need to wait until 2008 to get a fair hearing, along with 1990.

Thus, the jury's still out on what really mattered in the nineties; and as our journey through the highways and byways of rock'n'roll meanders closer to the now, it becomes increasingly difficult to predict what people will really care about by the time someone suggests a rewrite.

The nineties has been referred to as the greediest decade in world history, but sadly a play on decade-ence doesn't really work on the page... And although Maggie herself was soon to bow out, the effect of 1980s capitalism would continue slamming shockwaves through Scotland.

The first McDonalds opened in Moscow and the Soviet Union finally collapsed. Poll tax riots raged in England – we'd already had it for a year by then, complete with the promise of paying £206 per year for the foreseeable future (eleven months, apparently). Musically, Scotland's artists took two views – the fist or the finger. While there was a thoughful edge to a lot of the country's output, 'fuck it and dance' was an equally prevalent attitude.

Witness, then, Del Amitri's number eleven hit, *Nothing Ever Happens*, which represented everyone's New-Year hangover and much more besides. Not only did it snapshot the thoughts that were on almost everyone's mind at some level or another – it sent them round the world as big juicy stars. I should mention at this point that my wee brother Damien and I wrote a spoof of the track, which he still plays as part of his musical comedy set, and the chorus went like this:

What a world to live in, what a place to be born
The goldfish will float to the top of the bowl and be flushed down the loo by yer mum
And we'll all be steamin' tonight and greetin' tomorrow

Eh? *Eh?* Good, eh?

JUSTIN CURRIE, Del Amitri: I think that's a massive improvement – it's much less Peter Sarstedt and far more Arab Strap crossed with John Hegley. The futility of the goldfish being flushed down the toilet is positively Larkinesque – and it definitely scans.

Anyway... on a US promo tour we met four members of the Patridge Family over two weeks and in four separate cities. David was very nice but Danny was a freak. We later heard he'd only recently got out of jail for cocaine possession, and doing something unspeakable with a hooker in the back of his car. It may not be true – but having met the guy I wouldn't put it past him.

We were once asked by a radio DJ to hang about for fifteen minutes after our interview had finished because Eugene, the night DJ, was our biggest fan. 'Honestly guys, he'll flip out to see you guys – he really is your biggest fan...' Eugene arrived and he was a dwarf. No one at the station saw the irony in the words that had been used to describe him! Two of the band escaped to the parking lot while I was forced to contain myself, be pleasant, and sign things, and have my photograph taken with our biggest fan, Eugene. I've never forgiven those two band members.

On a similar note, we once had a famous one-legged groupie hang backstage at a club in Houston. In order to get some sympathy so she could hoover up our rider, she complained her boyfriend had stood her up... Here too, there was no trace of irony.

Fish's debut solo album, *Vigil in a Wilderness of Mirrors*, made it to number five. It had been two years since he'd left Marillion and the usual questions of whether he could do the do had been in many fans' heads. Fortunately, he could, did and has continued to. Aware of the advantages of independence and forced into action when he later fell out with EMI Records, Fish built his own studio at his Haddington farmhouse and then discovered it was haunted.

'Weird equipment failures, big heavy studio doors shutting by themselves, and even full-blown apparitions,' he recalled later. 'Eventually I called in a medium who said energies had been disturbed by all the building work. He told us to burn a little Italian sage in the studio, and that would sort it. Sure enough, it did. I found out later the original building had been home to Italian prisoners of war in the 1940s...'

Woo – ghosties. A different spirit began channelling through Primal Scream too, as Bobby Gillespie and Co. began experimenting with the newfangled DJ crossover stuff. Their top-twenty hit *Loaded* was the first result – it was based on *I'm Losing More than I'll Ever Have* from their previous LP, remixed by dance dood Andrew Weatherall. The resulting track was a dance groove and a rock song, and proved to be an important milestone in the development of the indie scene.

JOHN MARTIN: Bob G, the supposed psychedlic king himself, nearly freaked out for good one time in East Kilbride. The trip involved several members of Primal Scream and the Mary Chain – we dished out the tabs of acid like sweeties and went to hang out at an old factory by a golf course on the outskirts of town.

We had an old tape player full of psyched sounds like Love, the Elevators, the Seeds and all that. Just as we peaked, the batteries went low and that's when Bob started to freak for the first time... He was getting aggressive with Douglas so a few of us went to the golf course to chill out. Then we went for a stroll and Bob started heckling a couple of passing joggers. He was well on his way to losing his mind and putting a right bummer on our trip. We managed to drag him over a burn to settle him down. Then he freaked again – only this time he took off his trousers and pants and started to run round like a bunny rabbit!

Nearly everyone took off after that. But Paul and I were the most experienced drug-takers, so we realised the guy was now in big trouble. He was rolling about on the ground, covered in dirt, but we

Fish

managed to get his clothes back on. At that point Paul and I looked at each other and burst out laughing – it was ridiculous!

We thought we'd better head home and got a bus to Glasgow – only we were so ripped we got on a bus going the wrong way. We got off in the middle of a marching Orange band, then we finally caught the right bus. We got Bob safely home and merrily tripped into the small hours. But it was a long time before Bobby Gillespie listened to another psychedelic record... The Mary Chain got really freaked and burnt-out too. We'd known what to expect but the others didn't know what had hit them. To this day, though, it's been the most fantastically unreal day of my life. Without a doubt, Bob G would have been a dead man if we'd left him. It just shows the reality behind some of those rock'n'roll myths...

Another Bellshill band, Teenage Fanclub, debuted with their LP *A Catholic Education*. Former roadie Norman Blake proved himself to be an excellent singer and songwriter, and his band quickly acquired the nickname 'the Bellshill Beach Boys'. Meanwhile, ex-Screamer Jim Beattie formed a new band, Spirea X (which always makes me think of a chocolate bar, although I couldn't begin to guess why). That year was also the high point in the life of a young band called Foreign Country, one member of which went on to much bigger things.

TOMMY DEVLIN: Foreign Country were an okay band... but on his website, the actor Billy Boyd claims he played with the band at an Auchinlea Park rock concert in 1990. Wee fibber! He's five years too late – they stopped in 1985. What he actually played was the Balcurvie Road street party. The Auchinlea rock concert sounds better, doesn't it? The lead guitarist from Foreign Country – me! – did play Auchinlea in 1982, as part of Syndicate. We were one the youngest bands to play in Glasgow's Dial Inn – we were all around 16 when we did it.

Ayrshire's Trashcan Sinatras released *Cake*, an album which was to become viewed as a cult classic, in America at least. (There's a breathtaking photo on their website, from their *Weightlifting* album art, showing clothes hanging on a line above Loch Ness – unless it's gone by now.) The band spent time trying to make their US popularity work for them, and it may have affected their standing at home. They're still one of the very few bands to consist entirely of top-notch songwriters, mind – *Obscurity Knocks* was a spiffing debut.

So too was *Six to Wan (621)*, the first single by Hugh Reed and the Velvet Underpants. Inspired by the Sensational Alex Harvey Band and improv-rockers Edith and the Ladies, Hugh Reed O'Hagan put a band together and vowed to deliver songs about Glasgow in a Glaswegian style. At the same time, attention was paid to every facet of performance that could be applied, resulting in a madcap style of entertainment you'd have to see to believe. Quick-change costumes, audience interaction, comedy sketches, cleverly arranged video playbacks and latterly burlesque dancers have all been part of the show.

HUGH REED: The idea behind the band was that, in the way Lou Reed sang songs about New York street life, we'd do the same about Glasgow street life. We've always been a predominantly original band, with just the occasional cover song, but the rise of the tribute band meant we were often mistaken as a Lou Reed tribute band. So we had to change the name, to the Hugh Reed Explosion, and now we're a tribute to ourselves!

We used to do a cover of SAHB's *Framed*, and I used to run to a van outside and dress up as Jesus, complete with crown of thorns and full-size cross. It was always a mad dash getting back to the stage on time. One night, in my haste, instead of re-entering the pub I went into the restaurant next door... Imagine the faces! The band liked to play the wrong song as I walked up through the crowd,

The many faces of Hugh Reed

so I'd be coming back on to *Folsom Prison Blues* or *Jailhouse Rock*... Last time I played it was at the Royal Concert Hall when we were supporting Deborah Harry on her 1993 tour. When I came in from the back of the hall people actually booed – it was a family audience and I think they misunderstood my intention. Someone did shout, 'Give us Barabus!' which I thought was quite funny.

The best moment from the Underpants was duetting with Deborah on the last night of that tour – we sang the Velvet Underground number *Waiting for the Man*, and Deborah faxed Lou Reed to tell him she was singing with Hugh!

Glasgow was declared a City of Culture in 1990 – and not the kind you'd find in the finally historic outdoor cludgies. To celebrate, the biggest music event since the Loch Lomond rock festivals was put on. Called Glasgow's Big Day, it emptied many of the satellite towns and villages as an estimated quarter of a million people flocked to see the multi-stage extravaganza, headlined by Deacon Blue.

JILL: This is one of my happiest memories. Billy Bragg was supposed to be playing and rumours were going round that Michael Stipe was coming. People were all going, 'Do you think he's really coming?' But he did! It was before REM were that well known and before they'd really had any hits so it wan't a huge crowd. Stipe, Billy Bragg and Natalie Merchant played a three-song set together. Fantastic! I was besotted with Billy Bragg at the time and wasn't that bothered about Stipe, but I was totally won over after I saw him and heard that amaziing voice. REM remain my all-time favourite band to this day.

DWIGHT D EISENHOWER: Sheena Easton's transatlantic ned accent was the undoubted comedy highlight of the day – and the crowd just loved her. She got bottled off.

COLIN McBURNIE: I distinctly remember guys going through the crowd during Sheena's set, urging people to throw stuff at her. Some did. But I thought her set was excellent – very... Princey.

KENNY BONES: Big Country played to what felt like half the city on Glasgow Green. They were totally on form – one of the best shows I've ever seen.

TOMMY DEVLIN: I thought Deacon Blue were great too, even though it's always been popular to say you don't like them. I've always thought Ricky Ross was a good writer. I was blown away when I saw him do a solo version of *Beanoland* on the telly a few years ago.

Deacon Blue released an EP of four Bacharach and David songs, called the *Four Bacharach and David Songs EP*, which made number two – EPs still charted as singles then. KLF, featuring the Children of the Revolution, released *What Time Is Love*; the Wets did *Stay with Me Heartache*; Primal Scream did *Come Together*; Aztec Camera and Mick Jones did *Good Morning Britain*; Gun did *Shame on You*. The Cocteau Twins' seventh album, *Heaven or Las Vegas*, was yet another barrage of fine songwriting and superbly obscure delivery, and quite possibly their best.

Around lunchtime in early August, the date 12:34:56 - 7/8/90 went by. The Gulf War (the first one) began and Stevie Ray Vaughan died in a helicopter crash. Meantime, the Soup Dragons had completed their conversion from C86-ish Scots indie to something altogether more, em, baggy. Their single *I'm Free* is as much a Madchester anthem as anything to come out of the Hacienda Club.

SUSHIL K DADE, the Soup Dragons: We had a real blast making records. I really loved the tours where we had My Bloody Valentine open for us too. It was all pretty low-key but at least the Dragons had hotel rooms! The guys from MBV used to sneak in for a wash then head back to their Transit. Not glamorous – but it was pretty clear they would be big. They turned out to be one of the most creative bands of that period, and it was really special to witness that volcano about to explode.

A similar thing happened a few years later when a little unknown group called Oasis opened up for the BMX Bandits. We played in Worcester to about seventeen people, and I remember thinking, this band are going to be huge. They already sounded awesome at those early shows – and they were all sweet guys too... don't believe the hype.

Touring the States with the Dragons was incredible too. We usually travelled in sleeper coaches and we played everywhere from Hoboken in New York City to Madison Square Gardens, opening for INXS. Alice Cooper came backstage to say hello! We played at the club where Prince used to hang out and backstage that evening was a very hungry Alex Chilton, who cleaned up a fair portion of our fruit bowl – he's a healthy-living guy.

Hanging out with Dennis Hopper, doing the *David Letterman Show* with Darlene Love, touring with Tom Tom Club... Tina Weymouth taught me a lot about bass technique – she encouraged me not to use a plectrum and I've never used one since. She's an incredible bassist and storyteller.

I think the last show we played was in the Amphitheatre in LA. It was a benefit gig for the homeless, and it had a real varied bill – David Byrne, Suzanne Vega, Duran Duran... I remember we all joined the Farm on stage for the chorus of *All Together Now*. But touring for ten weeks had taken its toll – I had a headful of ideas that were driving me insane and I needed a vehicle for them. Soon after I got home I gave birth to our beautiful, bouncing darling baby called Future Pilot AKA.

When Nirvana played in Edinburgh in October 1990, Kurt Cobain asked local band the Vaselines to get back together to open the show. He'd been a huge fan of their three-year career, and Nirvana regularly played two of their songs, *Son of a Gun* and *Molly's Lips*. For the band's co-leading light Frances McKee, it was not a grand event.

FRANCES McKEE, the Vaselines: Aha! The Vaselines again. I'm a firehorse... Apparently the Chinese kill us as children or avoid having us, as we can be extremely unlucky – or extremely lucky. You decide which one.

The Vaselines were a joke. It was hard for us to hold our heads high at soundchecks – even at supermarket checks. We had no fans. Well... I had one. He cornered me in the laundrette while I was trying to stuff my dirty smalls into the machine. I never liked washing my laundry in public – then I went and dropped my pants trying to shove everything in too quickly.

I've only heard *Son of A Gun* once – it's never been my favourite song, so whatever anyone else did with it had to be a bonus. *Molly's Lips*, I can't even remember. I remember I had to give clearance for it to be put on a CD for children in America, and the guy asked if he could change it to *Mommy's Lips*. No problem, I thought – it would be nice for the toddlers to be singing not only about oral sex, but incest as well. Lovely. *Jesus Wants Me for a Sunbeam* was a big improvement, and sad as well.

We got back together for that last show with Nirvana. It was a bit strange – we hadn't played together for a long time, I hadn't played my guitar for a long time, and therefore I hadn't rehearsed for a long

**Sushil K Dade,
Future Pilot AKA**

time. The result was pretty bad – so I had to get very drunk to cover my embarrassment. I'd been teaching for about a year and I'm ashamed to admit it, but I didn't really undrstand who Nirvana were. My dad thought the guy's name was Kurt Cocaine... but they were all really sweet. We only really started to have fun about ten minutes before we got kicked out of the venue. I don't remember the rest – but I'm sure I didn't vomit on my way home – miracle!

I have no memory of any Vaselines shows, except having bottles thrown at us in the Barrowlands when we were supporting the Jesus and Mary Chain. Again, we hadn't rehearsed. I bumped into Stephen Pastel recently and he said that gig was the worst one he'd ever been to. Anyway, the bottles got thrown back at the audience – not nice...

By the end of 1990 I'd made a decision – it was the drums. I'd been in an all-keyboard school band, which I cringe to admit I called the Lords of Convention. I mean, how many ways can three words be so wrong? In my defence I'd just discovered a passion of Scots history, and I was trying to be, well, historic. But, no more synths for me – although I now own one of those (un)cool as fuck over-the-shoulder numbers, which looks (un)great on me. Nope – drums it was, because we'd discovered metal, and it was either that or bass, and string instruments and I had fallen out in primary school.

We called the band La Guerre – lager, get it? There were four of us unless we were doing a gig, in which case there were three because Alistair, whom we called Alice Dear, crapped out of gigging. Thus it was we became one of those bands to have the dubious pleasure of winning a talent show. Do not for a second think it was because we were good – it's because we were funny. As young lads, our definition of 'funny' was mobile, so that when I suggested we should shout 'Fix!' no matter who won, it didn't occur to me that the rest of them wouldn't shout it if we were shouting at ourselves. So I shouted 'Fix!' and looked like a complete prick, not for the first time in my life. Still, there was no evidence – the local paper's snapper, who'd dropped by before the show, hadn't bothered to take a photo of us because, hey, we were a rock band, so we couldn't win. It's like a whole big Scottish attitude in one wee new town!

Right, on to things you might want to read about... In 1991 KLF hit with *3 a.m. Eternal*, the IRA bombed Downing Street and the Gulf War (the first one) ended. Shamen released *Move Any Mountain*, which marked their crossover from an also-ran indie rock band to a global rave act. Tragically, founding member Will Sinnott drowned in Tenerife on a break from shooting the promo video.

MAX MAXWELL, Shamen: Will and I were at school together but I didn't get to know him until a party just as punk was taking off. We had similar tastes in music – we were both influenced by SAHB in particular. In fact, Will reminded me of Chris Glen in his stage performance.

My first band had been called The – everyone else was *the* Clash, *the* Damned – we were just *The*. Then along with Will I started a fifteen-piece band called the Nolan Brothers, which was a pastiche of every style of music, and we dressed up in costumes to suit what was being played. It was all very theatrical.

When I moved to Glasgow I used to drink in the Griffin and boast about how many bands I'd been in. One night, a promoter came up to me and said, 'You're in Edith and the Ladies, aren't you?' I said I was – it was one of the names I'd been bandying about but it didn't actually exist. He said, 'Great. You're playing at Joanna's next week!' So I phoned Shug Carlin and Will, and we did the gig, purely by making up songs on the spot. We relied on our tape machine, Edith, to provide random noises like hoovers and car engines. It worked – we developed a cult following and lasted from 1979 till 1986.

Will moved to Aberdeen, met Colin Angus and joined the Shamen. We kept in touch – in fact, just before he died he was talking about a solo album with me doing the lead vocals for him. But his death devastated me. Will was a very special person – not just a great creative musician, but so fantastically intelligent as well. He could have been anything he wanted to be.

Primal Scream's *Screamadelica* was their breakthrough moment, showcasing the completion of their move to a genre-crossing music machine. The LP has been voted the best Scottish album of all time at least three times. Meantime, the BMX Bandits' *Bandwagonesque* was that group's finest moment too, succeeding in generating a melting-pot feel and a whimsical production which warmly defined exactly what they were trying to achieve.

DONNIE MUNRO, Runrig: I'll never forget our show at Loch Lomond. It was just an amazing experience. I remember all these journalists backstage saying to me, 'Isn't it incredible, you playing to fifty thousand people?' But it wasn't – it hadn't happened overnight. We'd met every one of those people at village halls and clubs throughout the land over the previous ten years. It wasn't a gig, it was a gathering of friends, and that made it even more amazing.

We had a phenomenal year in 1991. Straight after Loch Lomond we did three sold-out shows at Edinburgh Castle, to something like eight thousand people a night. We invited the Gaelic poet Sorley Maclean to do a reading before one of those shows. Sorley was in his seventies and was used to doing readings to about three hundred people – but he did it. His amazing voice rolled out across this misty night on the castle rock... It felt as if the spirit of all the Gaels had come to reclaim the land.

Then we got hold of a circus tent and did a tour of the Highlands and islands, to crowds of three thousand a night. After that we did a spell in Europe and then came home in December for eleven sold-out gigs across Scotland. When I think about the percentage of the population we played to that year, it really is quite incredible.

Love and Money had been working on an album to be called *The Mother's Boy*, but James Grant changed his mind and the disc that got out was *Dogs in the Traffic*. It presented a back-to-basics vibe, allowing the songs and singing more space to breathe.

FREAKY TRIGGER: I was always surprised that Love and Money didn't repeat the divine ascension achieved by Texas – they were always a much superior act to Texas. I saw them a couple of times and they were fantastic. *Strange Kind of Love* was an excellent album – it sounds a bit dated now but *Jocelyn Square* and *Hallelujah Man* have still got what it takes.

Albums came from Fish (*Internal Exile*) and Hue & Cry (*Stars Crash Down*) while singles included Deacon Blue's *Twist and Shout*, Big Country's *Republican Party Reptile* and a re-release of the Waterboys' *Whole of the Moon*, which made number three this time round. At the end of the year, Freddie Mercury, Eric Carr (ex of Kiss) and newspaper thing Robert Maxwell all died, and the last fire was put out in Kuwait's oil fields.

The word 'diva' entered standard tabloid hackism in 1992, aided and abetted by Annie Lennox, who used it to title her first post-Eurythmics solo album. Guys, she was being sarcastic – but then, maybe you are too... 'Pop diva Kylie'? You *are*, aren't you? Well done. Annie scored a clutch of award nominations, along with hit singles *Why*, *Precious*, *Walking on Broken Glass* and *Cold*.

As time moved on from what seemed very much to have been a golden era, the English music scene seemed to be at increasingly at odds with the Scottish one. While we'd been keeping the standards of writing and creativity up high, the stink of stagnation in London led to the appearance of a visible north–south divide. It was a long time coming, when you think about it. The sounds bought in England were just a hell of a lot more throwaway – chart-toppers included Billy Ray Cyrus's *Achy Breaky Heart*, East 17's *House of Love*, and Take That, and Whitney Houston, and oh good lord end it now. While Scots outfits with an established following could keep charting, the chances of a new band being signed reduced to near zero.

TAM, Barky! Barky**:** There's a classic story about John Ottway releasing a single with a scanned Supertramp album label on it, and he's scored out their name and scrawled his own over it. Warners phoned up and said, 'You're not on our label – we didn't sign you,' and Ottway goes, 'No – I signed you!' That's kinda how the Barkies' second single, *Valentino*, came about... It was saidflorence's money that paid for it.

JIM, Barky! Barky**:** It's true... Bruce Finlay started coming to our gigs – a lovely guy who genuinely liked the band, and even better, he actually liked the fact that I ranted between the songs! He'd just finished with Simple Minds and wanted to start a new label. He got two million out of Sony for saidflorence so he spent some of it on us – got us a couple of high-profile gigs, and put us in a studio with Callum Malcolm, who'd produced the Blue Nile.

The problem was the stuff we were doing was starting to go out of fashion. Oasis wiped us out. There's been a brilliant time when you could get away with mixing up any kind of music, but when grunge and Britpop started happening anything with a drum machine was out of favour. It's a shame, because Bruce put a lot of effort in and so did we – but we were finished.

TAM: But I told Kit Cummings about using his saidflorence money. He was cool with it. Thanks, Kit!

It wasn't all bad news, of course. Shamen were on the up and led the even more dancy Time Frequency into the charts, while Gun were kicking hard and the Almighty followed them down the rocky road. By the end of 1992 Shamen's *Boss Drum* album had notched up a number three position while Gun's *Gallus* LP had reached fourteen.

You may remember the character *Ebeneezer Goode*, played by comedian Jerry Sadowitz in the Shamen's video. The controversy surrounding the lyrics – were they singing 'Es are good' or 'Eezer Goode'? – assured a number-one hit. Del Amitri also visited the singles chart thrice with scoops from their *Change Everything* album – *Be My Downfall* and *When You Were Young* were well-received, but it was *Always the Last to Know* (actually their first release from the LP) which became their best-known track, reaching number two.

MAX MAXWELL, Shamen**:** Colin Angus asked if I'd be interested in playing *Ebeneezer Goode* on stage. My role in the band was dancer and physical comedian – basically, I had to anything they were too embarrassed to do! For example, first time I did *Top of the Pops* I was dressed as a hookah-smoking caterpillar, sitting on a magic mushroom. Next time I was a shamanic caveman... I spent two years with Shamen, playing all over Britain and Europe, and doing all the big festivals.

JUSTIN CURRIE: Backstage we've been thanked for inventing golf. We've been invited to house parties where there was nobody there, no furniture, no food in the cupboards and no stereo. We've sat drunk in the back of strangers' pickup trucks and been taken, singing, to faraway suburbs where somebody's senile grandmother won't notice, to bars with no signs outside, pool halls full of insane rednecks, hotel rooms full of the wrong kind of people, the wrong kind of drugs and the wrong kind of music. We've woken up to find stowaways on the tour bus, all the furniture in our rooms gone, strange anonymous Polaroids of all sorts of sexual and chemical deviance pushed under our doors, and – most absurdly of all – we managed to sustain a mainstream career in pop music in the US and the UK on the thinnest of talents, the most meagre of ideas and the absence of cool.

God save rock'n'roll!

The World Trade Centre was bombed in early 1993, while actor Brandon Lee died in a bizarre shooting accident and the Branch Davidian sect died in a bizarre policing accident in Waco, Texas. But wee Marie Lawrie opened her year with a quite incredible comeback, hitting with *Independence* twenty-nine years after Lulu and the Luvvers had released *Shout!* There were four good strong-selling albums too: Deacon Blue's *Whatever You Say, Say Nothing* (number four), Runrig's *Amazing Things* (number two), a Midge Ure best-of and the Almighty's *Powertrippin'*.

One of the most intriguing recordings of the year would have to be One Dove's *Morning Dove White*. Jim McKinven, yet another ex-Altered Image, teamed up with Ian Carmichael and the seriously spooky voice of Dot Allison, and explored pop and dub soundscapes.

But there was an iron curtain descending – unless you were already in the door, you weren't getting in, except if you were Oasis. It was that time again– time for something to come along and turn all the heads. The attitude was 'You're not listening and therefore there's no point saying anything' and the soundtrack was Britpop. It was perfect for an abandoned generation and plenty of it was popular in Scotland, notably Oasis, who were discovered by Alan McGee playing Glasgow's King Tut's. Nevertheless, there weren't many Scots actually *playing* the stuff.

GIBBY: Once Robert was fully on board with Fastlayne, he suggested we change our image, and we did ourselves up as Wild West riverboat gamblers. Robert and Brian even staged replica gunfights during the show – I suppose you wouldn't be allowed to do that any more... We gigged everywhere in Britain and built up a huge fanbase, even though we never made any money at all.

Radio Clyde's Tom Russell was a big fan. He did a Sunday night in Sax in Cumbernauld, and the promoter, Mad Jock Barnson, was also a fan, so the place was like our second home. I remember one night I invited all my mates from a factory I'd worked in. We went down a storm that night and the crowd ended up stamping and chanting for encores. All my mates thought I must be a real star...

Mind you, that was the same night our other guitarist, Denis, thought he was going to get shot for real. There was a biker who always carried a real gun – I know, don't ask – and when he went into his inside pocket pay for an EP Denis saw the gun and shat himself... He started running away, but the biker hadn't paid for the EP yet so he went after him, waving nothing more dangerous than four pound notes!

We supported bands like Samson, Girlschool, Manny Charlton, Goodbye Mr Mackenzie and loads of others. We did Inverness Ice Rink with SAHB when they came back as the Party Boys with Stevie Doherty on vocals – we did a warm-up show in a pub that afternoon and Robert went out into the street with his radio mic, and held up the traffic while still doing the show! That got us a front-page story in the local paper and helped sell out our show.

The show was getting crazier – Robert was over the top by now. We captured the insanity when we did a video at Rosie O'Grady's in Falkirk. Our manager got the US Calendar Girls to appear and we

Fastlayne

had Vidal Sassoon stylists. Vanessa Warwick of MTV loved it, but the problem was the soundtrack had never been done properly. She said we'd get rotation if we re-recorded the soundtrack, but our manager disagreed, and another opportunity – and manager – was lost...

Robert knocked me out twice on stage: once he picked me up and dropped me on my head, and another time he bit me full-on with a solid antique chair. Both times, people say, I managed to keep playing – which means either no one ever listened to me or the bass is even easier to play than previously thought!

We used to get mobbed, Beatles-style, at the Seven Stars in Twyfford. When we went to play Tonypandy Naval Base, we were warned the crowd bottled you even if they liked you – we decided that wasn't going to happen to us, so the moment we opened the show, Robert ran towards the group of guys most likely to start it, jumped on to their table, booted their drinks on to the floor and let out his trademark air-raid scream. We had them from there – we didn't get bottled and we played some great shows there. One night, Robert took two bottles of beer off a guy and tanned them. What he didn't know was they'd both been spiked – and Robert doesn't even drink, never mind take acid. By the time we got back to the studio we were staying in, I'd been assigned to look after him, which consisted of spending the night under the mixing desk with him, agreeing that, yes, there was indeed a secret world just beyond the cable wallplate, but that instead of going through the tunnel to meet the inhabitants, we should wait for them to visit us...

The year 1994 was incredibly static in terms of breakthroughs. Wet Wet Wet's version of *Love is All Around*, from the movie *Four Weddings and a Funeral*, was the biggest-selling single of the year and spent fifteen weeks at number one, while Primal Scream's *Rocks* was possibly the most anthemic. Except, mind you, for Stiltskin. They were the first Scottish band to receive the intergalactic advert treatment, when the riff from their single *Inside* was used in a Levi's advert.

Now, you see, I've already fibbed to you about that; but in fact, the truth was a little difficult to come by. It would seem that the band and single had never actually existed. Stiltskin was invented by Peter Lawlor, who'd written the song and played all the instruments. Once it was picked up by the ad agency, he put a band together to maximise on its exposure. Singer Ray Wilson, 'twould seem, was recruited from an ad in *Melody Maker*. Can you guess what happened next, children? Can you? Well, I'll tell you. The single was a smash hit, the album was patchy at best, and when the band tried to tour it became obvious they weren't actually a band at all. Every member was a great musician, but that does not a good band make – they forgot to order in some passion, and it showed.

And you know, that's it. There were respectable chart entries from the Proclaimers (*Let's Get Married*), the Time Frequency (*Such a Phantasy*) Gun (*Word Up*, even though it was almost exactly the same as the Cameo original) and the Almighty (*Wrench*). But, aside from Stiltskin, there was not one single new Scottish band to have a hit in the UK charts. Talk about a walking advert for independence...

The live scene was experiencing mixed fortunes at the same time. It was now more or less impossible for any band to make even a pathetic living from the pub circuit. The notion of 'pay to play' had arrived, where bar owners bit the hands that fed them because MTV had pulled the carpet from the people with hands (the musicians). There was nowhere to learn your trade, and certainly no way to buy your education.

On the up side, though, a whole new generation of music fans were able to discover the joys of a big live vibe in the form of T in the Park, finally a successful Scottish festival which continues to go from strength to strength. The first event attracted twenty thousand punters to Strathclyde Park and gave them Primal Scream, Oasis, Blur and the Manic Street Preachers; at first glance it's maybe too Britpoppy, but it would have been impossible to make money otherwise and build into a more catholic-tasty event.

GAIL REDFERN: That first T in the Park was an amazing buzz... You couldn't believe you could get on a bus from George Square, and go and see Oasis and Primal Scream, have a big party, a huge day out with your pals, then get home for a couple of quid. I'm a mad festy-head now – I plan my holidays to make sure I can get to them all. I love the camping, living it rough, having a complete mess of a weekend with all your pals and all these great bands. I wouldn't have discovered that escape from boredom if it hadn't been for T in the Park. So, thanks, DF Concerts and Tennents!

PHIL HUNTER: I grew up in the knowledge you could always find a good band to watch. I didn't know that was a luxury – I didn't know you'd end up going into a pub and seeing a band trying to be Oasis, and failing badly. There's two things about that. Firstly, Oasis are a great band – I've seen them loads of times, including that first T in the Park. Secondly, the kids who were trying to be them didn't stand a chance – they didn't know how to use their guitars, they didn't know how to set up their sound, they didn't know how to put on a show. And the worst bit was there was nowhere for them to learn. I take my sons to T in the Park now and say, 'Watch and learn.' But that costs hundreds of quid, and it's one lesson a year. In my day you had a lesson every night for a couple of quid. I'm not knocking all these music courses, but I'm not sure how much use they are...

TOMMY ANDERSON: Tennents make good money out of T in the Park, and I've got no problem with that. But before that, they used to do a music magazine, *Tennents Live News*, and sponsor events all over Scotland. They've started doing a wee bit more of that again, right enough. I mean, you cannae say to Tennents, 'It's your job to support more live music than just your big money-making festivals...' But, fuck, *someone's* got to do it...

Elsewhere on the music scene, Shirley Manson left Angelfish and went to join Butch Vig's new band, Garbage, which was seeking to draw a line between techno and rock with MTV-age production values – and was to do so very well.

But a better way to end this transient period in Scottish rock'n'roll history would be to put on some kind of demonstration of wistful wanton waste, of self-questioning and re-evaluating; something so incredibly out there that it's either a hugely important thing to do, or the worst act of cultural vandalism since girlie poppers All Saints tried to claim they'd written the Red Hot Chili Peppers' *Under the Bridge*…

I've got it – let's get Bill Drummond and Jimmy Cauty of the K Foundation to burn a million pounds in a secluded spot on Jura, with only a movie camera for a witness. Surely the most expensive chapter-end in history – thanks, chaps.

(By the way, did you really do it? *Really*? Ah.)

13 THERE ARE THOUSANDS OF BANDS LIKE US

The word of 1995 was 'Freedom!' thanks to Mel Gibson's *Braveheart* movie. But Scottish rock'n'roll wasn't enjoying much of the stuff; while Britpop showed a new generation of kids how much fun live music could be, there was far less fun in playing it. We'd already been there, done that, given the T-shirt to Oxfam.

And if there was a convincing argument that said, 'Dear England, good luck with that retro thing you're doing... we did it fifteen years ago and we're waiting for you to catch up, love Scotland xxx', it was Edwyn Collins' *A Girl Like You*, which was quite simply everything Blur wanted to be, but better, cooler, suaver – and just better again.

Fred West killed himself ahead of being tried for killing other people; Russian president Boris Yeltsin considered killing us all when a Norwegian research rocket was mistaken for a nuclear attack; Nick Leeson killed Barings Bank when he lost $1.3 billion and Jonathan Schmitz killed his friend Scott Amedure after being confronted with Amedure's gay crush on him on a US TV chat show.

As cinema ticket sales led to conversations about Scottish independence, Runrig took another single into the top twenty. *An Ubhal As Airde* – translation, *The Highest Apple* – was another hit-out-of-advert moment; but in being the first hit to be sung entirely in Scots Gaelic, it was another first for the band. Attempts to hijack their success for political purposes, however, were frowned upon.

DONNIE MUNRO, Runrig: We were always identifiable as being very aware of our Scottishness, but we went to great lengths at that time to distance ourselves from political nationalism. In fact, the only time we complained about anything as a band was when the SNP used one of our instrumental pieces in a party political broadcast.

The only party we ever endorsed was the Scottish Labour Party. As a band we had a kind of general left-of-centre stance, broadly socialist. We'd done the Red Wedge tour with people like Billy Bragg and the Style Council, and we played the STUC Days for Scotland, and we played for Neil Kinnock when he was Labour leader. We wanted to make people think politically, because it mattered to us after our struggle to discover our own political history. Encouraging conversation is different from telling people how we think they should vote – the only time we did that was when we publicly endorsed Brian Wilson's SLP candidacy in the Western Isles.

But it was suggested to me recently that the height of our popularity was to do with anti-Thatcherist feelings – people wanted to move as far away from that as possible, and you couldn't get much further than Runrig. Perhaps there's some truth in that.

The Wets' album *Picture This* spawned the top ten hits *Julia Says*, *Don't Want to Forgive Me Now* and *Somewhere Somehow*, while fellow old hands Simple Minds hit with *She's a River* and *Hypnotised* from the album *Good News from the Next World*. Del Amitri's *Twisted* LP gave them the top-thirties *Here and Now*, *Roll to Me* and *Tell Her This*.

Mary Kiani and Jon Reid of the Nightcrawlers had once been an item, and now they spent a couple of weeks in the charts together – Mary with her solo hit *When I Call Your Name*, the Nightcrawlers with *Don't Let the Feeling Go*. The Crawlers also did an album, *Let's Push It*. Other chart action included Annie Lennox's haunting *No More I Love Yous* and *Whiter Shade of Pale*.

> **GIBBY:** We got signed to a label in Wales, but it very quickly became apparent that even Martin Kielty could have done a better job. Despite the best efforts of our producer, Terry, who'd invented the crossover system for Marshall, we did a runner back to Scotland. We thought we had at least enough material for a single, but Tom Russell and a lot of other people thought the name, *So Wrong*, was incredibly apt. We remixed it and Tom started playing it, but I think he'd lost interest in the band by then – maybe because we'd spent so much time down south, people in Scotland had started to forget about us.
>
> *Kerrang!* magazine tipped us as the next big thing and we were given a headline spot above Reef even though they'd already had two singles out – the promoter just thought we were a better band. Sadly the gig didn't happen... nor did our lucrative European tour, which would have made us a fortune – the promoter went bankrupt. The much-missed Paul Samson was a great help, and so were the Quireboys, Hothouse Flowers and Beki Bondage.
>
> But despite all this, we wound up with another shite label. They had a million pounds in backing, it seemed, until the Canary Wharf bomb in 1996 put their backers out of business. By that time, we were just shrugging our shoulders. It was par for the course, and it didn't matter any more how much of it had been true...
>
> Rab Andrew in particular thought we had good songs, but he was already looking after Gun, and he thought our commercial hard rock wasn't what the majors were looking for at the time. He told us to keep building on our live reputation. As we were leaving his office, his assistant, Emma Pollock, said we should start our own label in Scotland and concentrate on that. She was in the Delgados at the time, and of course, they did just that – they started Chemikal Underground.

First time I saw Fastlayne, I staggered into my local in Cumbernauld, pretty darned plastic already, and stopped in the doorway because everyone was staring at me. Well, they weren't – they were staring above me, where Gentleman Bob, the singer, was balanced precariously above the entrance, giving one of his songs laldy. I was a fan from that moment, even though I've never got rid of Gibby and Robert to this day...

I got a backstage pass for Donington in 1995 and I decided to wear a Fastlayne shirt – support the home troops and all that. What a mistake: I couldn't move all day for people wanting to say how great they were, did I know them, could I get in touch with them... I came back buzzing about the guys again – and that's sometimes tough when you've been trying to talk someone up for years. I really was convinced *this was it*. I couldn't understand why the band just nodded when I told them what had happened to me. We talked very idly at one point about me trying to manage them – I was, as they say, 'out of contract' because no one could be arsed with me playing drums behind them – but the truth was, they were already three-quarters down Split-up Street. Instead, my first management outing was with a band called Media Falls; and I apologise profusely for my part in their downfall... But they kept going and went on to reinvent themselves with a great line in courting controversy.

G MAN: That's a great story when you remember King Tut's claims to be the king of cool... We'd added another guitarist to the band to give us a harder edge and decided to relaunch the band with a new name. As a bit of an old schemie I decided to use the name the Tongs. It was an old gang name, very well-known around Glasgow, and I admit I was hoping for some publicity out of it. What I didn't expect was a phone call from Tut's boss Geoff Ellis, who was concerned that he might have a riot on his hands if we used the name. I thought, great – it's working!

I told him that since we'd hired the venue we could call ourselves what we liked, but he said he wouldn't let us play and we could have our deposit back. To say I was pissed off would be an understatement... But a few days later I was in Sax in Cumbernauld and I saw an old poster for a Chippendales-type troupe of male strippers, with bits of string hiding the lads' nuts. A light bulb went on in my head – I asked the venue for the poster and took it home, then phoned Geoff and said we'd call the band the *Thongs*. But my old punk roots weren't going to let them away that lightly – you could barely see the 'h' in 'Thongs' because I hid it behind the photo of the male strippers.

Still, we sold a lot of tickets, and went on with *Saturday Night's Alright for Fighting* and covered *Do Anything You Wanna Do*. I'm pretty sure there wasn't a riot – although someone spilled a drink...

Teenage Fanclub released *Grand Prix*, which silenced critics of their previous LP, *Thirteen*. They were still being that Bellshill way, but they were doing it with so much more of their own personality, as showcased in *Mellow Doubt* (geddit?) and *Neil Jung* (geddit, geddit?). Meanwhile, Shirley Manson's new band, Garbage, were something of a new Eurythmics: *Stupid Girl* from their self-titled first LP was just ahead of the pack in terms of arrangement and production, but not far enough for anyone to be unsure of them. It must have helped that they were regarded as an American band, right enough. They're *allowed*, you see.

Meantime, the Delgados' early releases on Chemikal Underground set them up beautifully. First came their own single, *Monica Webster*; then came *The First Big Weekend* by Arab Strap, which then featured in yet another beer ad (well, Guinness); and next up, 1996's *Kandy Pop* by Teen-C heroes Bis. They jumped into the limelight when *Top of the Pops* producer Ric Blaxill heard the track and put them on the show. They're reputed to be the first-ever unsigned act to appear – although some people like to question that without providing a backup argument, so shut it.

MANDA RIN, Bis: I was sixteen, John was fifteen and Stephen was seventeen when we started. They wanted someone to play keyboards so they could concentrate on guitars so I decided to give it a go. When we did our first gig at the 13th Note, I was incredibly shy – I think I spent most of the time with my head down, just playing. Then I wrote my first song and had to sing it... I was so shy I don't remember it at all, but everyone said it was brilliant, and I couldn't believe it.

That song, *Kill Your Boyfriend*, became our first single. We were writing fanzines, all those stories about the Teen-C revolution, and a guy from Spain thought he might like our song because he liked the music we wrote about. It was the first release on his label.

Things were going really well – John Williamson started managing us and he got us a four-week tour with Super Furry Animals. I'd just left school and I was supposed to be going to uni, to become a primary school teacher, but I decided to defer it for a year and see what happened with the band. My mum was outraged – but it was a different story when Polygram gave us a ninety-grand publishing deal... We lived off a tiny wage but we were still all with out parents so we didn't have much in the way of outgoings. We bought this tiny wee van and went off on tour with the Super Furries.

Half way through we got the call about *Top of the Pops* – the producer loved *Kandy Pop* and would we go on as an exclusive? I found a video of the performance in my parents' cellar recently, and I can't believe how awkward I looked. My voice had started to go on the tour so I'd been taking honey all day – we didn't even have a drink to relax before we went on. I do remember the dress I wore cost me a fiver from Virginia Galleries...

Kandy Pop went to number twenty-five so we went back on *Top of the Pops* just as the tour ended. The difference in our performance was night and day – we'd really grown in confidence.

Bablyon Zoo's *Spaceman* became the next Levi's advert hit in 1996, selling like billy-o despite the real track being about half the speed of the ad version. It was the year of Prodigy's *Firestarter* and the Spice Girls' *Wannabe*, while Oasis's *(What's the Story) Morning Glory* dominated the album chart, supported by Alanis Morisette's *Jagged Little Pill* and Kula Shaker's *K*.

The Dunblane massacre horrified the planet in March, and led to a fundraising version of *Knockin' on Heaven's Door* making number one when Christmas came. Dolly the sheep was cloned at the Roslin Institute, Prince Charles and Princess Diana divorced, and scientists announced they might have discovered primitive life on a meteorite from Mars.

The singles chart was changing – in the past songs had been 'growers', but the trend now, fuelled by new marketing strategies, was for discs to chart high then drop. It's no surprise that Scotland's quality songwriting didn't fare well in that environment. While Hawick dance act QFX hit with a cover of Moby's *Every Time You Touch Me* and Mary Kiani's *Let the Music Play* did well, the best chart position of the year by a Scots-related outfit was the number-ten appearance of *Don't Make Me Wait* by 911, three miniature dancers who were all English, but managed by Scottish outfit Backlash (which I had something to do with for a *very* short time and I was even sorry about it then...)

Two novelty singles attempted to support Scotland's short-lived Euro 96 football ambitions: Rod Stewart and the squad's *Purple Heather* made number sixteen while Primal Scream, Irvine Welsh and On-U got to seventeen with *The Big Man and the Scream Team Meet the Barmy Army Uptown*. Oh yeah. The Wets did *Morning* and Eddi Reader had *Town Without Pity*.

The semi-mythical Britpop war between Oasis and Blur had come to a head the previous year when they both released singles on the same day. Blur's *Country House* had made number one while the Gallaghers' *Roll with It* hadn't; but the latter track stayed in the charts longer and sold more copies. Oasis were officially the biggest band in the UK, and Scotland could relate in a big way, because they were brilliant live, as they demonstrated during two shows at Balloch Country Park in August.

ROABY K: What a weekend we had at Loch Lomond – the sun shone, the beer flowed and the vibe was mellow and cool. There were eighty thousand of Oasis's close friends all there to chill, and I didn't see any hassle at all from the Friday to the Sunday. Cast and the Bootleg Beatles were shit-hot, but I couldn't get into Ocean Colour Scene. Neither could my mates – we were like, 'Weller does that better than you!' I always said they only got signed because they were mates with Oasis and it was getting to be an embarrassment they didn't have a deal.

But there had been a lot of stuff in the papers about Liam being a lout, and he and Noel was always fighting, and Oasis were about to split up every other week. I didn't see a bar of it – when they went on stage they were all there to have a good time, and that's what they did.

Half way through *Whatever*, they went into a version of *Octopus's Garden*, and my mate Pebble was going to fling a bottle because he hated the Beatles. Imagine being into Oasis and not into the Beatles... But we slapped him down – everyone was in a party mood and the last thing you wanted was any hassle. Everything was too sweet. We still slag Pebble for that – every time something's going right, the football team's winning or whatever, it's like, 'I s'pose you want to throw a bottle now?'

Billy Mackenzie and Alan Rankine had split the Associates in 1990, and Rankine was in charge of a music industry course at Glasgow's Stow College. To make the experience as valid as possible, his students ran a real label, signed a real band and released a real album; and, famously, that was how Belle and Sebastian came to record the iconic Scottish album *Tigermilk*.

Only a thousand copies were made, with around four hundred being sent out as promos, meaning there were only ever six hundred on sale; but the band's leader Stuart Murdoch remembered they were tough to get rid of at first. 'Recording was very well planned,' he recalled in a rare interview later. 'Usually the college just did a single, but I reckoned we could do an album in the five days we had. I wrote the material then and there, and kept the arrangements simple so we could do it quickly. It became this underground classic, but not until much later – at first we quite literally couldn't give them away. I got one in my local record shop window and it sat there all summer, with the sleeve fading – I was so embarrassed...'

Six months later, they released *If You're Feeling Sinister*, continuing their policy of airy, vague and upbeat compositions. They also made a point of not *quite* co-operating for publicity, resulting in friends of theirs appearing in promo photos and suchlike. Soon, though, it was impossible to move in Scotland without hearing the band's name; and it wasn't long before someone came up with the concept of the 'twee' movement, in attempting to define the wilful return to childhood innocence featured in their music.

Meanwhile, Paul Buchanan and the Blue Nile released their *Peace at Last* LP, a continuation of their outta-the-blue contributions to musical culture.

ANDY P: *Family Life* from that album breaks my heart every time I hear it.

TOMMY DEVLIN: It's my favourite of theirs. I had the *Hats* album on my CD player non-stop for about a year. It's amazing how little promotion work they do – I had the pleasure of meeting Paul recently and he was surprised I recognised him, but he was delighted to speak to a fan.

FREAKY TRIGGER: *Walk Across the Rooftops* still sounds like nothing on earth, twenty years on. How do you even classify that album? Jangly ambient melancholia? There's a couple of great B-sides, one called *The Wires Are Down*, that isn't on any of the albums, and *Halfway to Paradise*, which I recall was the soundtrack for a TV programme of the same name.

Falkirk's Arab Strap ended up being glued on to that movement, but in fact their negative, downbeat songs sounded diametrically opposed to what Belle and Sebastian were doing. Their first album, *The Week Never*

Starts Around Here featured tracks like *Coming Down* and *I Work in a Saloon*. The work was rough-edged and had a DIY element, which helped reveal the underlying Scottish humour after a listen or three.

Still based in nearby Grangemouth, the Cocteau Twins released their *Milk and Kisses* LP. Love and Money's James Grant guested on Karen Mathieson's first solo album, *The Dreaming Sea*, in which she took the opportunity to explore soundscape ideas her vastly more trad band, Capercaillie, didn't want to touch. Meantime, a band formerly called Glass Onion changed their name to Travis and put out their first single, *All I Want to Do is Rock*.

> **MANDA RIN,** Bis**:** We started playing with people like Ash, the Foo Fighters, Rocket From The Crypt and the Cardigans. Doing the Barrowlands with Garbage was amazing! We also signed American and Japanese deals, and toured over there as much as possible. We were massive in Japan – I mean it – we sold a hundred thousand copies of our album in two weeks!
>
> I designed all our merchandise and record sleeves – I think it's a good way to connect with the fans. If I think about it, doing the fanzines helped with that. In fact, it was through the fanzines that we not only got to record our first single, but also play our first gig in London. I think in some ways it was like the internet is now – a great way to come to the attention of like-minded people.

Faced with the challenge of coming up with a promo video to help sell their singles from *A Happy Pocket*, the Trashcan Sinatras decided to go one better and made a concept movie based around characters from the album. *Spooktime* was set around a Glasgow pub and they referred to it as 'fifteen minutes of sex-sodden alcodelia'. It was shown in cinemas in Glasgow and London and at the Cannes Film Festival before being withdrawn by the censors – well, it *was* a bit adult. Charged that such an approach wouldn't help them with publicity, the band's Francis Reader said, 'It's no skin off my nose – no one plays our singles anyway...'

In 1997, as the domination of the Britpop thing subsided, Texas demonstrated a remarkable return to form with the number-one album *White on Blonde*. The singles *Say What You Want*, *Halo*, *Black Eyed Boy* and *Put Your Arms Around Me* re-energised their career – going right back to the start of Scottish rock'n'roll, they found a soul groove, sat in it, and stay there to this day; but as *Black Eyed Boy* in particular proved, they could really rock too.

Primal Scream's *Kowalski* went top-ten, from the LP *Vanishing Point*. Like Texas, it showed a successful reinvention; critics who hadn't liked *Give Out but Don't Give Up* were silenced as the band's energy levels went back up off the scale.

Also that year, Associate Billy MacKenzie failed to recover from his mum's death and took his own life.

Mary Kiani and QFX were back with *100%* and *Freedom 2*; and Wet Wet Wet released *If I Never See You Again* and *Yesterday*. Del Amitri, Teenage Fanclub and Gun had one hit apiece – *Not Where It's At*, *Ain't That Enough* and *Crazy You*. Travis made number thirty with *Tied to the 90s*, a song which they don't seem to talk much about.

> **JOANNE PATTISON:** I was in the 13th Note in Glasgow – when it was Glassford Street – and a couple of guys came in, really pissed, and started ordering bottles of champagne. They invited me and a barmaid who was just finishing to join them, asked us out and said they'd take us anywhere we wanted in the world. They said they'd just won the lottery, and they were really nice guys, but they got so pissed you couldn't talk to them any more and I went home. About two weeks later I was out

and about and these two guys were all over the record shop windows – it was a couple of guys from Travis. They must have been spending their advance... I wonder if the barmaid got lucky?

CLAIRE SWEENEY: I worked in the 13th Note when it was in Glassford Street, then when it became the cafe in King Street and the club on Clyde Street. Alex from Franz Ferdinand used to run a weekly gig called the 99p Club. I'll never forget seeing the Supernaturals... they were nice enough, fairly quiet guys – then they came on stage. The singer was wearing the maddest costume I've ever seen – his trousers and hat were all stars and stripes, and the whole show was amazing. They were one of the best bands I saw at the 99p Club... I saw a lot of shite ones.

JOHN AUSTIN: I still can't believe the Supernaturals didn't become superstars. They had two great singles, *Day Before Yesterday's Men* and *Smile* – you hear *Smile* on the ads for the online bank with the same name. But they were just an incredible fun band. The songs were good, solid pop, played like fuck – but it was the live show that got you. They'd just do whatever they liked. I remember one wee place in Edinburgh – all arches, but I can't remember its name – and the piano player wasn't in the song, so he got up and started walking around with a stupid robot walk, keeping the beat of the song, going into the audience to drink people's pints... I think they kept swapping instruments all night as well. You just got this feeling of greatness off them. I wasn't surprised when they got signed, but I was surprised when nothing came of it.

CLAIRE SWEENEY: The Note was really part of the music vibe in Glasgow. When it moved to King Street we started doing vegan-only food, so I think we got a reputation for being animal lovers and tree-huggers. One night, someone left their hamster there, with a wee note saying they couldn't look after it any more and could we find it a new home? Craig, the owner, could – he knew someone who specialised in caring for distressed hamsters, and the wee thing went away quite happily...

You know that thing you do with your pointer-finger and thumb, to show that everything's just right? If you look at it again, it could also mean 'zero' – and that's what it meant when my mates and I used it to crow about what happened to the Tories in Scotland. The Labour landslide election, which brought us Tony Blair, 'Cool Britannia' and all that kinda stuff, also made Scotland a Conservative-free zone and how good it felt too – little bit'o politics there.

It was a busy season for those of us unlucky enough to be working in newspapers – Princess Diana's death in Paris gave us all about ten days of fourteen-hour shifts; then we had the Scottish devolution referendum to keep us going for another couple of weeks; and in between times, Mother Theresa died too. I'd far rather have been a teacher – all those holidays, all that easy money, home early every day, sitting about in a class-room reading out lessons, getting the kids to read out the books for you or even just watching videos, then all those hours spent at home watching telly, drinking wine and knocking ashtrays over – bliss. (The page number and that sentence have been coloured up so my darling wife, a teacher herself, can find it easily when it's time for me to go to the spare room. Which gives me the last laugh, because I enjoy it there.)

DONNIE MUNRO, Runrig: It was time for me to go... I felt we were at the stage where we'd reached our peak. We were being looked on more as a 'business' than a creative force – things like units sold seemed to be more important than anything artistic. And I really felt it was time for a change in my life. I'd spoken to the band about it two years earlier, so it wouldn't have exactly come as a surprise.

Those farewell gigs at Stirling Castle gigs were very emotional. It really was the end of an era, and the audience reaction was very moving. There was a song we had way back from the early days called *Going Home*, and one called *Precious Years*, both fans' favourites, but of course that last night they had a special poignancy.

But I had a job to do, and my upbringing dictated that I do it with a certain amount of dignity – for me, for the band and for the audience. So I got on with that last encore, that last song, that last chorus, that last word, that last wave... The moment it got me was as I came off and went past the crew and people like Mark Green who'd been with me all the time. That's when it became personal.

I'm really happy Runrig have continued. The band was always based around Callum and Rory, and I've enjoyed their work over the last ten years. I think Bruce Guthrie is a great singer. Callum and Rory have always been interested in American country music and people like Neil Young. Bruce has brought that feel into the band, and I think it's great for them.

Fashion designer Versace was murdered and young nanny Louise Woodward was found guilty of shaking a baby to death. The Pastels put out a new album, *Illumination*; and as a big proportion of the record-buying public got into Radiohead's *OK Computer*, Mogwai released their first LP, *Mogwai Young Team*, which to many old bores could have sounded utterly incomprehensible.

MICHAEL GLENDINNING: I saw Mogwai start their set at King Tut's and I thought something was wrong – they were playing away and there was no sign of any singer and, by fuck, they needed something to sort out the mess. I waited to see what kind of character would arrive onstage, until it finally sunk in there wasn't going to be anybody. I would have left, but my mate's band was playing next so I had to hang around. One of the best things about Tut's in those days was, there was a place you could stand at the bar and see the whole show through a big mirror on the back wall. It was one of my favourite places to stand – and I admit I learned about it from Martin's *Big Noise* fanzine. Ta, Martin!

ME: Nae probs.

MICHAEL GLENDINNING: So I was watching them get on with it, pint in hand... when, suddenly, a revelation! I understood what they were doing! Vague memories from Higher Music came into my head, something about rondos and recitatives or shit like that, and I was like, 'These guys are playing a form of classical rock'n'roll...' Now, that sounds like a crap description, and it is, but I don't think their own label 'post-rock' is much better. But it was like what a gang of synth players might try, except using acoustic instruments. I loved it!

I went back toward the stage and got my head right into it. When they came off they must have been a bit bewildered to see this stupid old drunk idiot nodding and grinning and going, 'I get it! I get it!' I have to say I've never quite got into any of the other similar bands – Laika, Pram – but I've still got a soft spot for Mogwai.

After the demise of Barky! Barky, Jim Brady and friends were looking round for something a little more sedate to do and settled on a very relaxing semi-retirement hobby easy-listening vibe. The plan was to have a few mates playing cheesy lounge tracks, and to do it drunk; but it was so successful that the Johnny Seven found themselves taking it a little further than they'd originally planned.

TAM: We did a demo and started selling them at gigs. We came up with the idea of having them individually numbered, but we realised everyone would want either 001 or 007, so we had fifty of each made up... Someone would say, 'I'd really like number 007.' And then we'd say, 'You're in luck, mate – I think we've still got that one...'

JIM: We set out to tell the biggest lies right from the start and everyone just embraced it. We went, 'We're all millionaires, we've been doing this for years and we wrote all the Bond themes.' Everyone from Mogwai to Belle and Sebastian were just like, 'Aye, you did!' But then they'd tell other people and it would become true...

TAM: We told people we'd done the music for the movie *Boxing Helena* – nobody was ever going to watch it so nobody knew it was shite. What we said, I mean, not the movie, although it was shite an'all... So they believed that too!

JIM: And we lived in a penthouse flat in the Merchant City, with a fire pole in the middle that we slid down to get to the Sevenmobile! John Williamson got us some amazing gigs – I don't know whether he was using us to take the piss out of other bands or just taking the piss out of us! We were the only pop band to play in the art gallery.

TAM: We played at the opening of King Tut's – we wore false beards, and the crowd thought we were the Gyres in disguise...

JIM: Then we supported Justin Currie – or Derek Amitri, to give him his Sunday name – and started getting album launches and the like. Rolf Harris asked us to support him when he had his hit with *Stairway to Heaven*. The crowd were insane and we couldn't hear ourselves, but when we played the final tune, the theme from *Star Trek*, we held up our Stylophones and the place nearly exploded! We had four and Rolf didn't have one, so we gave him one of ours...

TAM: That was the gig when Rolf was talking to us about how it was a shame that some kids didn't do anything with their hands nowadays. 'You can do plenty,' he said as a girl walked by. 'Like, play with that sheila's minge!' I don't think I've ever been more astonished in my life – except for when I heard Glen Michael from Cartoon Cavalcade say 'bastard' in a bookies...

What's to say about 1998? Little as possible, if you ask me. All Saints, Aqua, B*Witched, Billie Piper, Cleopatra, Boyzone.... Och, just don't. And the Manic Street Preachers were really starting to tire out that 'we don't have another guitarist so we'll use a string section instead' routine. Still, top moments included Simple Minds with *Glitterball*, Texas featuring the Wu Tang Clan with *Say What You Want* and Travis's *More Than Us* EP. Derek Amitri did our World Cup anthem, *Don't Come Home Too Soon* – but they did, of course; and in a year that dripped with American input, Garbage hit with *I Think I'm Paranoid* and *Special*.

GIBBY: After Fastlayne ended I didn't stop playing bass for once, but fell straight into an indie band, Glass, which I'd done some session work for. My time with them included some superb sold-out gigs in Scotland and a showcase in London for Creation Records, who were interested in signing us. Jim and William Reid reappeared at this point, with advice on how best to deal with the A&R guy Paul Gallagher, who was Oasis's brother. I remember he left a message on our singer's answering machine: 'Love the tape, fookin' mad for it!' As Liam as you like – it was almost like us really saying, 'It's a braw bricht moonlicht nicht...'

On the night, though, the Gallaghers had had a family bereavement, so Paul's place was taken by a Canadian rep who 'didn't quite know what to make of us' – even though the owner of the venue kept saying we were the best band he'd ever seen and it would be a travesty if we didn't get a deal... Creation remained interested, but our singer in her wisdom decided that, from now on, anyone who wanted to talk would have to come to us, here in Glasgow. Fine if you're sixteen-year-old beauties, but not when you're thirtysomething indie-rockers...

Enough water was found on the moon to fuel a new space race; US president Bill Clinton began to get into trouble for messing about with the help, and the virtual age began to pick up steam with the introduction of the iMac, the launch of Google and the arrival of Sky Digital TV. Idlewild debuted with their *Hope Is Important* LP, while the Delgados released *Peloton* and Arab Strap presented *Philophobia*.

But the thing that's great, the thing that makes 1998 worth discussing even vaguely at all, is that Belle and Sebastian won the Best Newcomer award at the Brits. This, despite being two years old already; and despite Pete Waterman having done everything in his power to try and secure the award for his new dancy-prancy pop-shite act Steps. Sure, there was almost certainly a little dodginess going down, but who cares? Get it right fucking round you, London – give it some of that, heh-heh...

Turn, tu-uh-uh-urn, turn, turn turn turn... It was time for a wee change of direction for a music scene which had been moving towards an almost glam-like fascination with packaging. Songs had taken second place to delivery, and the split between musicians and performers hadn't been so clear for ages. If Belle and Seb had rapped knuckles upstairs, warning them they couldn't get away with it, then Travis took them by the luggie and made them wash the car while the good telly was on.

The Man Who is a marvellous pop album by any standards, with Fran Healy's ear for catchiness tuned to perfection. There were little elements of post-Britpop, touches of twee wistfulness, twinkles of soulful melody and buckets of beat-boom era construction. And when the band played a sun-baked Glastonbury Festival and it suddenly started to piss down as they played their anthem, they had the nation by the 'nads. They had two other hits that year, *Writing to Reach You* and *Turn* (hence the dodgy intro above).

MANDA RIN, Bis: We released three albums: *New Transistor Heroes*, *Social Dancing* and *Return to Central*. They were all different from each other and I'm very proud of them. But we took a major backlash from the music press... really bad, and I mean *horrible* bad! I was a bit upset when the music was criticised – after all it's your music, your baby – but then it started to get personal. I was being called fat and ugly, and for a teenage girl, that's just horrible.

There was a full page of letters in the *NME* just attacking us. There was one done in a ransom note style, saying something like 'Kill Bis now, or I will.' My parents were reading this stuff thinking, 'That's our wee daughter!'

At a gig in London with Ash, I got a pint tumbler thrown at me... I ended up with a big lump on my head and my keyboards were covered in beer. It even got into my contact lenses and I could hardly see. We had coins thrown at us when we played in Wales with the Foo Fighters – but Dave Grohl was really supportive. In fact, when they supported the Prodigy in Scotland, he dedicated a song to us, which was really nice of him. It was people like him that kept us going. Plus the fans – they were amazing – if it hadn't have been for them we might well have called it a day. But we'd grown up together and decided to stick it out.

DONNIE MUNRO: When I became rector at Edinburgh University I also became involved in a lot of politics – things like the right to education. It seemed natural to move into politics directly when the Labour Party approached me. Besides, I really wanted to go back into my own community, and this was something I could do there.

There are plenty of parallels to being in a band and being a politician. I remember speaking at a rally in the Usher Hall, along with Tony Blair and Richard Attenborough. I'd played there with Runrig, of course, so I knew the place, and I went to the dressing room I was sharing with Richard. He was asleep in a chair. I was thinking, 'Here's this really famous man... what the hell am I going to say when he wakes up?' Then Tony came in, and of course he used to go and see bands in the Usher Hall. So there we were: a politician trying to be a musician, and a musician trying to be a politician...

But both jobs require an understanding of presentation and delivery. There are some amazing performers in the political field, people like Tony Benn, and Blair himself. I remember the PA failed halfway through the night – he took of his jacket, rolled up his sleeves, went to the front of the stage and delivered an incredible address.

Idlewild reached number nineteen with *When I Argue I See Shapes* followed by *Little Discourage*, which made twenty-four. Texas made number four with *In Our Lifetime*, then five with *Summer Son*, then twelve with *When We Are Together*. The Eurythmics (I'm cool, I can type it now) returned with *I Saved the World Today*, and received a lifetime achievement award at the Brits.

Also in 1999, the Euro arrived, the Scottish parliamentary elections were held and the parliament reconvened for the first time since 1707, Napster began to change the world of music sales and the six-billionth person arrived on the planet.

SCOTT PIRRIE: My contribution to the Scottish music scene was slight, probably to the point of insignificance. I played in a band called the Answer in the unfashionable nineties, and for ten years or so we kicked around the pubs and clubs of the central belt, making no impact whatsoever.

There were thousands of bands like us – we were the guys no one quite remembered seeing, the forgettable first act on the three-band bill, the cannon fodder on the local scene, hanging around at the back of the dressing room full of awkward strangers. If they ever need a collective noun for musicians, I think it should be 'an insecurity'.

We had no business sense at all, save for blind enthusiasm, a modicum of talent and, like all the other hopefuls, a collective libido that required at least three trained handlers at times. But the small guys like us kept the whole machine in motion.

Of course, that's not to say we were in any way content with our lowly calling – it went without saying we'd have sold our grandmothers for the six-figure Sony deal, the tabloid courtship and the global female appreciation of our work.

Even though these things didn't happen, we still had a hell of a ride. From the unfettered enthusiasm of places like The Twa Corbies in Cumbernauld to the pretentious bollocks of King Tut's, our varied and sometimes itchy career included the inadvertent burning down of a night club in Blantyre, the electrocution of a guitarist, the loss of a perfectly good watch down a Cockermouth toilet, the loss of a perfectly good drummer in the Glasgow underground, enough chicken pakora to fill a small whaling trawler, three cylinder-head gaskets, one acrimonious divorce, one documented case of genital herpes and four chipped teeth – three due to the faithful old SM58 and one due to a kebab.

I suppose at times I hated it then – but I long for it now. So this goes out to the wee fish that made the big pond all the more inviting, the Transit van sleepovers, the questionable underwear, the venues that ranged from the palatial to the downright infectious, the fights, the beer, the broken hearts.

I'd recommend it to anyone.

14 IDOLS AND ICONS

Popularity polls distort with proximity – 'tis a fact, as well as a pleasantly alliterative phrase. John Lennon was *not* the man of the last millennium. He was a musician, and musicians are not the most important people on the planet. Nope, someone way back when – like the guy who discovered deadly nightshade was poisonous, or the bloke who suggested different wiping-sticks for each visitor to the toilet – someone like that was the man of the millennium.

Similarly, Belle and Sebastian are *not* the best Scottish band of all time. I don't mind them managing to win the national vote run by *The List* magazine but we all know it was bollox. SAHB were in the running and I'm not the only one who voted for them twice – B&S just cheated better than we did. So they stand up as winners of the contest; it's just, the prize was nonsense.

So, it's tough to try and work out what might have been the most important rock'n'roll events since the turn of the millennium; and indeed, the low level of response to my queries on the subject of 2000 onward shows how many people agree. With your permission, then, I'll spin through the last few years and just make a few suggestions. I'm prepared to stand corrected if you're buying.

Waking up to absolutely no Millennium Bug problems at all (is that because the Millennium Commission did its job or because it was all bobbins in the first place?), the Delgados released *The Great Eastern*. It's no insult to say their business interest, Chemikal Underground, has been as valuable as their musical creations; but there was time to sit back and enjoy a bit of cunningly crafted noise featuring some really wonderful orchestral arrangements lighting up damn fine songs such as *Make Your Move*.

Primal Scream changed their name to PRML SCRM for the release of XTRMNTR, underlining Gillespie and Co.'s ability to adjust their outlook to suit their output. The harsh titling tells you what to expect, and you get it in droves, notably in the single *Swastika Eyes*, and in *Kill All Hippies*.

GIBBY: Robert changed his name to Robert T Leonard, and he's become one of the country's top club entertainers, playing shows most nights of the week. I know what you're thinking, but don't – for a start, he always had the voice for it. Respectable bands like Gaberlunzie made the switch to the club circuit when the other work started drying up, and it's not done them any harm. Robert's shows are still as manic as ever – costume changes, audience interaction and great singing on top. I used to do some gigs with him and we had the audience in stitches. He used to strip me stark naked on stage, and I couldn't do anything about it because I was meant to be playing the keyboards...

Thing is I was miming, as you do – my job was to be part of the act rather than the music, and, okay, it's not playing bass in a rock band, but it was still a laugh. I remember one night in Dundee we had a big slow-motion dummy fight – it was me, Martin and Robert dressed as the evil emperor from *Star Wars*. Half the Dundee United team were in the audience, completely bewildered but killing themselves laughing...

Around the same time, Gary Mullen won *Stars in Their Eyes* as Freddie Mercury. I knew him from his rock band, Hellfire, who were brilliant. His mum had sent in the tape without him knowing, and he won! Suddenly he was selling out huge venues but he didn't have a band, so he got me in on keyboards to do what I'd been doing with Robert. I was still miming, but he'd introduce me as, 'Gibby, one of the world's greatest keyboard players!' Women really did throw knickers...

Peanuts creator Charles Schultz drew his last Charlie Brown, retired, and then died a week later. A French *Concorde* crashed in Paris and killed one hundred and fourteen people, bringing the supersonic era to an end. The Russian submarine *Kursk* sank with all hands, and fuel protests across the UK saw angry outbursts and blockaded roads.

Belle and Sebastian's *Tigermilk* had been re-released in 1999 and made number thirteen, and the follow-up, *Fold your Hands Child, You Walk like a Peasant* reached number ten. The single *Legal Man* got them on *Top of the Pops* too, opening up their whimsical world to a wider range of visitors. Teenage Fanclub's *Howdy!* and Idlewild's *100 Broken Windows* continued to reinforce the strength of the nation's pop scene. Possil's own Reverend D Wayne Love and his English counterparts in Alabama 3 received international attention when their bluesy-gospel track *Woke Up This Morning* was used as the theme for the US gangster show *The Sopranos*. To hear one A3 track is not to know enough about the wide range of influences they drag in and stack up; but the thick layers of humour and character are apparent from the start.

It was the year record companies began worrying about loss of sales due to online file-sharing. Just a few years later it seems strange that their first reaction was to try to wipe it out altogether – reminiscent of the Musicians' Union's attempts to ban the synthesiser in the eighties and *Melody Maker's* late-sixties efforts to make pop music illegal. Learning absolutely nothing over the previous fifty years, the suits with the City Fathers attitude honestly thought, 'How dare they?'

In 2001, the UK charts were completely dominated by girlies and boysies: S Club 7, Hear'Say, ex-Spice girls Geri Halliwell and Emma Bunton, Destiny's Child, Atomic Kitten, Five – and Limp Bizkit, whom folk must have thought were such an act, because *Rollin'* was the only number one that year with real drums.

Thank the good lord, then, for Travis's *The Invisible Band* and their singles *Sing*, *Side* and *Flowers in the Window*. The album title reflected their belief that the songs were more important than who performed them – an attitude clearly not shared by the Chart Fathers.

Mogwai's *Rock Action* showed a more mature approach to experimentalism, introducing a wider range of ideas but honing the constructions so there was more space for those ideas to breathe. The LP made number twenty-three, suggesting how many others agreed.

Colin MacIntyre decided to call himself Mull Historical Society when he signed a six-album deal. He grew up on Mull and the society's articles in the local paper had fuelled his imagination from an early age. So, too, had his uncle's band, when there was no radio signal on the island; and when his dad, respected broadcaster Kenny MacIntyre, died, he decided to call his first album *Loss*.

COLIN MacINTYRE: It was about being positive after experiencing loss. I got a £15,000 bank loan to do the album and live on – I'd been offered a publishing deal for the same amount but I decided to hold out for something better, and just used it as security against the bank loan. It was big risk, but the Bank of Scotland recognised my potential before Warners did... When the album came out I sent a copy to my bank business manager and invited him to any gig he wanted to come to.

Alex Higgins, the snooker player, was my obsession for a bit when I was young. He was a lovable rogue, always putting two fingers up at authority. So I wanted to use a photo of him on the cover of my second single, *I Tried*. In the end he'd only speak to me personally, so I called my childhood hero on his mobile. He was in a bar, not doing too well, although he kept calling me 'Mr MacIntyre'. In the end he wanted £5000 to use his picture – I think that might have bankrupted Rough Trade so I declined. He's still a legend as far as I'm concerned though.

Coincidentally, I was on Mull when the 9/11 attacks shocked the planet. I was on holiday and wasn't keeping up with the news. I went in to a pub for an afternoon pint and there it was on the telly. I think most people's experience was the same – it was tough to believe you weren't watching a movie, no matter how many times they looped the footage; and despite being surrounded by strangers there was a peculiarly close and muted conversation going on amongst us all. I remember being desperate to try and make a joke, which is my usual reaction in times of darkness, but even I realised it wouldn't be appropriate in this roomful of temporary family. Leaving the pub was actually more difficult than dealing with the headlines.

George W Bush was apparently president of the USA, Douglas Adams and George Harrison died, Labour won the general election – surprise, surprise – Jeffrey Archer was jailed, US energy company Enron collapsed and the iPod arrived. A few months later, in January 2002, a fifteen-year-old trainee pilot accidentally crashed a small plane into a Florida tower block, setting off a post 9/11 wave of terror; twelve thousand square miles of Antarctica disintegrated in four days; BBC Radio Six launched; the Queen Mother was finally laid to rest; and Brian May rather pompously played on the roof of Buckingham Palace to celebrate the Queen's silver jubilee.

It was the year when the TV talent show *Pop Idol* dominated the charts, with winner Will Young and runner-up Gareth Gates both spouting it out. Roddy Frame recorded the mainly acoustic *Surf*, a solo album, in his front room, successfully refocusing on his songwriting and flicking the V at critics of Aztec Camera's previous album *The North Star*. Idlewild hit with *You Held the World in Your Arms*, a triumphant slice of pop-rock that distanced itself from their previous heavy US guitar influences, a translation subtly referred to in the follow-up single *American English*. *The Remote Part* LP made number three. But one of the biggest events of the year, and one of the most underrated of all time, was the Frankie Miller tribute night in the Barrowlands Ballroom. Frankie had suffered a catastrophic brain hemorrhage which left him wheelchair-bound and unable to speak. In 2002 some of his friends and family got together to record a tribute album, and the tribute concert followed on. For some reason it was largely ignored by the media, but it wasn't by Scottish musicians, and it's the nearest thing the country ever had to a gala night.

GIBBY: There were some young bands who started the night, and that was okay, but things really got going when Robbo Robertson hit the stage – he was hailed like a returning messiah. He could still cut the mustard, and getting him back off was one of the major organisational feats of the night...

BRIAN ROBERTSON: I was in Frankie's band for ten years – I'd have played in quicksand for that man. I *had* to be there. It was very emotional, but I *had* to be there.

GIBBY: I ran into Stephen from the Cosmic Rough Riders and he said they were going on next with a surprise guest. Lo and behold, it was Joe Walsh from the Eagles. Joe had paid Frankie's medical bills in the States, so it made sense he was there. It must have been great for Stephen, standing on stage and getting to say, 'Ladies and gentlemen – Mister Joe Walsh!' Then Joe did his own set – *Rocky Mountain Way*, *Life's Been Good to Me*, but not *Pretty Maids all in a Row*, which was a shame.

Pat Kane did well, and Dean Ford from Marmalade was brilliant with his acoustic. Mary Kiani got plus and minus points – plus, she tried to do something a bit different with a Frankie song, and minus, she chose to do a dance version of *Be Good to Yourself*, which is my favourite Frankie track. Clare Grogan was good, Jackie Leven did a brilliant version of I would *Rather Go Blind*, and the BMX Bandits were good too.

Ray Wilson was a revelation. I'd heard him in Stiltskin and Genesis, and it was okay, but I think he won us all over that night. He did a gospel version of Frankie's *Good Time Love* – it blew us away.

Then Nazareth came on, and it really got rockin'. I hadn't seen them in years, and now Darrell Sweet had died I didn't know what to expect. But they had Pete Agnew's son on the drums and he put new life right through the band. *Broken Down Angel* had us all gobsmacked – Dan McCafferty is one of Scotland's best voices ever.

MARK MURDOCH: SAHB were without doubt the highlight of the night. The show had already over-run by hours, and the buses were off, but I was going nowhere without seeing them. No one even knew who was singing until Billy Rankin went up to the mic. He was incredible – I'd only ever heard him play guitar, when he was in Naz. I didn't know he could sing as well. They did *Faith Healer*, *Midnight Moses* and of course *Delilah*, and it was like being eighteen again. They could all still play like fuck and Zal was burstin' oot. I found out later on they hadn't played together in seven years – you could have fooled me.

CHRIS GLEN, SAHB: Aye, we were a wee bit nervous, but it's in your blood, and we'd been a band for more than thirty years by then – the odd year off here and there doesn't matter. And it was like old times. Our roadie Wee Tam, who was Sting's production manager by then, was looking after the stage, our sound man Davie Batchelor was at the desk, Nazareth's lighting man Ronnie was at his desk, and our old manager Eddie Tobin was in the crowd. The best thing about the night was Frankie, though – he wouldn't stop singing the chorus to *Delilah*. He's still doing it!

Jimmy Dewar, who'd been in Stone the Crows and Robin Trower's band, died that year, after a long illness. As well as having been close mates and bandmates with Frankie, he'd encouraged Scotland's biggest blues guitar legend to get on out there.

SHIFTY, Big George and the Business**:** We got going after Jimmy had to stop gigging. He and Big George remained very close friends, and George conducted his funeral service. He told a story about the night they'd finished a gig and gone back to Jimmy's for a wee refreshment. George went to put on a Ray Charles album, but Jimmy said, 'Frankie Miller's new album is there if you want to play it.' George said, 'I thought Ray was your favourite?' And Jimmy said, 'Well, to be honest, Frankie's the best singer I've ever heard – but don't you tell him that till after I'm dead, because you'll just give him a big heid.'

Frankie Miller's night: above, Dean Ford from Marmalade and Dougie MacLean, writer of Caledonia; below, Dean, Billy Rankin and SAHB; top right, Ray Wilson, Alan Mair from the Beatstalkers and Only Ones, with Zal Cleminson; centre, Robbo Robertson and the BMX Bandits; bottom, Dean Ford and SAHB soundchecking

Frankie Miller's night: above, Dan McCafferty with Nazareth and Billy Rankin with the house band; below, the grand finale; top right, the lyrics for Darlin' are quickly handed round; bottom, Frankie in action; and, inset, the football trophy he showed me last time we met – I thought you might like to see it too.

DAVE ARCARI, Radiotones**:** It was Big George who got me into music, guitars and blues. I used to join in with a country duo in the Ben Nevis who encouraged me to grab the Tele and play some Dylan or whatever else I'd been learning. The guy on pedal steel was a complete alky – he was magnificent, but I could never work out how he could play so well and not be able to stand or speak… One night they weren't there so as I wandered back towards Partick I saw there was live music in the Exchequer. Big George and Jimmy Dewar were on – I discovered the blues and it changed my life.

SHIFTY: We'd played just about everywhere so it was time to do an album. We went to Shabby Road Studios in Kilmarnock and it was recorded and mixed in just two days. Then there was a hefty delay in getting it mastered and pressed because one of the band had to be at the high court… So one night, a punter shouted, 'When's this alleged album coming out?' We didn't have a title up to then, so we called it *The Alleged Album*.

In keeping with the back-to-basics feel of the whole project, we ordered one thousand plain white covers, two thousand 'Alleged Album' stickers – one for the front and one for the back – and one thousand inner sleeves. The band and crew then proceeded to insert discs into inners, inners into covers, and put stickers on the front and back. A few had squinty stickers and hidden messages to relieve the tedium. Then we hand-delivered them to local shops all over the place, and they sold out in the first few days.
Fluff Freeman praised it on his Radio One rock show.

STEF MILLS: They're alleged to have pulled a dead-wide trick to promote the album – they sent their mates into record shops to ask about it before it was out, so the owner wouldn't know anything about it. Then after there'd been a dozen people asking, the band would go in and say, 'Would you like to stock our album?' Course they would!

George, of course, is a legend. Among the many stories, lots of which seem to include shite, is my personal favourite, which goes like this. His rider is very simple – 'A bottle of Southern Comfort whenever I shout for one' – and he'll happily down three during the course of an evening. One night he must have done unusually well, for he staggered into a taxi, bellowed, 'Bangkok, my man!' and feel asleep. The cab driver took him to Banknock and kicked him out.

SHIFTY: There was a short-circuit on stage once and I was electrocuted – I was flung across the stage and landed in the drumkit. George realised what was happening and kicked the bass out of my grip, breaking the circuit. He came over to check I was alright and shouted for Richie the roadie to get me a treble Southern Comfort. Richie came back and George drank it… well, he'd had a stressful moment! I had burns on my hands but I was okay…

In 2003 Biffy Clyro began to rise towards the heights, Mull Historical Society released the *Us* album and David Sneddon became famous after winning the *Fame Academy* reality talent show. That broke up the first band I'd ever actually been in with Gibby…

GIBBY: I was asked to join pop-rock band the Martians, which had Martin's wee brother John and Davie Sneddon in it. We recorded a great live EP at CaVa Studios in Glasgow and played at the Spirit Aid after-show party, where a highly-perceptive Ian McCullough of Echo and the Bunnymen declared us a 'superb band'. Then we did a spoof version of *War of the Worlds* at the Edinburgh Festival, and ended up doing a big show at the Bedlam Theatre, where we got a standing ovation.The problem was, Davie Sneddon went and auditioned for *Fame Academy*, and he got in when someone else fell ill. He'd only done it because he was getting hassle from the dole. It got us a fair amount of publicity – they even interviewed me on the show, where I revealed I didn't watch it because I didn't have a telly!

We did another demo, featuring Michelle Cassidy, who was in the comedy-drama *Teachers* – she had a great voice.

ME: My heart was in my mouth that final night. I didn't want him to win – I knew it would be the end of the band, and I'd only really just got into it. But how can you wish the worst on someone like that? After a lot of thought I decided not to vote, and to let everything spin out as it would. Of course, the besstert won, and that was that. Within days radio stations were being told if they continued giving us publicity they wouldn't be allowed access to Davie. I'd had this cunning plan – on the back of all the interest we'd get a development deal for, say, £50,000, split it five ways and fuck off, then get back together with a new name. Of course, it didn't happen.

DAVID SNEDDON: That first single, *Stop Living the Lie*, was handed to me as a done job. They'd recorded some jam sessions I was doing earlier in the series, then when I won they said, 'Here's your first single.' I don't listen to it...

ME: My stupid sense of humour nearly got us killed, again. First time the boys were all back together was when Davie and John were doing a lightning tour of Scotland – something like ten shows in ten hours or an equally silly prank. They wound up at the Garage in Glasgow for the finale, and Davie got his first gold disc on stage. We were in the crowd among all these girly-boppers, screaming mad for Davie. He went to do one of our songs and said, 'I used to be in this band, the Martians...' and they all went ballistic, cheering and shouting. I booed at the absolute top of my voice, and suddenly silence fell around us and we were like the cowboys facing the Indians...

GIBBY: We got through to the final of a newspaper battle of the bands. They didn't know about the Davie connection, and they'd even asked him to be a judge. On top of that, Martin worked at the newspaper in question at the time – so when the night came, the judges announced that no way would we be allowed to win, for fear of it being called a fix.

ME: Which made it a fix, didn't it?

GIBBY: We did a good gig, though. But in the end John went off to join Davie's new band, do *Top of the Pops* and support Elton John and all that. And I was back on the dole again, but concentrating on writing my own songs.

ME: And what happened to me? Oh...

The end of 2003 brought another talent show thingy, *Pop Idol 2*, won by another Scot, Michelle McManus. The result was controversial simply because Michelle was a big girl; judge Pete Waterman, for one, wasn't going to stand for it. The story goes he left the studio before the announcement was made. Good on you, Pete, for believing in something. We, meanwhile, will stick with having friends and being nice people, and recognising someone who can sing when we hear one.

The Hugh Trowsers band, the Martians (with David Sneddon) and Robert T Leonard. Tips for the future? Nah – just people I expect beer from.

I've said it before and I'll say it again – steer clear of these things unless you're getting as much out of it as the other guy... Mere weeks before Sneddy went into *Fame Academy*, I had a row with wee brother John when we ended up doing a silly wee pay-to-play band battle. What was the best we could get out of it? The chance to pay to be in the quarter-final too. 'But it's publicity,' I heard someone whine. 'No, it's playing in front of people who don't care about you, except the pals you've brought,' said I. (We won, of course, but that's neither here nor there, and I didn't shout, 'Fix!' because I already knew it was...) And I think I'll take this opportunity to try embarrassing John by telling the world he used to be known as 'Flower' and 'Jinglebop' in our house. Ask him why – go on, do. Shut it, Damien... you were 'Moog' and 'Earways'.

It was also the year Franz Ferdinand arrived, with what was called a Jam-type new-mod sound, but which could clearly be seen to be a follow-on from Edinburgh's Postcard bands from the early eighties. *Take Me Out* made number three and so did their self-titled album.

CLAIRE SWEENEY: I couldn't have been happier for Alex. He'd spent years on the scene, putting on nights for other bands and helping everyone out. He really deserved it. Even once he was huge, he'd invite me in for a cup of tea because we lived quite close to each other in Dennistoun. I never had time, but the offer was always genuine. I'm glad genuine can still work out...

It was the twentieth anniversary of Band Aid, and the result was Band Aid 20 with a modern pop version of the song, which just showed how different things were, nuff said. That year I had the pleasure of attending an awards ceremony as part of the now-reformed SAHB; they sat us at a table with the Darkness, which was top fun. We were there to accept a lifetime achievement award (well, SAHB were – what did I have to do with it?) and the Darkness were getting a special award for having been the first band ever to open a festival one year and headline it the next. Only, SAHB did it back in the seventies... Ach, well, the champagne was free.

KT Tunstall exploded onto the scene in 2005 with her number-three album *Eye to the Telescope* and her singles *Other Side of the World* and *Suddenly I See*. It marked a great achievement for someone who'd been plugging away for years, trying to be a wee bit mainstream and a wee bit special, and believing all the time in the sheer beauty of songs – as, I suggest, most of us Scots do. Franz Ferdinand made number one with their second LP, *You Could Have It So Much Better*, having put an even stronger spin on their modern retro vibe, and picking up a whole host of copyists on the way.

Which brings us to 2006, fifty years after Lonnie Donegan changed the world. Belle and Sebastian reached number eight with their *Life Pursuit* LP. Primal Scream changed their sound again with the *Riot City Blues* album and the number-five single *Country Girl*, which saw them moving back towards basics again. (Is it just these old ears or is *Country Girl* remarkably similar to Queen's *Fat Bottomed Girls*?) Bert Jansch received the *Mojo* Merit Award for his successful career, and during the ceremony Elton John and Bernie Taupin talked about the days they used to sit around listening to Bert's records and wishing they could be as good as him. Sandi Thom hit with *I Wish I Was a Punk Rocker with Flowers in my Hair*, a surprise strike, it's claimed, via a series of internet webcasts. And *Top of the Pops* ended after forty-two years. Whatever next?

I'll borrow a tradition from a highly-regarded old sports journalist, and say this: my predictions for the next ten years in Scottish rock'n'roll are in an envelope, sealed and stored in the sight of my colleagues, to be opened in 2016. I'm confident I'll have been proved correct – that's because there's ninety different envelopes.

SIGNOFF

This book has more or less managed to be another edition of *Big Noise*. The principles have been the same from the start – let people say what they want to say, try not to get in the way, but stitch it together so that it makes sense, and hope there's an underlying truth in there. And, looking back over this fifty-year journey, I think there is.

Scots are selfish sharers. If something new comes along, I want to play with it myself for a while, then when I've come up with a couple of tricks I'll share them with you, then you do it too. Scottish music works best when there's the facility to apply one's own character, as well as one's own musical talent. Scottish musicians on the whole are more than just musically creative. Maybe that's true of the rest of the world too, but they can work it out for themselves...

But is being Scottish important? I'd have to say yes, and I'd suggest the sheer quantity of talent backs the position up. I also can't see how being Scottish could fail to affect your attitudes and therefore your art. I do get why some bands don't want to make an issue of it. Texas and Travis, for example, like Annie Lennox before them, are trying to be something altogether more global. In some circles there's a fear of being labelled 'too parochial' and it's better to suppress the issue. But ultimately, if you don't know where you came from, how can you know where you're going?

And it's getting more important, despite all this globalisation malarkey. The web has changed everything, and if it remains as vibrant as it's been, the changes will become more and more focused on personality.

Sandi Thom's webcast concept is great, although it's a lot more expensive than her PR people would have you believe. I did one with the Hugh Trowsers band and I could see the advantages immediately – but also the drawbacks. There's just no substitute for being in the room as someone does the do. Until they can plug you into bad smells, barstaff clatters and the distraction of that cute bird in the corner, it's not rock'n'roll for me. But then, thirty years ago you went to a gig and didn't drink. I can't even begin to think of watching a show now without a pint in my hand.

The web, as well, has brought many bands out of retirement – because none of them realised until the email age how big their fanbases had been. In the mid-sixties the Beatstalkers sold eighty thousand records and the paperwork said they'd sold five thousand. Translation – for every fan they had, there were at least fifteen they didn't know about. And back then, the label bosses could shake their heads and shut the office door. Nowadays, we can *prove* they don't know what they're talking about. They're just banks – we only need their money. Because, the thing is, you can now create your own product to a more-than-adequate standard. You just can't afford to publicise it.

There will never be another John Peel, which isn't to do down the folk all over everywhere who play the part of mini-Peels. But perhaps we won't need a new on – the newfangled electrickery is moving us all towards monocasting. Back in the day, you could sit in front of the TV camera, or at the broadcast mic, or behind the typewriter, and tell thousands or millions of people what you thought. It was a great deal of hassle for them to tell you back. With MySpace, YouTube and blogging, and whatever comes next, it's as easy for me to talk to you as it is for you to talk to me. News services are struggling because the facts are easy to get hold of, and they always subsisted on selling you facts. The great argument for authoritative delivery style in the printed press was, 'People want to be told things.' In 2006 they know everything before it can be put on the page and punted.

So what matters instead? It's what always mattered – character. It's what drove anyone who ever changed anything to get up and get it done. And, this time round, it's increasingly more difficult to control.

Sure, there'll be less money to be made in future, because there'll be much more product to compete with. But it only fuels creativity – how much money is enough anyway? – and as music makers and music fans we can't lose. The only people with anything to worry about are the ones who've hidden behind a corporate mask because they just don't have enough personality and attitude. Someone will probably fuck it up for us, but we're approaching that individualist level playing field that is the proper definition of anarchy.

So that's my prediction for the future – character as currency. And we have more than most – bottle the stuff and we'd be as rich as if we had oil – oh, shit... Ach, someone will sort it out. And they'll probably be Scottish.

Fuck, that's last orders. Do you want another?

Ch;M.

Notes